WHAT LIES BENEATH MATTERS

A WORKBOOK FOR TWEENS AND TEENS WITH ADHD

GRACE DA CAMARA | PSYCHOLOGIST
& MADALENA BENNETT | GENERAL PRACTITIONER

First published in 2023 by

UWA Publishing, Crawley, Western Australia 6009

www.uwap.uwa.edu.au

UWAP is an imprint of UWA Publishing, a division of The University of Western Australia.

The information and strategies in this workbook are based on the author's interpretations of the books that she has read, on her experiences as a mother of a child with ADHD and the results of her personal experiences in her clinical work, as a psychologist, working with children and adults with ADHD and their families.

Requests for information should be addressed to: SafeZone Counselling, szcounselling@gmail.com

ISBN: 9781760802585

Editor: Valerie Latimour
Proofreader: Euan Lloyd and Stephanie Lu
Illustrations: Anne-Marie Douse
Cover design: Taloula Press
Contributions: Brooke Penny (Nutrition); Euan Lloyd (Executive Function).
Printed by Lightning Source

This book is dedicated to all children around the world who courageously struggle each day to cope with their ADHD challenges – and the parents who support them unconditionally.

This book belongs to

____

Grace Da Camara & Madalena Bennett

This unique mother/daughter combination brings together the knowledge and experience of a psychologist who specialises in working with children, adolescents, adults and families affected by ADHD; and a general practitioner with a focus on a multidisciplinary approach to treatment.

Grace employs a range of therapeutic approaches, including Cognitive Behaviour Therapy, Rational Emotive Behaviour Therapy, Interpersonal Psychotherapy and Acceptance Commitment Therapy. She adopts an eclectic approach on the basis that each client is unique and has their own particular presentation. Her overriding focus is to help the client develop a better understanding of their challenges and grow in a personally meaningful way.

As a GP, Madalena recognises and acknowledges the need for education on ADHD for mental health professionals, including GPs. She is a member of the RACGP specific-interest ADHD, ASD, and neurodiversity group and has engaged in upskilling for fellow GP colleagues in this area.

Both Grace and Madalena support and endorse the need for greater knowledge and education about the condition, with a focus on interventions targeted to individuals and families living with ADHD.

ACKNOWLEDGMENTS

First and foremost, I want to thank all the children who have participated in OnTrac over the past five years. Your participation influenced the content of this workbook, how OnTrac looks today and the entire, What Lies Beneath Matters, series. You've taught us so much about best practices in working with children with ADHD, especially in group settings. Many parents opened their hearts to us before, during and after each program, giving us valuable feedback on how each child was experiencing the program and the exercises/activities that they found useful. The responsibility parents shoulder in advocating for the needs of their child with ADHD is not taken lightly, and we appreciate their confidence in us.

Our eternal gratitude to the wonderful group of third-year medical students from the University of Western Australia who have chosen OnTrac as their Services Learning Project. Through their dedication, support and continuous constructive feedback, this workbook and program have come to fruition. I hope that this experience met your objectives and contributed to your learning and personal development in preparation for your careers as medical doctors.

To Euan, a postgraduate psychology student, in recognition of all your input in the final layout of the modules, as well as for creating the mind maps. Your 'can-do' attitude and commitment to making this workbook as tween/teen friendly as possible is much appreciated. Lucky are those that you will serve one day as a psychologist.

To Stephanie, in thanks for the beautiful artwork and cover designs. My appreciation for always making yourself available to assist me, in the midst of your own studies.

To Valerie, my editor, my thanks for your ongoing support in all my projects. Your ability to put my thinking and ideas into words was fundamental to this work.

To the professional Q&A panel, thank you for the precious gift of your time to answer the many questions raised by the children and their parents as each program was delivered.

To ADHD WA, my ongoing gratitude for facilitating the delivery of the program.

My deepest gratitude to my family, especially my son who has ADHD – in your struggles I found the strength to persevere even when challenged by my critical inner voice.

Contents

Introduction

Children who have been diagnosed with ADHD often have little to no knowledge or education about their diagnosis. Many tell me, 'I was told that I had ADHD and that the medication would help me manage it'. 'I was told that I needed to take these vitamins so that I could do better at school, but I never really knew what I was supposed to do better.'

Often there is a lack of education for youth about their diagnosis, a lack of support for educators to teach children with ADHD, and a lack of support for parents of children with ADHD. ADHD is a lifelong diagnosis, and children need people with knowledge of the condition to help them understand their diagnosis, learn to identify their symptoms and advocate for themselves.

Children living with ADHD often get negatively labelled. They may experience difficulties in several areas of their lives, which can cause feelings of shame, fear and self-doubt. Parents want their children to be happy, to be liked and to fit in at school; to become independent and responsible adults; and to succeed in their chosen careers and relationships. Parents need to recognise when their children are experiencing ridicule, isolation and frustration.

When a child has ADHD, parents have additional challenges: a meltdown, a bad report card, a 10-minute worksheet that turns into an evening-long struggle. Parents must always be 'on', and this can be exhausting. 'How can we give ourselves a break?' some ask. A parent of a child with ADHD needs extra patience, dedication, compassion and the know-how to advocate for their child. Despite how tiring and challenging their child can be at times, parents still hurt and become defensive when others criticise their child, especially when only the negative aspects get attention. Children with ADHD can be sweet, funny, loving and creative, but it can be difficult to recognise these positive traits when they are buried under power struggles, episodes of acting out, shame, worry and guilt.

It is important to be realistic about what constitutes the perfect family. Don't waste your time and effort striving to structure your family in the way that your extended family and friends view as 'ideal'. Spend your energy doing what works for your family. Stay focused on the long-term goal. Yes, you want your child to learn the skills they need to succeed in life, but you also want to have a loving family, with parents and children who feel good about themselves.

Let them know that you are in their corner and love them no matter what, and together you will get through the smooth and the rough times.

A Note for You

If you are a young person with ADHD, you may at times get overactive and struggle to sustain attention during lessons. This makes it hard for you in school. Many of the young people that I work with tell me that they don't like school, that it is difficult and that they get into trouble more often than the other children in their class.

They tell me that they get into trouble for actions that they cannot really control, like fidgeting, forgetting things and daydreaming during class. The most common concern, however, is related to peer relationships. Most children with ADHD tell me they don't have friends and feel left out during group work, recess and get-togethers outside of school.

'Teachers are always saying, "Why aren't you paying attention? Stop dreaming. Stop fidgeting; just get on task"', reported a 15-year-old with ADHD, predominantly inattentive type. 'The truth is that I was paying attention, just not to what I was expected to be paying attention to. I just want to run out of the classroom and never return, I hate feeling so embarrassed and ashamed.'

Some behaviours associated with ADHD can make you seem rude and disrespectful to people who don't understand the condition. When teachers don't have enough training on ADHD, they can think that you make the choice not to listen and do as you are told.

This workbook draws upon my experiences working with children and families to help you understand the most common problems children with ADHD report. Filled with lots of facts, activities and quizzes, you will learn to handle different aspects of your ADHD a little better. But like most things in life, practice is needed, and the more you practice, the better you will get at it.

Some activities you can do on your own, while others require help from another person, such as a parent, teacher, mentor or counsellor.

My hope is that this workbook will become your go-to resource to help manage your everyday challenges.

Remember these three simple truths:

- If you do not ask, the answer will always be **no.**
- If you do not go after what you want, you'll never **have it.**
- If you do not step out, you will always be in the **same place.**

ADHD Overview

Worldwide, ADHD prevalence in children aged 18 and under is estimated to be around 7.2% (Thomas et al. 2015).

In the United States

The 2016 National Survey of Children's Health (NSCH) interviewed parents and reports the following ADHD prevalence data among children ages 2–17 (Danielson et al. 2018):

- 5.4 million children (8.4%) have a current diagnosis of ADHD. This includes:
    - About 335,000 young children ages 2–5 (2.1% in this age group)
    - 2.2 million school-age children ages 6–11 (8.9% in this age group)
    - 2.9 million adolescents ages 12–17 (11.9% in this age group).
- Severity of ADHD among children ages 2–17:
    - 14.5% had severe ADHD
    - 43.7% had moderate ADHD
    - 41.8% had mild ADHD.
- Co-existing conditions (children ages 2–17):
    - Two out of three children (63.8%) had at least one co-existing condition.
    - Half of all children (51.5 %) had behavioural or conduct problems.
    - One out of three children (32.7%) had anxiety problems.
    - One out of six children (16.8%) had depression.
    - About one out of seven children (13.7%) had autism spectrum disorder.
    - About one out of 80 children (1.2%) had Tourette syndrome.
    - One in 100 adolescents (1%) had a substance abuse disorder.

The same study found the rate of ADHD diagnosis increased from 7% in 1997–1999 to 10.2% in 2012–2014. This increase remains to be understood, and common perceptions that ADHD is over-diagnosed in the US persist. Previous studies conducted in the United Kingdom have also observed a significant increase in ADHD prevalence, although the prevalence estimates were substantially lower than those in the United States.

It remains to be understood how much of the reported increase in diagnoses in the US can be attributed to etiologic factors; ADHD has a genetic component with an estimated heritability of 70–80%. In addition to genetic risk factors, environmental risk factors are believed to contribute to the development of ADHD. Prenatal and perinatal risk factors, including premature birth, low birth weight, maternal cigarette smoking, and maternal use of certain medications or illicit substances during pregnancy, have been associated with ADHD risk.

Environmental contamination, such as lead and pesticide exposure during prenatal and/or postnatal periods, is also a possible risk factor for ADHD.

ADHD in Australia Today

A National Survey conducted by ADHD Australia in 2020 to identify and clarify the key issues faced by people living with ADHD, reported that as many as 7% of children and about 2.5% adults have ADHD. Among many findings, the following three key areas of concern stood out in the survey results:

1. the cost of life of living with ADHD
2. the need for schools to truly accommodate, empathise with and understand children with ADHD to help them meet the unique challenges they face
3. the need for awareness and understanding of the challenges people at all ages with ADHD face in day-to-day aspects of work, social and family life.

Funding is essential to establishing all three of the above areas. Funding for families of children with ADHD and individuals with ADHD; funding school support and resourcing; and funding to raise awareness of ADHD.

For all of the survey participants, the number one difficulty in regard to ADHD was the everyday challenges of living with ADHD. These included, but were not limited to, the challenges of living with one or more co-existing conditions; dealing with the impact of ADHD in school and employment; the impact of ADHD on social and relationship matters; and the impact on the family unit.

These challenges were exacerbated by a lack of awareness and understanding in the general Australian population about the ADHD community and their needs. The full survey is available on ADHD Australia's website: www.adhdaustralia.org.au

Managing ADHD Beyond Stimulant Medications

Despite there being standardised guidelines for ADHD treatment, not everyone will respond to a treatment in the same way. What works for one person might not work for another. This is because the brain is like a fingerprint, everyone has a unique genetic makeup that dictates how they will respond to a particular treatment.

There are many effective non-stimulant treatment options for managing ADHD symptoms. Before recommending a specific treatment regimen, a healthcare provider will thoroughly evaluate a person's past medical and family history during an initial consultation. Working with an ADHD specialist who can help navigate the available treatment options is vital for a person's success in managing ADHD symptoms.

With this brief understanding of what we know about ADHD in 2022, this workbook endeavours to help you cope with the negative feelings and dysfunctional behaviour patterns that are often part and parcel of ADHD. Ultimately, the aim is to help you live a more fulfilled life and be successful in your personal, family, school and social life.

This workbook...

- is based on the latest research
- helps you understand how ADHD presents for you
- shows you what Executive Functions are and how they affect you
- teaches you strategies to implement in your day-to-day life to help you manage daily challenges better
- guides you through a process of bringing about change to improve your life.

The many activities and exercises will help you apply these ideas, and challenge the barriers that have gotten in your way before, so that you can be more consistent and effective.

How to get the most out of this workbook and why you should expect results:

1. The focus of the workbook is on doing and not just knowing. The book includes many thought-provoking exercises and reflections. You don't have to do any of the exercises, but – like much in life – the more you put in, the more you get out. You may find that some of the exercises resonate with you more than others do. This is normal – after all, ADHD has many faces and presentations.
2. The development of this workbook happened in real life, while delivering its content to tweens and teens with ADHD in groups and in individual settings: questioning, adapting, testing and making the necessary changes over a period of four years. This means that all the exercises have been actively tried and tested before the decision was made to include them. The challenge was to include a range of content to serve the many ADHD presentations. My hope is that you will give it a fair go.
3. There's a lot of good information out there about time management, organisation, to-do lists, procrastination, remembering things better, etc. for children with ADHD. These important topics affect how you live your day-to-day life. In this workbook, I highlight the need to till the soil before sowing the seeds. In the context of ADHD, this means understanding what lies beneath,

especially the roles of adaptive thinking and Executive Function deficits. Understanding these concepts helps you change negative thought patterns, so you can choose the most effective strategies for you, apply them consistently and stick with them until you get results.

4. The good news about this workbook is that you can jump around. You don't have to start on page 1 and work diligently through to the end. Feel free to jump around and complete the exercises that are important to you and your challenges with ADHD.

Never Forget that 'You Are More Than Your ADHD'

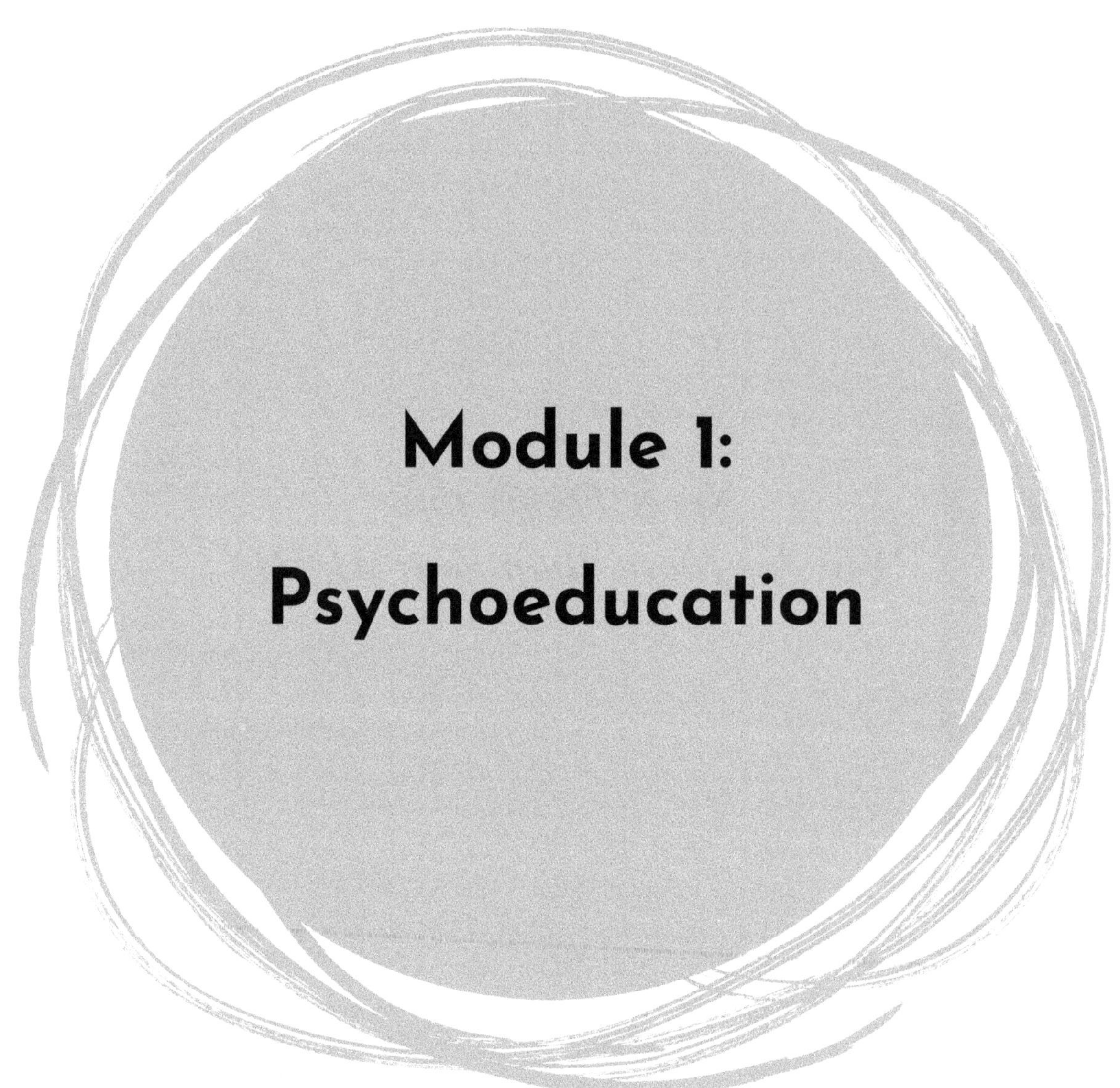

Module 1:

Psychoeducation

Topic 1: What is ADHD?

Affecting approximately 7% of children and about 2.5% of adults, ADHD is characterised by a pattern of inattention, hyperactivity, restlessness and impulsivity. Prevalent and long-lasting but treatable, ADHD is a neurodevelopmental (brain based) disorder with strong genetic factors. Studies suggest that the genetic contribution of ADHD ranges from 60–90%. This means that if you have ADHD, there is probably someone in your family who has it too.

Brain imaging has shown that individuals with ADHD have less dopamine available in the brain's reward networks. Because of this, they do not get the same level of satisfaction from doing ordinary tasks. This is felt as boredom, and it depletes a person's motivation to persevere or even get started.

Although many questions remain unanswered, what we know is that:

- a child with ADHD is four times more likely to have a relative with ADHD
- we do not know the exact causes of the disorder
- there is no cure for ADHD
- treatment manages symptoms and is an ongoing process
- treatment should be multimodal: a combination of treatments that may or may not include medication
- parents should be active in a child's treatment
- ADHD affects Executive Functioning (EF) development
- ADHD affects Emotional Dysregulation (ED) and anger
- ADHD affects motivation
- ADHD seldom exists in isolation.

What Lies Beneath ADHD?

For a person diagnosed with ADHD, they must meet certain criteria. These criteria are described in two manuals: *The Diagnostic and Statistical Manual of Mental Disorders, Fifth Edition* (DSM-5) and *International Statistical Classification of Diseases and Related Health Problems* (ICD). To meet the diagnostic criteria, problem behaviours need to:

- occur in more than one setting
- cause impairment in major life activities, and
- start before the age of 12.

The DSM-5 criteria for ADHD can be found in **Appendix A.**

Although the diagnostic criteria doesn't include difficulty regulating emotions, clinicians have a growing interest in this, as it is commonly found in ADHD.

Since ADHD seldom exists in isolation, clinicians need to evaluate for additional co-morbid conditions, such as anxiety, depression, learning disorders and oppositional defiant disorder. These will guide treatment options.

Medication is currently the first line of treatment for ADHD, and the most extensively studied. Stimulant medication has been used effectively in the treatment of ADHD for many years and can reduce the core symptoms of ADHD: inattention, hyperactivity, and impulsivity. However, there is ongoing debate about this treatment, and it does not work for everyone. In addition, medications do not provide individuals with practical skills for long-term management of their ADHD. Disruptions to overall quality of life, such as underachievement at school, poor peer relationships, conflict at home and relationship difficulties, all call for treatment that is multimodal in nature.

ADHD is not a simple behavioural disorder. It is a complex condition affecting the brain's management system. This system, called Executive Functions, operates below the surface in every aspect of our lives. ADHD delays the development of Executive Functions skills. What others see is but a fraction of the issue. Like an iceberg, where 90% of its mass sits under the water, many facets of ADHD lie under the surface. The 10% that we see, the core symptoms of inattention, impulsivity, and hyperactivity, are important, but do not explain the whole picture.

Exercise: What Does Your ADHD Iceberg Look Like?

Circle the symptoms/issues that are true for you. Add any other symptoms that you experience that are not listed. If you would rather fill in your own iceberg, a blank one is provided on the next page.

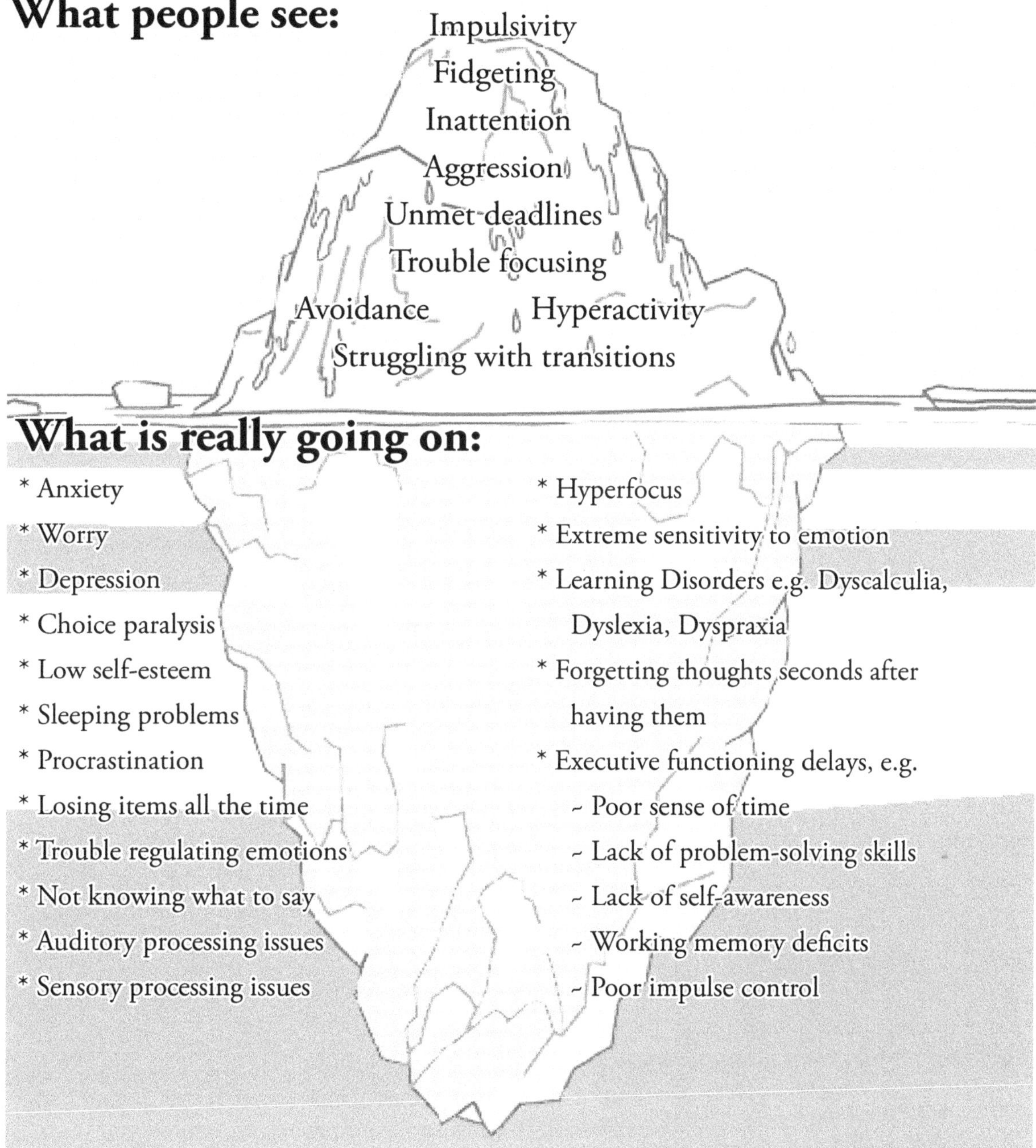

Adapted from chrisdendy.com

Exercise: ADHD Iceberg

Use this blank iceberg to identify your own visible symptoms, and the hidden layers that lie beneath the surface. Refer to the list on the previous page for guidance and ideas.

Personal ADHD Checklist

Below is a list of typical things that individuals with ADHD report. Go through the list and check the ones that apply to you.

Home

- ☐ My room is a mess.
- ☐ I find it difficult to follow the rules.
- ☐ I forget to do things my parents tell me to do.
- ☐ It's hard to start my homework.
- ☐ I often interrupt family members.
- ☐ I have trouble getting ready for school on time.
- ☐ I get easily distracted.
- ☐ I get angry if I cannot have screen time.

Friends

- ☐ A lot of my friends are younger than me.
- ☐ I don't think I am as smart as other children.
- ☐ I get into fights or become upset with my friends easily.
- ☐ It's hard to make friends/sometimes other children don't want to be friends with me.
- ☐ I don't get invited to birthdays or get-togethers.
- ☐ I am mean to my classmates.
- ☐ I am bossy in play.

School

- ☐ I can't find my homework to turn in at school.
- ☐ I always want to finish my work as fast as I can, and I end up making a lot of mistakes.
- ☐ I'm often told to calm down or slow down by my teachers.
- ☐ I blurt things out in the middle of class.
- ☐ I have trouble paying attention during class.

Add up the checks in each section. **HOME** _____ **FRIENDS** _____ **SCHOOL** _____

The section with the most checks may be the area that needs the most attention. Identify a goal in this area that you would like to work on.

My goal is: ____

____

Exercise: How Happy Are You?

Rate your level of satisfaction in the different areas of your life, where 0 means always very unhappy and 10 means always very happy, then join the dots.

0
2
4
6
8
10
Always very unhappy
Fairly happy
Always very happy

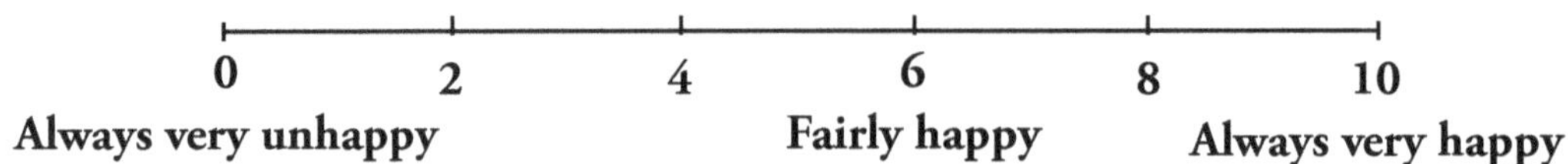

How happy are you with how you...

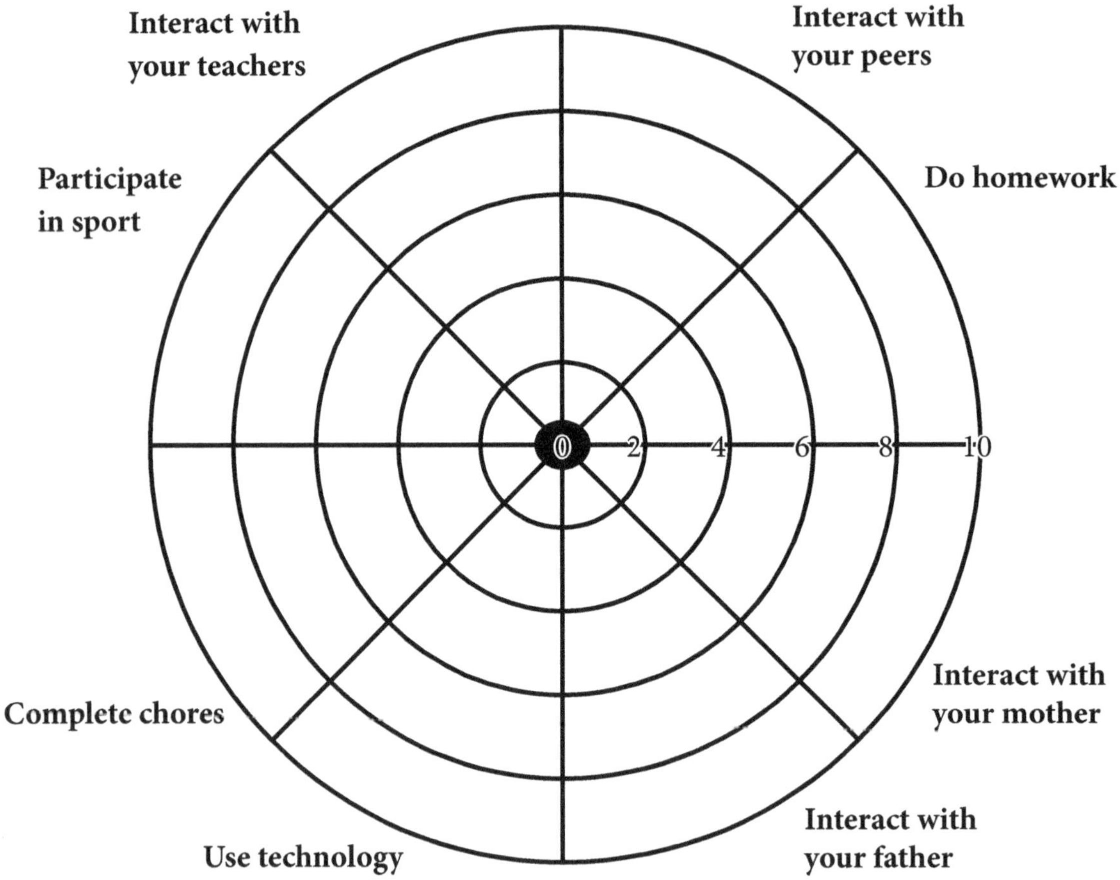

Interact with your teachers
Interact with your peers
Participate in sport
Do homework
0
2
4
6
8
10
Complete chores
Interact with your mother
Use technology
Interact with your father

In which areas of your life would you like to make changes?

____

What can you start doing today to bring about change?

____

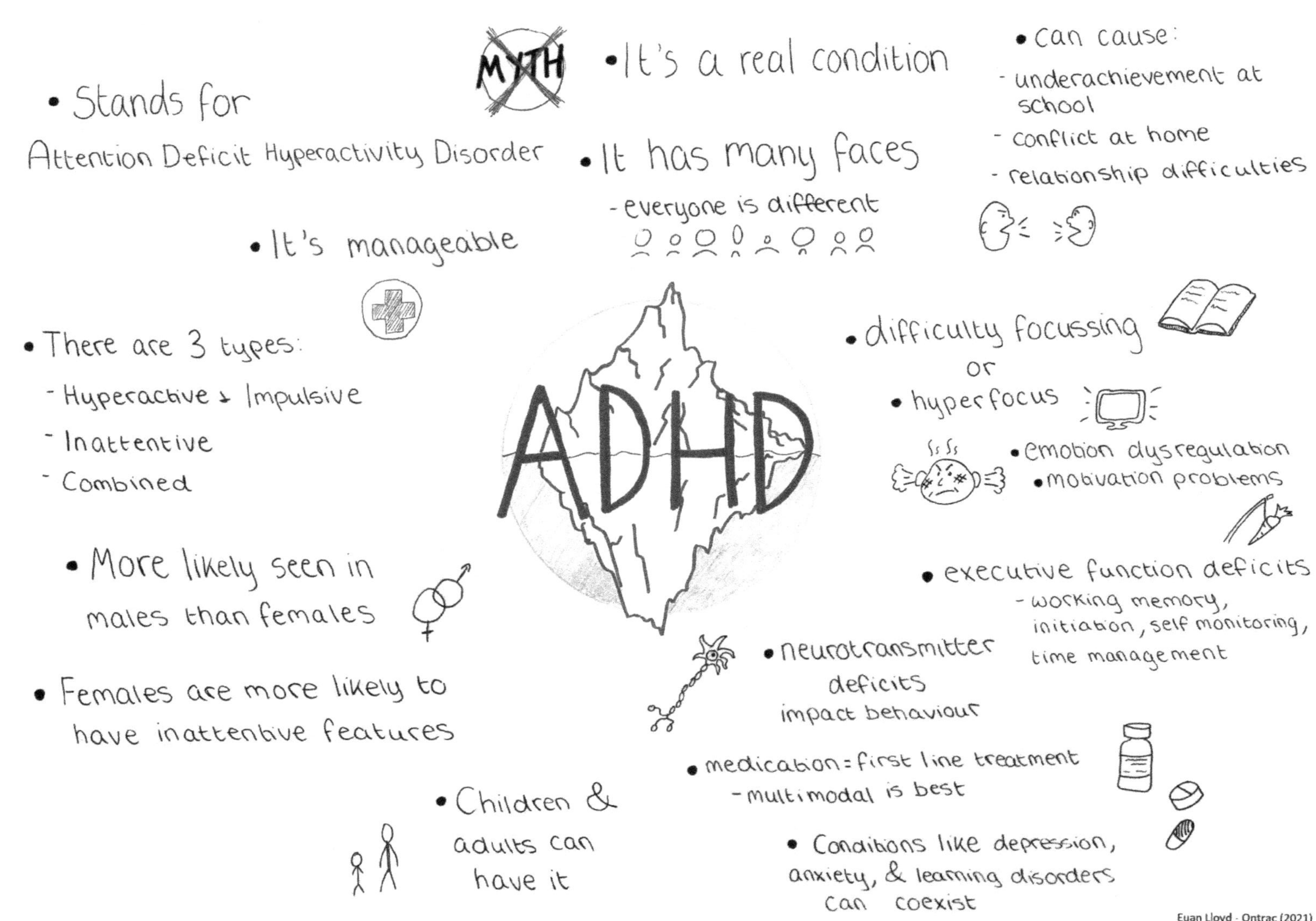
ADHD
MYTH
• Stands for
Attention Deficit Hyperactivity Disorder
• It's a real condition
• It has many faces
- everyone is different
• It's manageable
• There are 3 types:
- Hyperactive & Impulsive
- Inattentive
- Combined
• More likely seen in males than females
• Females are more likely to have inattentive features
• Children & adults can have it
• can cause:
- underachievement at school
- conflict at home
- relationship difficulties
• difficulty focussing
or
• hyperfocus
• emotion dysregulation
• motivation problems
• executive function deficits
- working memory, initiation, self monitoring, time management
• neurotransmitter deficits impact behaviour
• medication = first line treatment
- multimodal is best
• Conditions like depression, anxiety, & learning disorders can coexist
Euan Lloyd - Ontrac (2021)

Did You Know? Having ADHD means that you learn and pay attention differently. Your teachers and parents may comment that you struggle to focus on schoolwork, and that you often daydream and struggle to 'get on task'. Others may say that you can't slow down, and that you are disruptive. Your own emotions may also vary. ADHD can cause strong feelings inside you: anger, frustration, feeling overwhelmed and misunderstood. It can affect your sleep and how you feel about yourself. One thing is clear: although being a child with ADHD is challenging, the key is to be willing to learn as much as you can about what your biggest struggles are, so that interventions can target those struggles and help you manage them better.

What led to your diagnosis of ADHD?

____

____

____

How do you feel about your diagnosis?

____

____

____

What was the best and the worst thing about your diagnosis?

____

____

____

Many myths exist about ADHD, and people will have their own opinions about this condition. What do you think about the following statements?

1) ADHD is simply a label for behavioural problems; children with ADHD just refuse to sit still and are unwilling to listen to teachers or parents.

____

____

____

2) ADHD is just a lack of willpower. Children with ADHD focus well on things that interest them; they could focus on any other tasks if they really wanted to.

____

____

____

Do you think that comments like the ones above stop people from disclosing their ADHD and seeking help? Give reasons for your answer.

____

____

____

Important Points to Remember about ADHD

ADHD is not:

- a learned behaviour
- a discipline problem
- a spoiled child
- a temper tantrum
- 'the easy way out'
- a willpower issue
- an inability to willingly control oneself

ADHD is a:

- medical condition
- chemical imbalance
- war between brain and body
- struggle to fit in
- struggle to develop relationships
- battle to maintain self-esteem and self confidence
- big deal to those who suffer with it

ADHD Is a Real Condition!

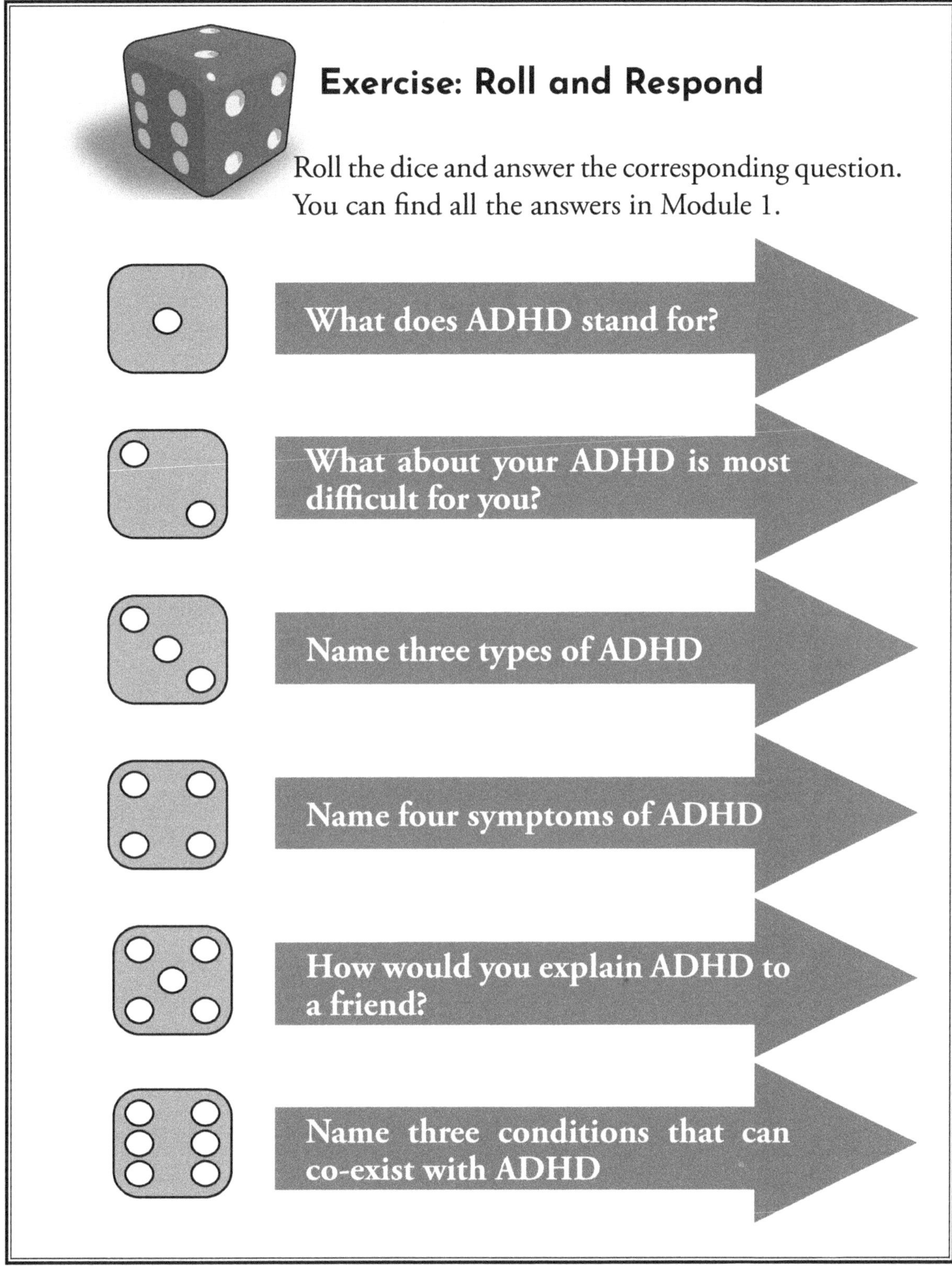
Exercise: Roll and Respond
Roll the dice and answer the corresponding question. You can find all the answers in Module 1.
What does ADHD stand for?
What about your ADHD is most difficult for you?
Name three types of ADHD
Name four symptoms of ADHD
How would you explain ADHD to a friend?
Name three conditions that can co-exist with ADHD

Topic 2: Executive Functions

Did You Know? Executive functions (EFs) are a group of cognitive processes and mental skills that help coordinate almost every activity in our daily life. EFs are the brain processes that make us human, and are some of the last brain systems to develop, only fully maturing around age 30.

To succeed in school, at work and in life itself, your EFs need to be developed and working well. You need to be able to reason, creatively problem-solve, think before you speak or act, stay focused and concentrate, exercise self-control and resist temptations, and exercise the flexibility to see things from different perspectives and adapt to change. The good news is that EFs can be improved at any age. In dealing with your EF skills delays, first identify where your gaps lie. Once the gaps are identified you can choose from the many activities available to help you manage and strengthen your skills in those areas.

Stress, even mild, seriously impairs EFs. Mindfulness practices that involve movement, such as judo, tai chi and taekwondo, are helpful to improve EFs.

Most activities will improve EFs if they challenge you and you enjoy the activity enough to keep working at it. A supportive mentor who believes in you is critical to the success of any program in improving EFs.

EFs are managed in the prefrontal cortex of the brain, as shown in the diagram.

Executive Functioning Challenges

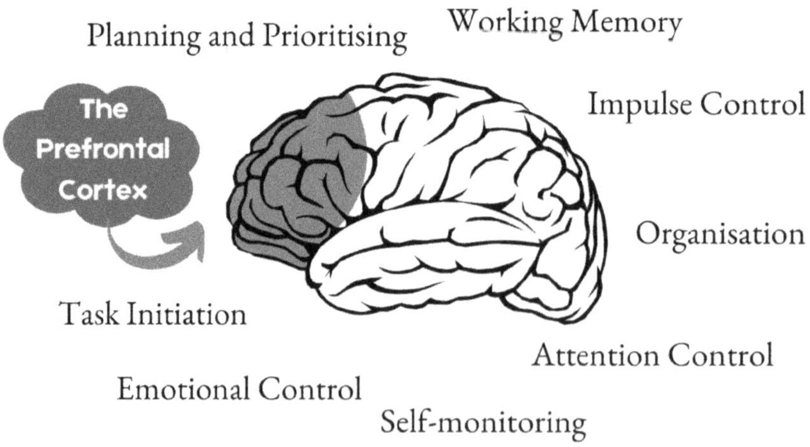

Executive Functions Checklist

If you have EFs delays, you may struggle with some or all of the following.

Tick the ones that apply to you.

	Skill	What it means	How it may look
	Impulse Control	Helps you think before you act	Blurting out inappropriate things or engaging in risky behaviour
	Emotional Control	Helps you keep your feelings in check	Overreacting; having trouble dealing with criticism and regrouping when something goes wrong
	Flexible Thinking	Allows you to adjust to the unexpected/change	Not being able to 'roll with the punches' or getting frustrated if asked to think about something from different angles; also known as taking perspective
	Working Memory	Helps you keep information in mind while manipulating it	Having trouble remembering directions and instructions
	Self-Monitoring	Helps you have self-awareness and evaluate how you are doing	Being surprised by a bad grade or negative feedback
	Planning and Prioritisation	Helps you work consistently towards achieving your goals and planning to meet them	Not knowing which parts of a project are most important and where to start
	Task Initiation	Helps you take action and get started	Freezing up/procrastinating because you have no idea where to start
	Time Management	Accurately estimate how long a task will take; the ability to use time efficiently	Under/overestimating how long a task will take; getting side-tracked and struggling to sit still or pay attention; a struggle to estimate time e.g. 'How long is 20 minutes really?' or 'How much can be done in 20 minutes?'
	Organisation	Skills that help you keep track of things physically and mentally	Losing your belongings, homework or even a train of thought

	Attention	Staying focused on a task or person for a period of time and shifting that attention when needed	Struggling to give enough attention to a task or forgetting what you were supposed to be doing
	Persistence	Sticking with a boring/ challenging task from start to finish	Struggling to complete tasks that are boring or challenging

Of the weaknesses that you identified with in the table above, which two or three cause you the most problems?

____

____

What struggles do these weaknesses cause for you?

____

____

Scenario

JP has ADHD. He is super friendly, kind, polite and considerate. He always says 'please' and 'thank you'. He does his chores at home, and at school he always picks up rubbish in the playground and throws it in the bin. He knows that litter is no good for the environment.

Unfortunately, because of his ADHD, JP has problems completing assignments and, at times, he is impulsive and speaks out of turn at home and in class. Sometimes JP gets mad and can't express what he's feeling and what's bothering him.

His father can relate to JP because he has ADHD too and often says, 'It does not help when you just sulk around, mate. Trust me, I know.'

JP's mother found him a mentor, an older cousin, and slowly JP's ability to name his emotions increased, and he became better at expressing his feelings.

Everyone is patient with JP because he is a nice person.

Use the EFs checklist to help JP identify his EFs skills deficits. Write them below:

____

____

Identifying the Gaps

The following steps will help you identify and manage EFs skills deficits.

Ask 'Which EFs are challenging for me? Where do my gaps lie?'

Brainstorm the solutions you would like to try

Choose the best solution

Do it!

Evaluate

The most important step in this process is to identify and accept that you have an EFs problem, and to be specific about where the weaknesses are. Once the exact problem is identified, you can brainstorm the various options, choose the most suitable solution and take on the responsibility to do it.

Ways to Improve EF in Different Settings

Impulse Control

School. Activities that give immediate rewards can be more appealing than schoolwork. Finding ways to give yourself small, regular, immediate rewards can help to stay on task.

Home. Make sure your parents understand your struggles with impulsive behaviour. Negotiate a rewards program that aims to fix one behaviour at a time.

Social. Count the number of times you interrupt a conversation – set a goal to not go over a certain number of times. Ask a close and non-judgmental friend to help you identify when you are being impulsive.

Emotional Control

School. Allow yourself to have breaks and opportunities to disengage from stressful tasks to stop things becoming too frustrating.

Home. If you are getting worked up in an argument, remove yourself from it and come back later with a cooler head. This can be difficult at the time, but will pay off later and increase the likelihood of a win-win outcome.

Social. Using 'I' statements to communicate your feelings to your friends means they can fully understand your needs and not feel attacked. For example: 'I feel sad when you don't want to hang out with me because I value your friendship.'

Flexible Thinking

School. Modify your environment – if you're switching from a collaborative project to writing an essay, move to a quiet space to get you 'in the zone' for writing.

Home. Keep a daily plan available – knowing what needs to be done next (e.g. an appointment, sport after school, dinner) will better prepare you to flow into it.

Social. Practice thinking about other people's perspectives. This means understanding their values and interests, as well as what they are currently doing; for example, it might not be a good time to talk to your friend if they are running late for class!

Working Memory

School. Use palm cards to physically arrange information on your desk, rather than entirely in your head. Your teacher may be able to help you break things down into key points.

Home. Remembering lots of information is hard for everyone, and especially so for people with working memory deficits. Use lists when shopping or getting ready to go out.

Social. Use a calendar to keep track of when and where you are hanging out with friends. People will be appreciative when you arrive on time.

Self-monitoring

School. Place checklists on the corner of your desk or inside your pencil case. Make a habit of engaging in self-monitoring whenever you see them.

Home. Ask yourself, 'Am I doing what I am supposed to be doing?' If not, start immediately. You may need to ask yourself this many times before the task is finished, but with time, you will improve and need to use it less and less.

Social. Monitor your speech volume, others' personal space, and whether you are dominating the conversation. Working on one of these at a time is easier than trying all at once.

Planning and Prioritisation

School. When you first receive an assignment or project, immediately identify the main parts that need to be done (e.g. researching), as well as the smaller parts (e.g. fixing the font/titles). Prioritise the main parts.

Home. Planning is something that becomes a habit but can be really tough the first time. Use a diary with hours/minutes already printed to help with this transition.

Social. Maintaining a balance between social activities, solitary activities (e.g. watching TV), homework and chores comes with good prioritising. If seeing friends is getting in the way of homework, maybe they are prioritised too highly.

Task Initiation

School. Doing a stimulating activity before beginning a task can scratch your brain's itch for excitement, making it easier to focus. Talk with your teacher to find a short activity you enjoy that won't distract others in the class.

Home. Everyone procrastinates for different reasons. Identifying **why** you procrastinate allows you to address that problem and begin working on that task.

Social. If you have trouble starting conversations, try practicing with your best friend or someone who you think is friendly. When you feel comfortable, try with someone else.

Time Management

School. Having a watch that beeps at certain times can help you keep track of time (and how much of it you have spent on one activity).

Home. Simply put a post-it-note on your bathroom mirror with the time you need to leave for school written on it. This serves to visualise the time and acts as a reminder.

Social. When putting appointments into your schedule, include travel time on either side when deciding how long it will take.

Organisation

School. Having a single notebook with a section for each subject means that you only need to remember one notebook each day.

Home. Create a 'launch pad' at home. This can be an area in your room or by the front door where you keep everything that you need to take to school each day.

Social. Sometimes we have so many things to say to someone, we can't even remember them all. Try to remain mentally organised during a conversation, but also accept that it is okay to forget things and that there will always be another opportunity to ask something.

Attention

School. Ask if you can sit in a seat with less distractions. This might be at the front or away from a window.

Home. Time how long your attention normally lasts before you get distracted. Now set a timer when you are doing homework and take a five-minute break when your 'attention timer' goes off.

Social. Meditating and practicing mindfulness at home before social outings can increase your attention and focus when you go out.

Persistence

School. Set a goal and check your progress towards it. Seeing that you are making progress creates motivation.

Home. Have a system of small, immediate rewards for boring tasks.

Social. Positive self-talk can defeat unhelpful thinking styles. For example, tell yourself that it isn't the end of the world if you think someone doesn't like you.

Which of the above strategies have you tried?

____

Did they work?

____

Which one/s could you try next?

____

____

Accommodations

Here are some examples of modifications that you can ask for at your school and use at home to help compensate for any EFs deficits. Talk to your teacher and parents to see which accommodations you are entitled to. Check the ones that you think could be helpful to you.

General Accommodations	
☐ Additional time for assignments	☐ Computerised spell-check support
☐ Review sessions	☐ Reworded questions in simpler language
☐ Have student restate information	☐ Projects instead of written reports
☐ Space for movement or breaks	☐ Modified time demands
☐ Study sheets and teacher outlines	☐ Pass/no pass option
☐ Alteration of the classroom arrangement	☐ Modified grades based on independent education plan
☐ Hands-on activities	☐ Highlight important words/phrases
☐ Immediate feedback	☐ Work-in-progress check

Testing and Assessment Accommodations	Behaviour Modifications
☐ Additional time	☐ Breaks between tasks
☐ Untimed tests	☐ Daily feedback to student
☐ Oral instead of written projects	☐ Have contingency plans
☐ Read test and directions to student	☐ Use de-escalating strategies
☐ Provide study guides prior to tests	☐ Use positive reinforcement
☐ Highlight key directions	☐ Use peer supports and mentoring
☐ Test in alternative site	☐ Model expected behaviour by adults
☐ Use of calculator or word processor	☐ Have parent sign homework
☐ Pace long-term projects	☐ Set and post class rules

Other Ways to Manage Your EFs

Many children with EFs challenges thrive on out-of-the-box interests. Find different activities to pursue and keep all options open for consideration.

Sports and games like tag or laser tag require you to monitor yourself and others all at once. Yoga and meditation encourage mindfulness and are especially helpful for impulse and emotional control.

Music demands attention as well as a good working memory.

Theatre and dance engage working memory and impulse control as you have to remember lines or dance routines and stay in character the entire time.

Card games heavily use working memory and flexible thinking. Games with complex decisions, such as chess, poker, Sudoku and Rubik's cubes, also rely on many EFs.

Computer games that involve keeping track of a large, open world require not only working memory but also organisation and planning. Fast-paced games require good impulse control. However, these games alone will not give you good EFs skills and should be played as part of a balanced lifestyle.

Your parents may initially serve as your external 'frontal lobe' – providing the scaffolding you need to be successful. However, the objective should be for you to learn and internalise the skills to become an independent learner with the full range of EFs.

You might see your parents as nagging or controlling, but as you improve your EFs skills they will invariably step back and give you more control. Accepting the challenge and addressing your problems often leads to an increase in responsibility and self-advocacy. This empowerment, in turn, leads to increased self-esteem and confidence.

Share this information about your EFs gaps with your parents and teachers so they will be better equipped to help you. However, it is a two-way street, which means you need to prove to them that you are making an effort to change. It all starts with asking for help and then persevering.

Word Finder: Executive Functioning

EFs are the cognitive abilities that control and regulate most of what we do in day-to-day life. EFs include the ability to initiate, plan and organise, solve problems, regulate emotions and monitor behaviour. The terms below are additional functions of our EF system. Find them in the word finder and colour them in.

D	G	F	G	O	E	W	S	Y	F	X	Y	H	Z	P
I	N	F	M	N	V	M	L	L	X	I	P	P	R	W
S	I	L	H	G	I	O	I	Q	Y	G	U	O	F	O
O	N	O	D	B	S	N	X	T	M	N	C	G	S	L
R	O	K	V	I	E	N	E	P	C	R	N	N	J	S
G	I	U	N	D	E	R	S	T	A	N	D	I	N	G
A	T	G	I	G	X	O	U	S	S	W	T	W	E	Q
N	I	H	Q	M	I	A	T	Q	N	I	I	O	S	K
I	S	R	V	B	L	I	I	B	P	J	L	L	T	D
S	N	P	E	I	N	Y	S	S	E	M	K	L	A	U
E	A	T	T	A	X	Y	E	P	I	W	D	O	R	X
D	R	Y	T	P	L	A	N	N	I	N	G	F	T	C
Y	T	I	L	I	B	I	T	C	A	R	T	S	I	D
S	O	D	L	U	F	T	E	G	R	O	F	I	N	Z
N	Y	K	D	A	T	L	X	F	U	O	T	D	G	W

Disorganised
Distractibility
Following
Forgetful
Listening

Losing
Messy
Planning
Procrastination
Punctuality

Slow
Starting
Time
Transitioning
Understanding

*See **Appendix B** for the answer key.*

Topic 3: ADHD and Emotions

See a child differently, you see a different child.
~Dr Stuart Shanter

Did You Know? Individuals with ADHD experience emotions differently to others. They often report experiencing:

- fast-building, high-intensity and short-lived emotions
- difficulties recognising emotions in themselves and others
- extremes of empathising completely with others or reacting with a lack of empathy to others
- experiencing many more emotions simultaneously than a typical person might.

Experiencing multiple – often contradictory – emotions at the same time can be difficult to understand. For example, it is not uncommon for someone with ADHD to say they feel excited, happy, frustrated and nervous all at once, where a neurotypical person is likely to only be experiencing one or two emotions.

Children with ADHD can also be more prone to 'meltdowns' than others, when extreme emotional build up causes them to act out, often crying, laughing, yelling and moving all at once, driven by difficult emotions they struggle to understand or regulate.

Emotional Dysregulation (ED)

ED refers to difficulty managing emotional responses, such as sadness, anger, irritability and frustration. In general, ED involves having emotions that are overly intense in comparison to the situation that triggered them. It might mean that you feel confused and guilty about your emotions or are overwhelmed to the point that you can't make decisions or manage your behaviour. This might look like temper tantrums, outbursts, crying, yelling, swearing and even physical abuse. The degree and severity of these behaviours can differ significantly from person to person.

History Stuff: Is Emotional Dysregulation Part of ADHD?

Emotional dysregulation used to be considered a core part of ADHD and was included in many descriptions of ADHD over the decades, such as 'mental restlessness', 'hyperactive child syndrome' and 'hyperkinetic impulse disorder', before the term ADHD was adopted. In all of these early conceptualisations, ED was considered a key part of ADHD and physicians sought to treat patients and mediate the impact that ED had on someone's life.

Measuring ED was more challenging and, as such, it was phased out of medical descriptions of ADHD. Recently there has been debate whether to include ED as a core symptom of ADHD alongside inattention, hyperactivity and impulsivity.

Current Knowledge about ED and ADHD

ED is increasingly recognised as a core feature of ADHD. Studies show that up to 70-80% of children with ADHD struggle with ED. Inappropriate responses may be both internalised (e.g. the individual may be withdrawn, moody or sad) or externalised (e.g. they may be emotionally volatile, aggressive and combative). Early life emotional regulation is managed largely extrinsically (e.g. parents organising their child's daily routine), but as children grow older, they need to develop their own regulatory processes.

According to Barkley (2015), ED is a core symptom of ADHD and refers to deficiencies in areas including the ability to:

- stop inappropriate behaviour triggered by strong emotions. This is illustrated by low frustration tolerance, impatience, being quick to anger, aggression, greater emotional excitability – all of which are related to the impulsivity dimension of ADHD
- self soothe and down-regulate a strong emotion
- refocus attention from exciting or upsetting events.

ED consistently predicts:

- social rejection in children with ADHD
- greater parenting stress and family conflict in parents of children with ADHD; greater stress in parents with ADHD

- impulse buying; poor finances
- interpersonal hostility in adults with ADHD
- job dismissals and workplace interpersonal problems
- relationship conflict
- road rage, drink driving and crash risks.

How ADHD Amplifies Emotions

Emotions try to get your attention – if you don't listen, they will keep trying! However, if you recognise and name the emotion that you are feeling, the intensity of the emotion actually reduces by itself.

Understanding why you feel the way you do is an important step to taking back control of your emotions. Let's look at an example:

John is sitting quietly, listening to the teacher. The teacher hears whispering in the class. She turns to John and Anna, who is sitting next to John, and says, 'Sit quietly, or I will send you to the office!'

Neither John nor Anna were whispering. Anna does not respond to the teacher. John, however, says sarcastically to the teacher, 'I wasn't the one talking!'.

The teacher reprimands John yet again, this time for being disrespectful. This results in John being further agitated and accusing the teacher of always picking on him. 'You should be sure about what you're saying before you falsely accuse people!' The escalation continues until John gets sent to the principal's office and is in serious trouble.

John felt extremely angry and frustrated in response to what he saw as unfair treatment. This, combined with the inability to self-regulate and think about the long-term consequences of his behaviour, led to his reaction.

In addition to difficulties with managing negative emotions, some children with ADHD also experience difficulties with managing positive emotions.

For example, a 14-year-old boy with ADHD might respond to an announcement of a fun group activity by spontaneously jumping up from his chair and sitting back down repeatedly, clapping and raising his voice with excitement. His peers will likely perceive him as childish, immature and odd. Repeated instances of this type of behaviour may lead to social rejection.

Studies suggest that children with ADHD are prone to excessive displays of both negative and positive emotions. These include descriptions of children being emotionally immature, overly boisterous, rowdy and having low tolerance for anger and frustration. This is thought to impact an individual with ADHD's well-being and self-esteem far more that the core symptoms associated with ADHD (hyperactivity, impulsivity and inattention).

Managing Amplified/Intense Emotional Episodes

Did You Know? Most children with ADHD experience intense emotional episodes. One minute they feel fine, but then it's as if a storm hits. They might become frustrated, angry, overwhelmed, or want to hurt themselves or someone else. They may not understand why this happens or be able to predict when these outbursts will occur. It might seem like little things trigger the episodes. They feel as if their life is a 24/7 emotional roller coaster. Is this you? If so, keep reading.

Think of emotional regulation as a backpack of emotions. We all have an emotional backpack, but not every backpack is the same size or shape. You may have a big backpack with many pockets for all the emotions that you experience, or you may have a small backpack with limited space for emotions. Stressors throughout the day add different emotions to our backpack. If we have well-developed emotional regulation skills, we are better able to prevent running out of space in our backpack. On the other hand, if we have underdeveloped emotional regulation, our backpack may run out of space because we don't have the skills to hold everything together.

Both under-regulation and over-regulation can have negative consequences. With over-regulation, you may withdraw, avoid, become easily upset or shut down. With under-regulation you may have trouble containing intense emotions.

How big is your backpack?

____

____

How many pockets does it have and are they all the same size?

____

____

____

How heavy is it?

____

____

____

What is the heaviest thing in your backpack?

____

____

____

Who do you give permission to put stuff in your backpack?

____

____

____

Who can help you to re-pack/arrange your backpack?

____

____

Ways to Deal with Emotional Storms

- **Identify warning signs.** When are you most vulnerable? For example, when you are arguing with your parents, hungry, tired, lonely or experiencing difficulties at school.
- **Notice triggers.** Pay attention to events or things that trigger/set off an episode. Identifying patterns is helpful to deal with episodes before they happen or get out of control; for example, certain topics might upset you.
- **Preventative actions.** There are things you can do to protect yourself. For example, you might choose to avoid certain people or places when you know you are vulnerable to an episode. You might take extra time to take care of yourself by getting more rest, exercising or distracting yourself by watching a movie.

On the table below keep track of your intense emotional episodes. Write down the date, the situation, what triggered or set you off and your warning signs and triggers. Describe what you did to manage the episode, and then reflect and write down what you might do differently next time.

Date	Situation that set off the episode	Warning signs or triggers	How did you manage the episode?	What can you do differently next time?

Now that you know more about your emotional episodes, follow the action plan below to start managing your emotions and improve your quality of life.

What do you need to stop doing?

____

____

____

What do you need to do less of?

____

____

____

What do you need to start doing?

____

____

____

What do you need to do more of?

____

____

____

Who can help you follow through with your plan?

____

____

____

Treatment Considerations

Treatment for ADHD has been focused mostly on regulating the core symptoms. Only recently has research looked at ways to manage other issues, including ED. For some people, ADHD medication alone works to both control symptoms and help with the management of responsibilities. Most people, however, will need a combination of treatments to get the best effect. It has often been said that 'pills don't teach skills'. Medication combined with other treatments, such as cognative behavioural therapy (CBT), helps with the wide-ranging effects of ADHD. CBT seems to pick up where the medication leaves off, helping to manage those symptoms still present when medication has done all it can.

Similarly, parent behavioural training programs focus on teaching parents what it means when children behave the way they do, and how to develop parenting solutions that make sense for their family. This can help avoid power struggles and conflict escalation. Parental ADHD, especially if undiagnosed and untreated, can lead to poor emotional control and engaging in emotionally provocative behaviour.

Childhood is an important time for developing an understanding of emotions, and behaviour-based treatments like CBT can help. We are not born knowing how to manage our emotions; this means that we have to learn. We learn from all kinds of experiences and people, including parents, friends, teachers and society in general.

Emotions are neither good nor bad – feelings just **are**. Just remember, there is a difference between having an emotion and acting on that emotion. When a strong emotion comes, you do not have to act on that feeling, all you have to do is recognise that you are feeling the emotion. You cannot get rid of emotions because they serve important survival functions. Acknowledge and work through it – respond, don't react.

Domains Of Self-Regulation

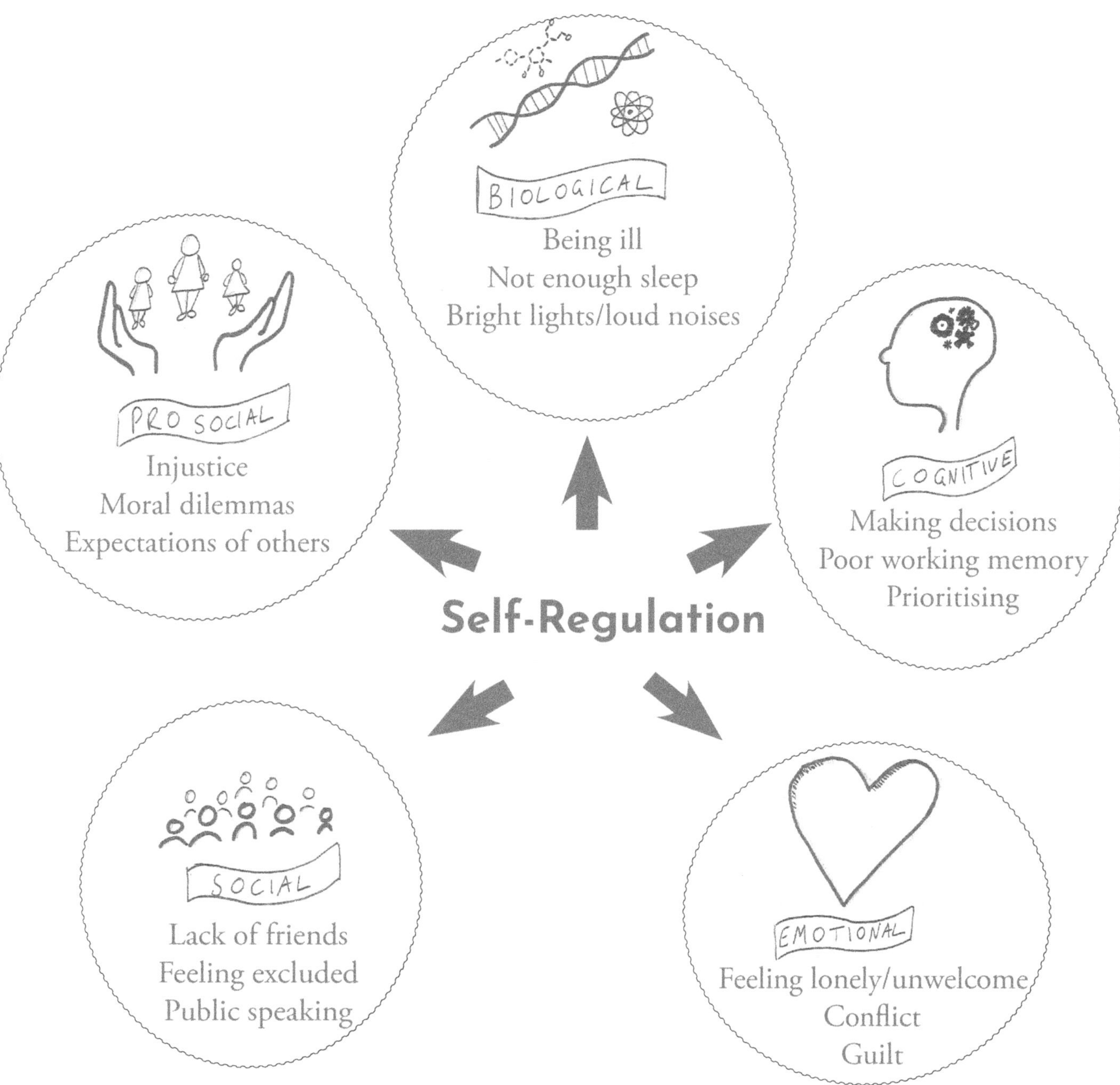

- Each domain has its own stressors
- Each domain interacts with the others
- We need to be 'stress detectives' for all five domains

Managing Anger

> ***The children who need the most love will ask for it in the most unloving of ways.***

Did You Know? Of all the emotions, anger is the one that gets children into most trouble. Suspension, expulsion, exclusion from peer groups, family conflict and, in extreme cases, trouble with the law, are reported.

For many people, anger is used to mask other feelings. Like an iceberg, the anger is only the tip above the water's surface – what people see and judge. Beneath the surface lies what really matters and what needs to be addressed: sadness, helplessness, hurt, guilt, shame, rejection, loneliness, feeling overwhelmed, humiliation, and lack of understanding of self and others. People need to understand what lies beneath their anger in order to cope better with their emotions.

These emotional difficulties only add to the burdens of having ADHD. Learning to manage your anger can help ease these burdens and improve your relationships with parents, friends and teachers.

What do others see you do when you are angry?

____

____

____

____

Have these behaviours become repetitive? In others words, do you engage in the same behaviours every time you become angry?

____

____

____

____

What Does Your Anger Iceberg Look Like?

Think about a time when you felt angry. What other things were you feeling under the surface? Circle the ones that apply to you.

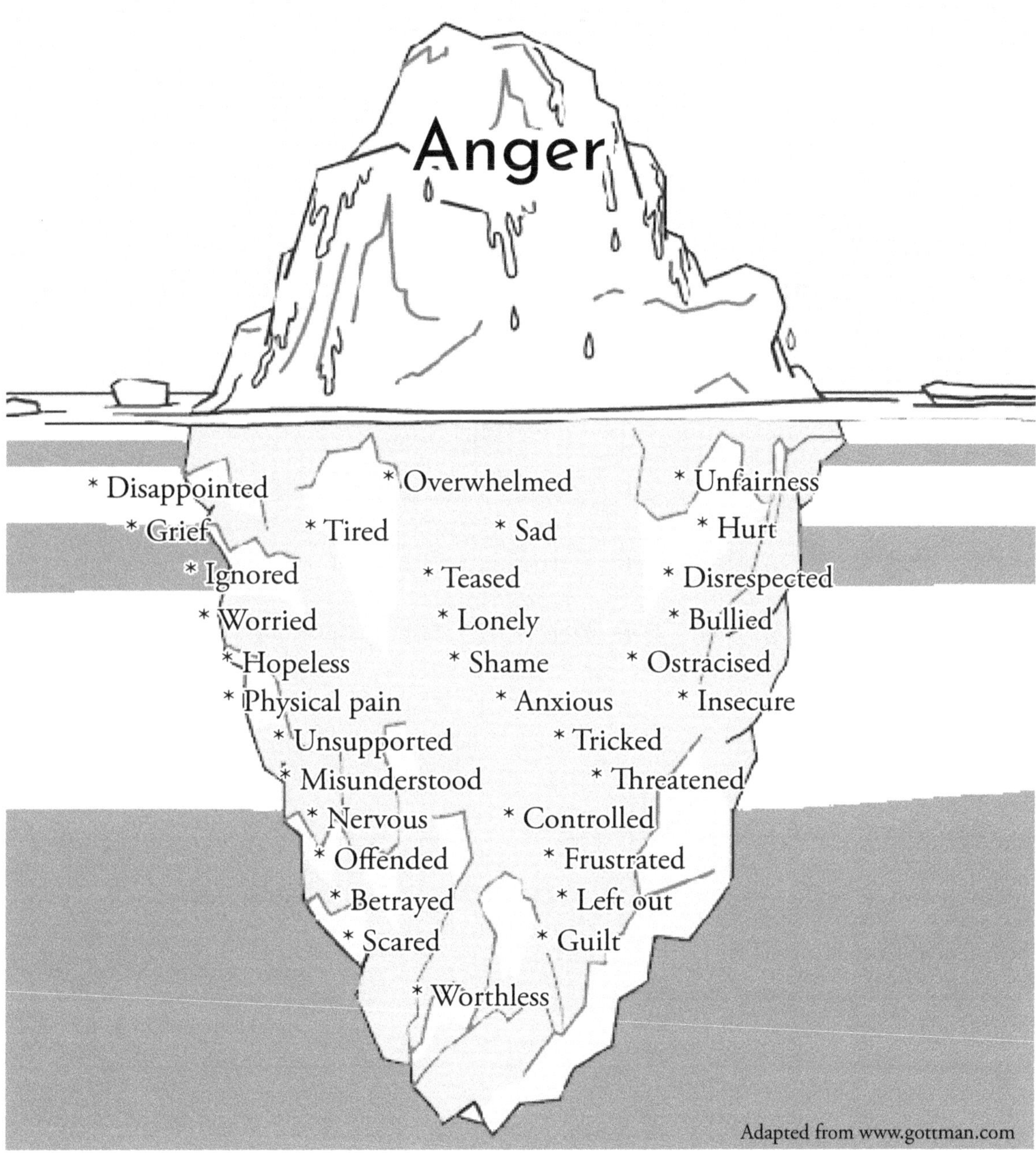

JP got sent to the principal's office for arguing with his English teacher. The principal suspended him for a week because this was not the first time that JP had engaged in this type of behaviour. JP's suspension means that he is going to miss his basketball game. He is clearly angry about the suspension and runs out of the principal's office, slamming the door behind him. This behaviour gets him suspended for an additional two days.

JP is angry. What else might he be feeling?

____

____

Jane's parents are divorced. When she was visiting her dad, he told her that her mum was to blame for their divorce. When Jane returns home, her mum asks her whether she got her homework done. Jane screams at her mum, telling her to leave her alone, goes into her room and locks the door.

Jane is angry. What else might she be feeling?

____

____

Think of a situation where you were angry and got abusive towards another person. Describe the situation and name the feelings that you experienced besides anger.

What happened?

____

____

What did you say and do?

____

____

____

Besides anger, what other feelings did you have?

____

____

Anger is often misdirected, taken out on the people around us, even though it stems from unfair criticisms/events in the past. Is this statement true or false?

Why?

____

____

____

Can you be angry and respectful at the same time? If yes, how?

____

____

____

The Stages of Anger

1.Triggering Event

The situation that starts your anger

2.Negative Thoughts

Irrational thoughts that occur because of the triggering event

3.Emotional Response

Negative emotions that come from negative thoughts

4.Physical Symptoms

Your body automatically responds to anger with things like:

- A racing heart
- Clenched fists
- Sweating
- Shaking

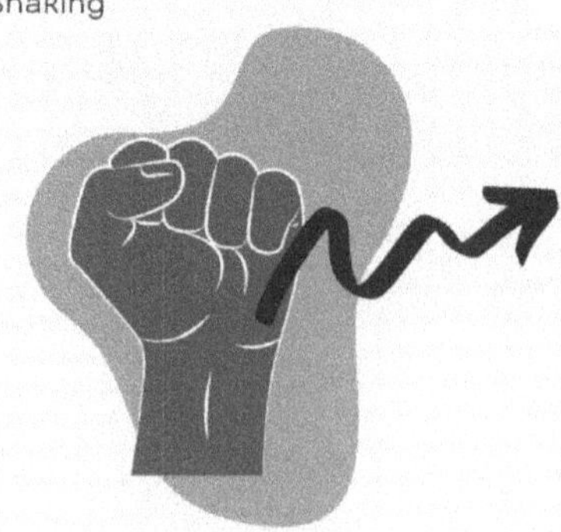

5.Behavioural Response

Reacting based on your thoughts, feelings and physical symptoms by:

- Yelling
- Arguing
- Throwing things
- Fighting

Anger Warning Signs

Did You Know? Anger signs are clues that our body uses to let us know our anger is increasing. These clues start to appear while our anger is still manageable. If we notice them in time, we can hit the brakes, and take control of our anger before we 'flip our lid' and get into trouble. We all have our own anger warning signs. It's important to learn what they are, so we can spot them before our anger gets out of control.

Read the anger warning signs below. Underline any that you have noticed in yourself, and add any others you experience at the bottom.

Common Anger Warning Signs		
My face feels hot	I start to shake	I raise my voice
I go quiet	My eyes get watery	I try to bother people
I want to hit something	I feel annoyed	I can't think straight
I feel like I'm going to explode	I'm boiling over	I want to run away

My Anger Triggers

Exercise: Rank how each item makes you feel from 1–10 using the scale below.

1	2	3	4	5	6	7	8	9	10

Calm Frustrated Angry Very Angry

Home:

__ My parents yell at me
__ I get treated unfairly
__ Someone calls me names
__ I get told 'no'
__ I get ignored
__ I get blamed unfairly
__ I get grounded
__ I lose at a game or activity
__ My parents argue
__ Someone breaks a promise
__ I have to stop playing
__ My siblings touch my things

School

__ I get treated unfairly
__ Someone lies to me
__ I don't understand the instructions
__ Someone tells me what to do
__ I have too much work to do
__ Someone touches my stuff
__ The teacher does not call on me when I put my hand up
__ People talk about me behind my back
__ Someone steals my things
__ I don't get picked for group activities
__ I lose during a game or activity
__ I get called a name I don't like
__ The work is too hard for me
__ I get a bad grade on a test
__ I get into trouble for something I didn't do

Social settings

__ I get excluded from social gatherings
__ I get criticised for my performance
__ I don't perform well in a game
__ Someone talks bad about my family
__ Someone spreads lies about me
__ I lose a game or activity
__ I'm talked about behind my back
__ No one tells me 'good job'
__ No one values my opinion

Which of these three environments have the most triggers for you? What can you start doing today to manage the triggers that you identified?

____

____

____

Exercise: What Makes You Angry?

Circle the things that make you angry.

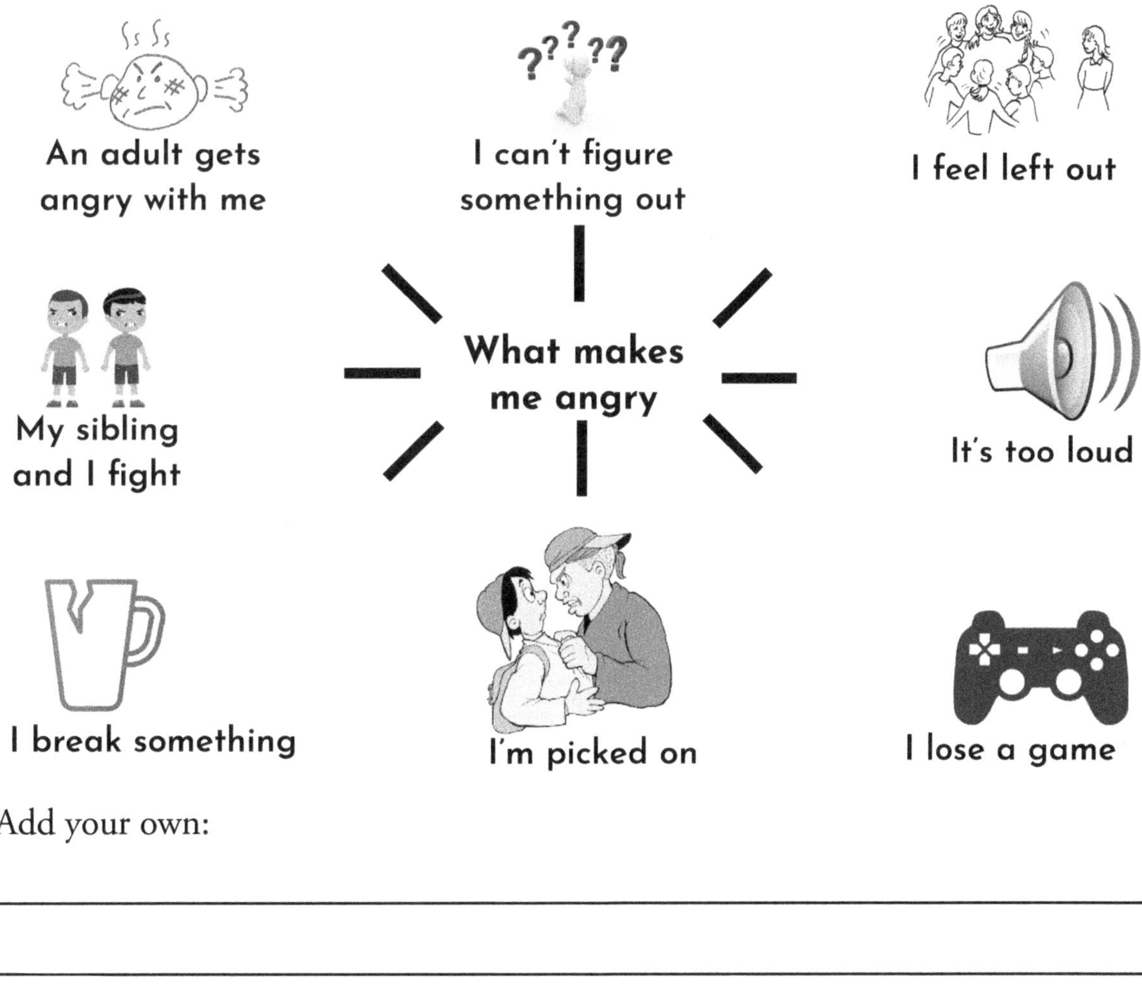

Add your own:

____

____

____

Strategies to Cope with Anger

Firstly, it is important to understand that anger is a human emotion like any other and that we should not deny ourselves the right to be angry. Anger is a natural, valid emotion that responds to threats and injustice, and if expressed in a reasonable way, does not harm others or ourselves. When we communicate anger clearly and allow its motivating force to fan our passion, we can use anger to motivate positive change.

Below is a list of healthy strategies to manage anger. Check the ones that you already use, and circle the ones that you would like to try.

- ☐ Express how you feel, clearly and consistently.
- ☐ Notice your early signs of anger so that you can stop it from escalating. Take time out, at least 30 minutes to calm down.
- ☐ Find healthy outlets and make amends by acknowledging abusive anger and apologising.
- ☐ Take a deep breath in through your nose, hold and breathe out through your mouth as if blowing through a straw.
- ☐ Go for a walk/run in nature.
- ☐ Hug a tree.
- ☐ Name the good things in your life.
- ☐ Colour in or draw.
- ☐ Read a book.
- ☐ Play with your pet/take your dog for a walk.
- ☐ Listen to your choice of music or a motivational podcast.
- ☐ Speak to your parents or an adult you trust.
- ☐ Play board games with your family.
- ☐ Work in the garden.

Add your own:

____

____

Anger Diary

Anger has a way of sneaking up and taking control of our thoughts and behaviours before we realise what is happening. With practice you can get better at monitoring your warning signs before anger takes over. Keeping an anger diary can be helpful.

Instructions: A few hours after you've become calm, or at the end of the day, take a few moments to reflect on when you felt angry or even a bit frustrated. Complete your diary following the example below. Record as many situations as possible.

Example:

Situation: Mum told me off for tracking mud all over the carpet without noticing.

Trigger: Getting told off.

Warning Signs: Before I got angry, I noticed my hands clenching and I became combative.

Anger Response: I called Mum a 'clean freak' and kicked the dustbin out of the way. I couldn't stop thinking how unfair she was, because I hadn't done it on purpose.

Outcome: Mum ended up getting really angry too and I lost my gaming time that day. I felt angry for the way Mum treated me and mad for losing my gaming time. I went to bed feeling angry and sad.

Situation: ____

____

Trigger: ____

____

Warning Signs: ____

____

Anger Response: ____

____

Outcome: ____

Situation: ____

____

Trigger: ____

____

Warning Signs: ____

____

Anger Response: ____

____

Outcome: ____

What patterns are you noticing in relation to how you manage your anger?

____

____

Flipping Your Lid

When we 'flip our lid', the connection between the thinking brain and the limbic system (lizard brain) is interrupted. This is when we do things on impulse or behave in ways that may get us into trouble, such as yelling, hitting, swearing etc.

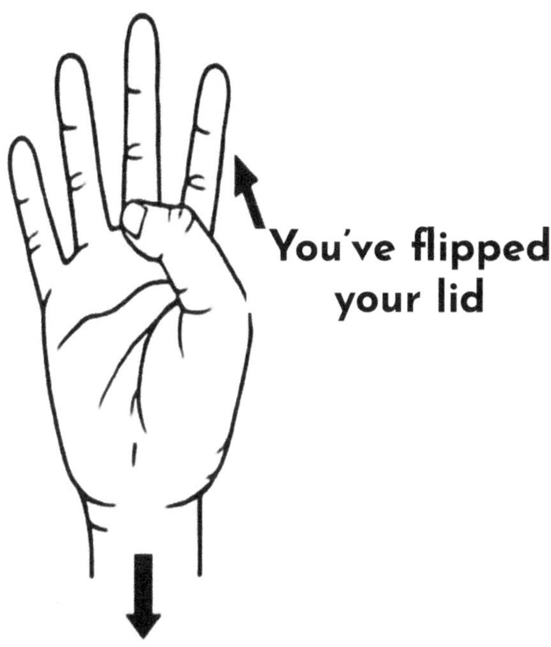

Prefrontal Cortex (thinking brain)

- Language of thought and verbal expression
- Reasoning
- Problem-solving
- Decision-making

Limbic system or Lizard Brain

- Deals with big emotions, like anger, fear and anxiety
- Alarm centre, acts on instinct: fight, flight or freeze

Adapted from Sharon Selby (2015)

For more information on the Fight or Flight reflex, see **Appendix C.**

Scenario

Peter had a friend over and, as usual, his younger brother was a pain! He hung around them and would interrupt their conversations and play. Peter would scream at him to get lost and to stop being a pest. Peter was concerned that his friends would not want to come and play again if his brother kept on being such a nuisance. This made him angry.

Once, Peter threw the footy against the mirror in the hallway and shattered it to pieces. On a number of occasions, he has been punished for 'flipping his lid', like when he called his mother stupid and spat peas on his brother's plate during dinner.

Because Peter's father is a FIFO worker, he is seldom home, and Peter really misses having him around.

One morning when his father was home, Peter's brother was annoying him, and he slammed his bedroom door so hard that the handle fell off. His father knocked, then came in and asked, 'Why are you so mad all the time, mate?'

Peter burst into tears, saying, 'I hate living here. Everyone is against me.'

'No one is against you', his father said, reaching out to give him a hug. Peter pulled away and ran out of his room. Whenever someone spoke to Peter about his attitude or behaviour, he would shut down and blame others for his miserable life.

Do you sometimes flip your lid and become disrespectful? Or have you experienced someone flipping their lid? What was the situation?

____

____

____

Think of a time you were really upset. Did you do something that you later regretted?

____

____

The diagrams below show the difference between showing respect and disrespect in relationships with family members. The respect diagram behaviours acknowledge other people's values and are behaviours we should strive to engage in.

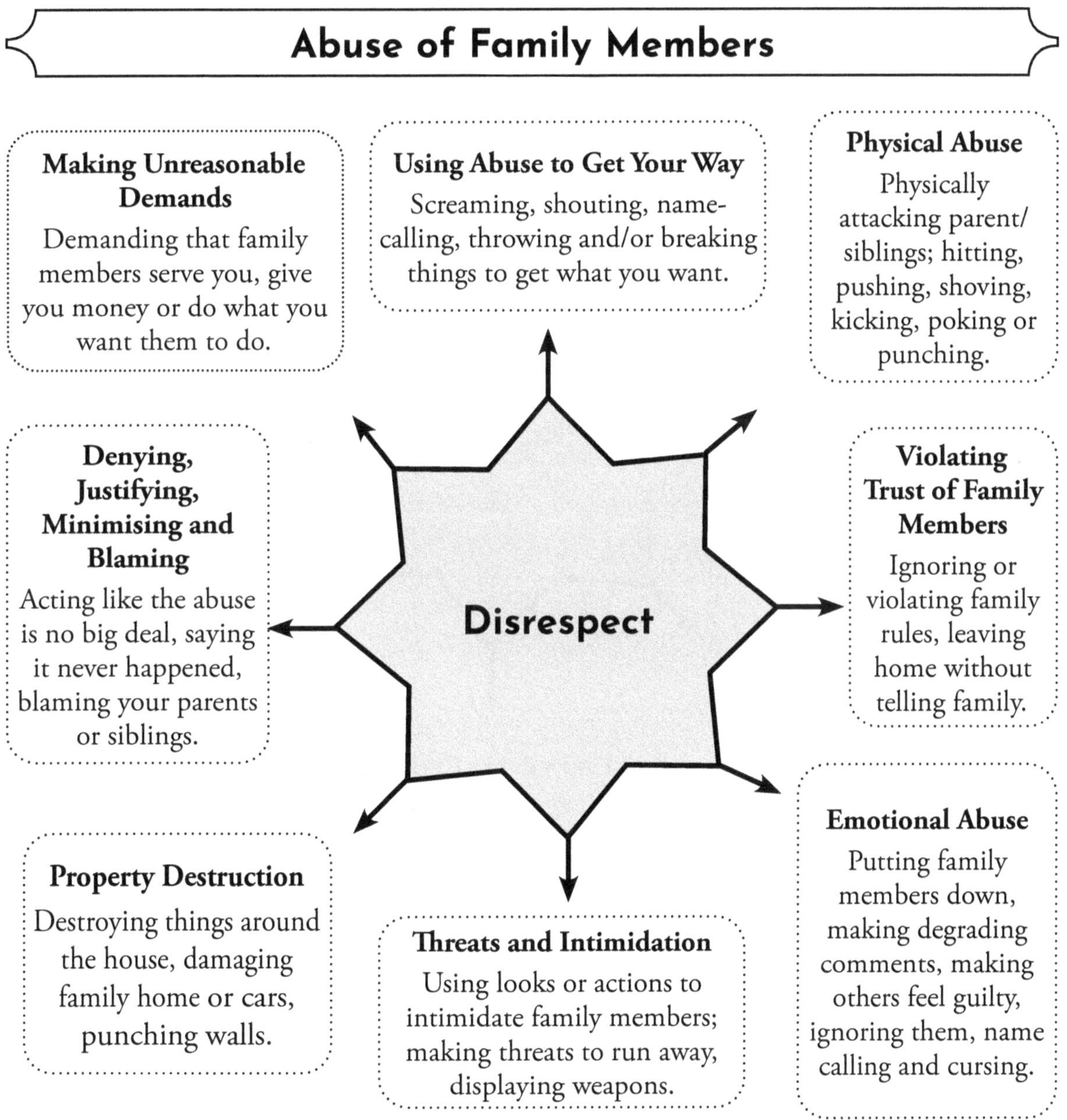

Mutual Respect

Respect

Choosing to Stay Non-Violent
Stopping yourself when you feel like hurting a family member, staying respectful when you have conflict.

Non-Aggressive Behaviour
Talking and acting so that all family members feel safe and comfortable expressing themselves and doing things.

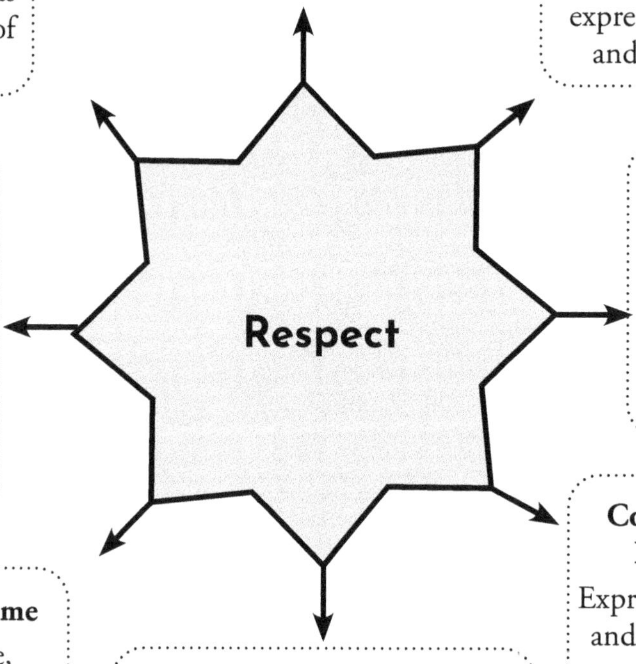

Being Trustworthy
Developing and accepting guidelines, being reliable and honest.

Communicating Respectfully
Expressing your needs and feelings directly and respectfully: being willing to compromise.

Problem-Solving Respectfully
Being willing to listen, to value each other's position and to work towards a compromise.

Respecting Your Home
Valuing your home, respecting other family members' property, contributing to care of home.

Being Accountable to Family
Accepting responsibility for your behaviour, admitting being wrong, communicating truthfully.

Respecting Other Family Members' Needs
Thinking through how your behaviour affects others, being aware of others' needs.

If you engaged in a behaviour on the Abuse/Disrespect diagram, what could you have done differently to remain respectful?

____

____

____

Choose one of the behaviours you did on the Respect diagram. What helped you stay respectful? What skill did you use?

____

____

____

Scenario

Sam is a 12-year-old boy with ADHD who has been suspended from school. His father stays at home with him but insists that Sam does a number of homework exercises. Sam understands the necessity and is doing the work, but becomes increasingly frustrated by the amount of work.

Sam thinks he is doing the last exercise when his father indicates there is one more page of maths to do. Sam's head starts to hurt and he feels agitated. Just then the telephone rings; it is the school principal wishing to speak to Sam's dad about the suspension and what will happen next. Sam can only hear a little of the conversation but, already agitated, he becomes increasingly angry. His face turns red and he begins to throw things, first around the house then in his room. He yells and screams, disrupting the telephone call, and kicks his father in a rage.

Finally, he storms out the door and hides under a bush in the garden.

Can you relate to Sam in the above scenario? If so, explain the situation that you were in.

____

____

____

Take responsibility for your behaviour using the following steps

If you have been abusive toward family members or property, or made threats to do so, answer the following questions.

Who was hurt by my behaviour?

____

____

What was the harm, damage or loss caused by my behaviour?

____

____

How did my behaviour affect each person (including me)? How did it impact our relationship?

____

____

____

____

What do I need to do to repair the hurt or problems caused?

____

____

____

What do I need to do to restore the relationship?

____

____

What could I have done differently? What can I do to keep from repeating the behaviour?

____

____

Interventions for Children with Anger Issues

Cognitive Behavioural Therapy (CBT): Some children with anger issues have a tendency to over-perceive threat – they overreact to an unclear or ambiguous situation. For these children, CBT can help the child to understand that something ambiguous isn't necessarily threatening. It also helps the children learn how to tolerate normal frustrations and develop better coping strategies.

Parent Counselling/Parenting Training: Parents have a role in how a child's anger manifests. A parent's angry reaction can lead to mutual escalation, such that parents and children both start to lose their balance. This can form a negative loop. With counselling and training, parents can develop a better understanding of their child's behaviour and respond accordingly.

Medication: Regular stimulant medication for ADHD helps symptoms much of the time, but is only about half as helpful with anger problems. Selective Serotonin Re-uptake Inhibitors (SSRIs) may be an option for treating severe anger problems. While further research is needed, there is some evidence that when mainstream stimulant medications are not working, and severe anger problems are a core issue, adding an SSRI may be a reasonable step.

Other treatment options: Mindfulness and physical exercise are increasingly showing to be beneficial for children with anger-related issues. Omega-3 supplements also appear to have a small effect in improving emotional self-control in children with ADHD.

Anger may indicate an associated mood disorder but often is just part of the ADHD. Either way, a multimodal intervention will ultimately give the best outcome.

Word Finder: Emotions Underlying Anger

Often, when we experience anger, there are other emotions hidden below the surface. The terms below represent emotions underlying anger. Find them in the word finder and colour them in.

L	O	N	E	L	Y	E	D	Q	E	R	T	Y	U	A	O	P	A	S
F	F	E	M	B	A	R	R	A	S	S	E	D	R	F	Z	L	X	C
A	F	R	U	S	T	R	A	T	E	D	U	I	O	R	M	N	B	V
F	E	V	J	A	R	L	N	S	C	A	D	E	Y	A	R	T	E	B
A	N	O	F	I	I	H	X	J	K	L	I	V	C	I	B	N	M	L
J	D	U	F	D	C	A	I	Q	W	E	S	I	A	D	U	I	O	P
K	E	S	N	B	K	C	O	X	Z	A	R	S	T	F	G	H	K	L
Q	D	G	H	J	E	L	U	M	N	B	E	N	T	D	R	G	K	L
T	R	O	U	B	D	E	S	N	M	V	S	H	A	M	E	F	U	L
U	N	I	M	P	O	R	T	A	N	T	P	H	C	R	J	E	N	H
N	S	R	T	Y	I	O	E	F	J	P	E	E	K	Q	E	G	S	D
A	B	A	N	D	O	N	E	D	E	J	C	R	E	D	C	D	U	A
E	F	J	G	K	L	A	F	H	U	R	T	P	D	E	T	E	T	A
W	O	R	T	H	L	E	S	S	A	W	E	P	E	W	E	N	P	U
D	I	S	B	E	L	I	E	F	D	T	D	A	N	X	D	O	U	S
D	F	G	U	I	L	T	Y	G	R	E	W	Q	E	R	T	R	R	I
U	N	S	U	P	P	O	R	T	E	D	B	O	T	T	E	D	E	D

Abandoned
Afraid
Anxious
Attacked
Betrayed
Disbelief
Disrespected
Embarrassed
Frustrated
Guilty
Hurt
Lonely
Nervous
Offended
Rejected
Shameful
Tricked
Unimportant
Unsupported
Worthless

See **Appendix D** for answer key.

Topic 4: Motivation and ADHD

> ***You can motivate by fear, and you can motivate by reward. But both those methods are only temporary. The only lasting thing is self-motivation.***
> ***~Homer Rice***

Did You Know? Feeling unmotivated is a big obstacle for children and adults with ADHD. Inconsistency in motivation and performance is one of the most puzzling aspects of ADHD. Teachers and parents struggle to understand why children show strong motivation for some tasks, and not for other things they consider more important. This inconsistency can appear as lacking willpower or defiance. 'If you can do that, why can't you do the same for this, which is even more important?' parents may ask.

This too-common tale in ADHD often gets children labelled as unmotivated, lazy or even apathetic. These negative labels are unfair and hurtful.

Instead of simple laziness or a lack of motivation, this immobility or sluggishness happens because of EFs skills gaps that can be associated with ADHD. Understanding this is crucial to correct misperceptions about ADHD.

The reality is that ADHD behaviours are not a matter of willpower. They are a result of a problems with the dynamics and chemistry of the brain.

When individuals with ADHD are faced with a task that is interesting to them – not because someone told them it is important – that perception changes the chemistry of the brain instantly. This process is not under voluntary control.

ADHD, Motivation and Executive Functions

Motivation plays an important role in goal-directed behaviour, but it can be hard to understand, especially for those with ADHD. Rewarding tasks motivate us; however, in school, students are faced with tasks that are not rewarding or motivating, but still need to be done. This requires effort, and effort requires motivation.

Behaviours that require effort need EF, such as attention, cognitive control, emotional control and motor control. Studies have shown that one reason people with ADHD are able to utilise EFs and focus on some tasks, while being chronically unable to focus adequately on other tasks, is due to neural transmission.

Dopamine is a neurotransmitter, or chemical messenger, in the brain that plays a big part in EFs, as well as our ability to feel pleasure. People with ADHD tend to have less release and re-uptake of dopamine. Treatment with stimulant medications improves neural communication, but it's important to remember that this process is not under voluntary control. Heightened interest – and the resulting increase in motivation – that comes from dopamine release only happens when the task is either interesting and pleasurable, or invokes fear of a negative result.

Types of Motivation

In psychology, the two main types of motivation are intrinsic and extrinsic.

'Intrinsic' refers to something coming from within. It is the inner drive that propels a person to pursue an activity, not for external rewards but because the action itself is enjoyable. 'Extrinsic' motivation, on the other hand, refers to doing an activity to attain some separable outcome, such as earning a reward or avoiding a punishment.

Intrinsic Vs. Extrinsic Motivation: Why We Do what We Do

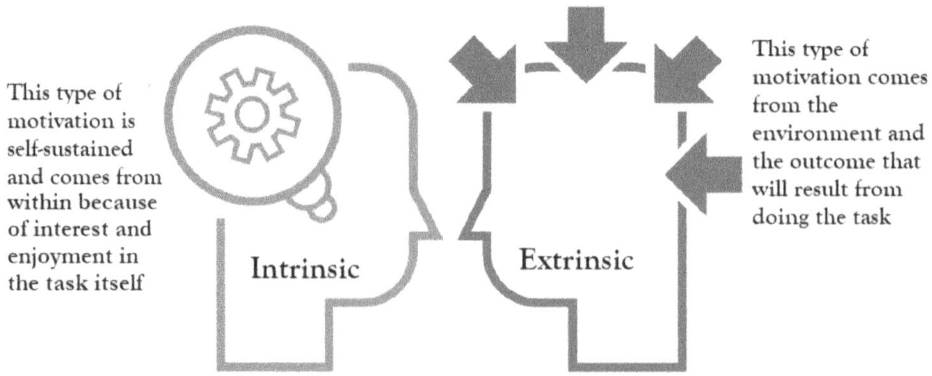

Adapted from Ryan & Deci 2000

Exercise: What Makes You Act the Way You Do?

Read the questions below and circle the option that you would most likely choose.

1. **You are offered two roles in the school play. Which one will you choose?**
   A. The lead role, which is glamorous and gets you a lot of attention
   B. Another part that's less glamorous but lets you use more of your acting skills
2. **You are offered two jobs. Which one will you choose?**
   A. The one that pays very good money
   B. The one you'd really love doing, even though the pay isn't very good
3. **You are choosing between two classes. Which one will you choose?**
   A. The easier one
   B. The more interesting and challenging one
4. **You must read at least one book this semester. Which one will you choose?**
   A. One book from the list the teacher has given you
   B. Five books of your choosing that are just as long
5. **Two people have invited you out. Which one will you choose?**
   A. The person who is fashionable to be seen with
   B. The more interesting but less popular person
6. **Which do you feel you learn more from?**
   A. Studying for a class so you can get an A
   B. Studying for a class because you're interested in it

7. **In deciding between two sports, which one will you choose?**

   A. The one that gives trophies to the best players at the end of the season

   B. The one that is the most fun

8. **Which feels better to you?**

   A. Cleaning your room so that you will get your allowance

   B. Cleaning your room because you want to

9. **In general, which is more important to your decision-making?**

   A. Appearances

   B. Meaning

10. **In general, which are you more interested in?**

   A. Quantity

   B. Quality

Total your As and Bs: A __ B __

- If you scored 8 or more As, you're probably motivated from the outside. You care a lot about what people think of you.
- If you score 8 or more Bs, you're probably motivated from the inside. You care more about your own opinion than the opinions of others.

Sometimes it helps you to be motivated from both inside and outside. For example, you can care about what others think but still be true to yourself.

Why Is it so Hard to Motivate Children with ADHD?

ADHD brains differ from neurotypical ones in ways that impact motivation. For example:

- The parts of the brain that manage EFs and emotions have different levels of activity.
- Electrical activity differences make it harder for ADHD brains to filter out irrelevant stimuli and focus on the task at hand.
- ADHD is linked to low dopamine activity, which impacts desire and reactions to rewards, success and failure.

These differences mean that children with ADHD have to work harder to acquire information and pay attention. That can mean that children with ADHD experience more frustration and failure than they do success, which negatively affects self-perception and increases stress, further paralysing the brain. Issues include:

- **Lack of desire:** 'I don't want to do this.'
- **Relevance:** 'This has no meaning/value for me!'
- **Shame avoidance:** 'If I do this I will look/feel stupid (again).'
- **Success avoidance:** 'If I do this boring task as expected, I'll just get more of it.'
- **Desire to retain control:** 'You can't make me do it.'

A child's negative perceptions about their ability to complete a task may become a barrier to getting started, and result in less helpful processing because all that stress makes the brain shut down. Children with ADHD require a different approach to process, stimulation, momentum, motivation and managing the emotional effects of their challenges. This is not because they are lazy or have a bad attitude, but because of their neurobiology.

How to Identify Motivational Problems

Fixing motivation is a long process that begins by understanding your brain chemistry and the challenges it creates. You can use the following three steps to help you:

1. **Name it:** Make sure you know that your condition can make certain situations more difficult or challenging. Understand that ADHD is real, but you can learn to manage the challenges.
2. **Understand your presentation:** Know that certain challenges are related to your ADHD; for example, getting organised, starting a task (initiating), keeping a flow of competing thoughts in the background or completing a task.
3. **Meaning in the context of your life:** Your motivational difficulties are not related to intelligence. ADHD is a neurological difference. This doesn't mean you're not smart, it means your brain works differently. ADHD can present a challenge, but it doesn't have to be a disability. It's a skill deficit that can and must be managed if you want to achieve success and live up to your fullest potential.

For children with ADHD to successfully tap into their motivation, they must have/develop self-awareness and self-advocacy. This means being able to say the following:

- I have ADHD.
- I can explain my condition to other people, and that what looks like poor motivation is often related to my ADHD.
- I understand that ADHD impacts me in a unique way.
- ADHD makes tasks that are manageable for others challenging for me.
- I may be more motivated by some tasks than others. This has to do with my history of experience with the task, and my mindset.
- Yes, I want to strengthen my ability in this area. I want to get better at this thing.

The above awareness ultimately leads to acceptance of your ADHD, and an understanding that you need to keep learning and developing new strategies to manage the many transitions inherent to adolescence. For most children, this is not an easy process – understanding, guidance and education are paramount.

Increasing Your Motivation

> ***Nothing we can do can change the past, but everything we do changes the future.***
> ***~Ashleigh Brilliant***

It is easier to stay motivated when you have clear and purposeful goals and a plan to achieve them. Here's how!

1. **Set SMART goals.** Set goals that are in service of your values. Make sure that these are:
    - **Specific**: What is your goal? How often or how much? Where will it take place?
    - **Measurable**: How will you measure your goal? How will you know that you are making progress?
    - **Attainable**: Is this a goal that you think you can actually reach?
    - **Realistic**: Is your time frame realistic for the specific goal?
    - **Time-bound**: When do you think you'll be able to reach your goal?
2. **Tell someone in your Circle of Support about your plans.** Get their support and feedback.
3. **Acknowledge success, and reward yourself when you reach each step.** Review each day. Every morning, ask, 'What can I do today?' At the end of each day, ask, 'What have I achieved today, however small?' Write it down.
4. **Acknowledge and be mindful of unhelpful or negative thoughts and feelings.**
    - Give up the struggle of trying to stop unhelpful thoughts.
    - 'That's how the mind and body work, it's what it does'.
    - Use positive and encouraging self-talk – be your own coach.
    - Practice self-compassion instead of self-criticism.
    - Keep the focus on your values.

5. **Visualise success.** Use your imagination. See yourself in your mind's eye starting out on your first steps, seeing things through and achieving your goal. Imagine how that would feel. Imagine the feedback from others.

   Choose someone from your Circle of Support to act as a role model. Imagine yourself acting in the character of that person, living your values and achieving your goals. In spite of your thoughts or feelings:

   - take action
   - maintain an 'I can do it' attitude
   - stick with it.

6. **Get Active.** Inertia tells us that an object in motion tends to stay in motion and an object at rest tends to stay at rest. Exercising releases dopamine in your body. Exercising makes you feel better overall and helps you want to be more active. If you don't know where to start to get motivated, start by going for a run or going to the gym. Physical activity improves ADHD symptoms and helps build motivation. Just the action of movement will produce inertia towards more and more movement. By getting out, you will want to go and accomplish more. Getting active will change your outlook and get you back on track towards being productive.

   Stop unhelpful habits and form new ones. Create a balanced daily routine. Create a healthy balance of work, rest and play.

7. **Get Help.** ADHD and lack of motivation won't go away without effort and work. It will be difficult if not impossible to do it all on your own.

   Your friends and family want to see you succeed. Ask someone in your Circle of Support to help you be accountable. Let them know when you are feeling particularly down or unmotivated. They know you the best and can encourage you to follow through on your goals.

   The solution to a lack of motivation is to modify and adjust the learning environment rather than trying to change the person.

   Lastly, learn the value of honest self-appraisal, and how to accept and use feedback from other people. Compare your current performance and use of skills to your previous efforts. Then use the skills you've learned in the past to drive you further in the future.

Develop a growth mindset: **I can, I will, I can't just yet**, vs **I can't, so I won't**. Externalise what your brain is saying to you at the beginning of the task and challenge your negative self-talk.

Staying Motivated in the Classroom

Success in school requires children to pay attention to assigned tasks and expectations. Children with ADHD have difficulty sustaining their attention, particularly during repetitious or prolonged tasks that are not entertaining or stimulating. The expectations of the classroom are in direct conflict with the limitations of a child with ADHD.

Children with ADHD may be continually blamed, reprimanded and censured for behaviour that is beyond their control. They begin to feel angry, resentful and frustrated. This frustration is exacerbated by the fact that children with ADHD are often exceedingly bright, and they are well aware of the discrepancy between their potential and their performance.

The table on the next page shows some of the ways that ADHD symptoms conflict with classroom expectations.

Consider the following expectations:

ADHD Symptom	Classroom Expectations Affected
Impulsivity	• Wait until you are called on • Keep your hands to yourself • Take your time • Read the directions carefully
Hyperactivity	• No pencil tapping • Stay in your seat • Play/talk/work quietly
Organisational problems	• Keep your desk/book bag orderly • File your homework • Where's your pen/pencil/ruler/glasses?
Low frustration level	• Repetitive learning tasks • If at first you don't succeed… • Be patient
Inability to learn from experience	• How many times have I told you… • Do you remember what happened last time?
Impaired sense of time	• Arrive on time • Hand things in on time • Estimate how long it will take you to…
Difficulty with sequencing, prioritising, analysing, synthesising	• Figure it out yourself • How would you solve this problem? • What's your solution?
Memory deficits	• Don't forget to… • Always remember to… • The due date was… • Come prepared
Inattention	• Watch those careless mistakes • Listen closely • Pay attention • Follow the main idea
Inability to sustain effort	• You should have finished that by now • Great start, but then you fell apart • Unacceptable handwriting

> ***If a child cannot learn in the way we teach,***
> ***we must teach in the way they learn***
> ***~Ignacio Estrada***

Because of your ADHD, your performance and motivation are influenced by three major factors:

1. degree of interest in the activity
2. difficulty of the activity
3. duration of the task.

You may have significant difficulty with tasks that require organisation, planning, inhibition, self-monitoring and sustained effort.

It is easy to see that many traditional classroom activities will be inappropriate for you. Included among these are:

- heavy emphasis on work sheets
- independent work
- long-term assignments
- extended silent reading
- multi-step tasks.

As much as possible, the curriculum should be stimulating and relevant to the life experiences of the children. Research has shown that a curriculum that is irrelevant to the student's social and economic interests generally results in disruptive behaviour, poor academic performance, limited progress and dropping out.

Children with ADHD live very much in the present. Therefore, long-term goals and rewards (e.g. grades and report cards) are often ineffective motivators.

Children with ADHD respond more positively to a curriculum that allows choices and options. They are also more likely to participate actively in tasks when there is a degree of creativity and novelty. In order to maintain the motivation, the teacher should simultaneously consider what is being taught and how it is being taught. The content should be stimulating and relevant; the presentation should be creative, multimodal and enjoyable.

What does your teacher do in the classroom that helps you stay motivated?

____

____

____

Name one thing that you would change in school that would increase your motivation.

____

____

____

How would a motivating teacher teach?

____

____

____

What affects your motivation at home?

____

____

____

What could you start doing today to increase your motivation?

____

____

____

Getting Motivated
What motivates you?
money
Extrinsic
praise
attain a separable outcome
avoid punishment
grades
A+
or
pride
achievement
Intrinsic
the fun or satisfaction attached to the activity
interest
curiosity
Growth Mindset
Use other people!
tell someone close to you
- your circle of support
get their support
+
feedback
act like your role model
Goals
-the bigger picture-
why am I doing this?
- is it in line with my values?
SMART Goals
where do I want to be in ___ years time?
Acknowledge unhelpful thoughts
self compassion vs self criticism
trick yourself into starting
break tasks into small chunks
CHOC
Visualise Success
See yourself finishing
How will I feel?
How will others respond?
Euan Lloyd - Ontrac (2021)

Developing a GROWTH MINDSET

A mind is like a parachute. It doesn't work if it is not open.
~Frank Zappa

People with a growth mindset believe that their abilities can improve over time, that things can always get better, that problems are challenges that can help them improve. A small change in thinking can mean big changes in your life.

Instead of...	**Try Thinking...**
This is too hard	This may take some time and effort
I can't make this any better	I can always improve so I will keep trying
I will never be that smart	I will learn how to do this
I give up	I will use some of the strategies that I have learned
My friend can do it	I will watch how they do it, so that I can try it
I just can't do this	I need help understanding this
I am not good at this	What am I missing?
It's good enough	Is this really my best work?
I made a mistake	Mistakes are opportunities to learn
Plan A didn't work	There is always plan B
This task is too big	I can tackle anything I put my mind to
I don't understand this	I don't understand this **yet**

Do you already have a growth mindset?

____

How does having a growth mindset help you achieve your goals?

____

____

____

Topic 5: When ADHD Is Not the Only Problem

> ***You may encounter many defeats, but you must not be defeated. In fact, it may be necessary to encounter the defeats, so you can know who you are, what you can rise from, how you can still come out of it.***
> ***~Maya Angelou***

ADHD itself is challenging, but when you have other coexisting conditions, the difficulty increases. A landmark study by the National Institute of Mental Health showed that up to two-thirds of individuals with ADHD have at least one other coexisting condition. The symptoms of ADHD (constantly on the go, fidgeting, interrupting and blurting out, difficulty sitting still and need for constant reminders, etc.) may overshadow these other disorders. Sometimes these conditions are secondary, meaning that they came about as a result of dealing with the daily challenges of ADHD. When this is the case, once ADHD is managed, the symptoms of the secondary condition may resolve themselves. In other cases, these conditions are separate and need to be treated separately from ADHD.

Several disorders can coexist with ADHD, but some disorders tend to occur more commonly with ADHD.

Disruptive Behaviour Disorders

As many as 40% of individuals with ADHD have oppositional defiant disorder (ODD). This condition involves a pattern of arguing, losing one's temper, refusing to follow rules, blaming others, deliberately annoying others, and being angry, resentful, spiteful and vindictive.

Among individuals with ADHD, conduct disorder (CD) may also be present, occurring in about 27% of children and 45% to 50% of adolescents with ADHD. Children with CD may be aggressive to people or animals, destroy property, lie or steal things from others, run away, skip school or break curfews.

Mood Disorders

Mood disorders are characterised by extreme changes in mood. Children with mood disorders may seem to be in a bad mood often. They may cry daily or be frequently irritable with others for no apparent reason. Mood disorders include depression, mania and bipolar disorder. Approximately 14% of children with ADHD also have depression, whereas only 1% of children without ADHD have depression. In adults with ADHD, around 47% also have depression. Typically, ADHD occurs first and depression occurs later. Both environmental and genetic factors may contribute.

Anxiety Disorders

Up to 30% of children with ADHD also have an anxiety disorder. Individuals with anxiety disorders often worry excessively about a number of things (school, work, friendships etc.) and may feel stressed out, tired and tense, and have trouble getting restful sleep.

Tics and Tourette Syndrome

Tics involve sudden, rapid, involuntary movements or vocalisations. Tourette Syndrome is a much rarer, but more severe tic disorder, where individuals may make noises, such as barking a word or sound, and movements, such as repetitive flinching or eye blinking, on an almost daily basis for many years. Less than 10% of those with ADHD have tics or Tourette Syndrome, but between 60% and 80% of those with Tourette Syndrome have ADHD.

Sleep Disorders

Up to 50% of parents of children with ADHD report that their children suffer from a sleep problem, especially difficulties with falling asleep and staying asleep. Sleep problems can be a symptom of ADHD, may be made worse by ADHD or may make the symptoms of ADHD worse.

Substance Abuse

Research suggests that youths with ADHD are at increased risk for very early cigarette use, followed by alcohol and then drug abuse. Cigarette smoking is more common in adolescents with ADHD, and adults with ADHD have elevated rates of smoking and report particular difficulty in quitting. Youth with ADHD are twice as likely to become addicted to nicotine as individuals without ADHD.

Some fear that stimulant medication for ADHD may make people more likely to abuse stimulants later, but research has shown this is not the case. In fact, adolescents who are prescribed stimulant medication for their ADHD are less likely to subsequently use illegal drugs than children with ADHD who are not prescribed medication.

Learning Disorders

Learning disorders can cause problems with how individuals acquire or use new information. The most common learning disorders are dyslexia and dyscalculia, affecting reading and calculcating. Up to 50% of children with ADHD have a co-existing learning disorder, whereas only 5% of children without ADHD have learning disorders. In addition, 12% of children with ADHD have speech problems, compared to 3% of those without ADHD.

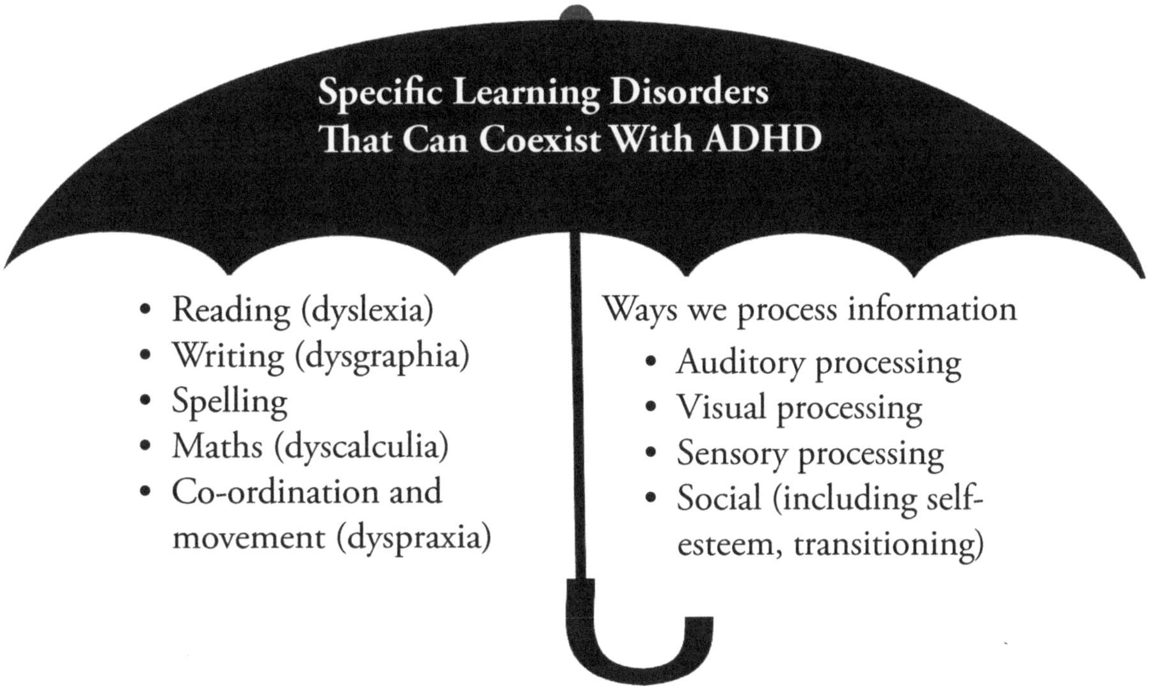

Specific Learning Disorders That Can Coexist With ADHD

- Reading (dyslexia)
- Writing (dysgraphia)
- Spelling
- Maths (dyscalculia)
- Co-ordination and movement (dyspraxia)

Ways we process information

- Auditory processing
- Visual processing
- Sensory processing
- Social (including self-esteem, transitioning)

Treatment of Coexisting Conditions

If you have coexisting conditions, your medical team should work with you and your family to establish an individually tailored treatment plan. Which condition they treat first will depend on which one is causing the greatest difficulty in your life. Your healthcare professional may choose to treat the ADHD first, as this may reduce stress, improve attentional resources and even enhance your ability to deal with the symptoms of the other condition.

Treatment options for ADHD include behaviour therapy, medication, skills training, counselling and school supports and accommodations. Treatment plans are ongoing and should be reviewed at least once a year to check how well they're working and adjust them if necessary.

Were you diagnosed with ADHD as well as one or more of the conditions described here? If so, which one and how is it being managed?

____

____

____

Scenario

Jane jumped when the teacher called her name, even though she knew she was next. She stood up and wiped her sweaty hands on the front of her jeans, then picked up her notes and walked to the front of the class. Her mouth was dry, and she tried to swallow past the lump in her throat. After a panicked glance at the sea of faces in front of her, she looked back at her notes, blinking several times to make the blurriness go away. As she started her talk, her voice sounded shaky and weak. She asked her teacher to give her a minute. She returned to her desk, had a sip of water, and took a deep breath. Feeling steadier, Jane walked back to the front of the class, picked up her notes and delivered her presentation.

What could be affecting Jane other than ADHD?

____

____

Did Jane do the right thing in this situation?

____

What else could Jane have done?

____

____

Topic 6: Multimodal Treatment

> ***If you understand how your own unique brain wiring works, you won't suffer, you will learn how to thrive.***
> ***-ADD Coach Academy***

Neurotransmitters Involved in ADHD

To understand ADHD, it's important to understand a little bit about the brain and the nervous system. Your body moves in response to messages from your brain. These messages are carried from neurons in the brain to the central nervous system by chemical messengers called neurotransmitters. Thoughts and feelings also rely on neurotransmitter activity.

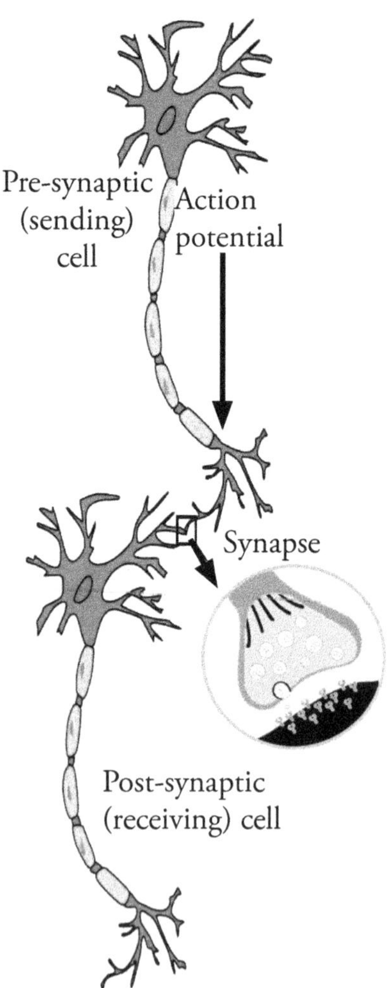

The synapse, as shown in the diagram, is where neurotransmitters cross from one nerve's axon (called the pre-synaptic side) to the next nerve's dendrite. The other side of the synapse is called the post-synaptic or receiving cell, where the neurotransmitters latch onto the receptors of the next neuron. When enough neurotransmitters attach to the post-synaptic neuron, the nerve fires, and it releases neurotransmitters at its own pre-synaptic end. This process continually repeats. The neurotransmitters implicated in ADHD include:

Dopamine controls impulsivity, paying attention and memory. Dopamine is an excitatory chemical, which means that it helps the nerve cells fire off impulses to communicate with one another.

Norepinephrine/ Noradrenaline helps with paying attention.

Serotonin is involved with sleep and mood. If you don't have enough of this chemical, you may have sleeping problems and get depressed more easily.

The primary role of ADHD medication is to treat ADHD symptoms by balancing neurotransmitter availability in the brain. However, finding the best medication and dose is not always easy and you have to be willing to persevere. When you finally do get it right, it's like a 'wow' moment, when you tell yourself 'this is really helping me'. The message is, 'just because you tried a medication once and it did not seem to work, don't give up on medication altogether'. When you start a new medication, it is a good idea to keep track of how the medication is working by keeping a medication side-effects rating scale. Take the results to your doctor for a discussion on whether this medication is giving you the best outcome, and whether it needs some adjusting in terms of the dosage.

We know that when managing ADHD, no treatment is sufficient on its own. A multimodal approach (a variety of interventions that target the individual's needs) has shown to be the most effective. Because ADHD is a condition that impacts the child in most areas of their life, interventions need to be designed for home and school. For example:

At home	At school
Morning routine	Classroom
Afterschool routine	Playground
Homework routine	Recess
Chores	Team activities
Dinner	Sport events
Bath	Assembly
Bedtime	Excursions

Intervention options include:

- Medication
- Behaviour modification
- Social skills group therapy
- Individual therapy
- Family therapy
- Parenting courses
- Special education
- Tutoring
- Coaching
- Mentoring
- Executive skills training, e.g. time management, organisation, problem-solving as well as distractibility and procrastination.

Although these are not treatments for ADHD *per se*, we also cannot disregard the importance of healthy eating, physical exercise, adequate sleep and proper hygiene in keeping a healthy mind and a healthy body.

Is It OK to Take Medication?

Many children who have ADHD take medication. If you are taking medication, you have probably tried different kinds and dosages to find one that works for you.

Medication for ADHD is like a pair of eyeglasses. Just as your glasses sharpen fuzzy vision, medication helps your brain focus. They work as long as they are active in your body. Some are good for a few hours, while others can last most of the day.

Scenario

Xavier did not like taking medication at school. He was increasingly refusing to go to the school nurse during lunch to get the second dose of his medication. His mother spoke to the paediatrician and Xavier was given a different medication for his ADHD. 'You only need to take this medication in the morning instead of twice a day', his paediatrician said.

Unfortunately, within a week of taking the new medication, Xavier started feeling nauseous and having stomach pains. His mother read the information on the leaflet and saw that what Xavier was experiencing was one of the side effects of medication. Xavier worried that he might have to go back to the old medication and wanted to stop taking medication altogether.

His mother was very understanding and reminded Xavier of how his medication had helped him. His grades had improved, his relationship with his older brother was better and he seemed happier. Xavier agreed that the medication was helping and went back to the paediatrician with his mother for another opinion.

Can you relate to Xavier in this scenario? Have you had to try different medication and adjust the dosage? Tell us your story.

____

____

____

____

____

____

The list below explains the benefits of ADHD medication in helping you to manage your symptoms of ADHD.

Cognitive Effects

- Improves attention to tasks and schoolwork, and reduces distractibility
- Improves short-term memory
- Decreases impulsivity
- Increases academic productivity and accuracy

Motor Activity and Coordination Effects

- Decreases excessive talking and disruption in the classroom
- Improves handwriting and overall neatness of written work
- Improves fine-motor control

Social Behaviour Effects

- Reduces daydreaming during class
- Decreases aggression and improves self-regulation
- Improves ability to concentrate and participate in organised sports
- Improves interaction with peers
- Improves interactions with parents
- Improves interactions with teachers

Common Side Effects

Sometimes medication that helps with your ADHD can have other effects, such as:

- Reduced appetite
- Weight gain
- Insomnia (unable to sleep)
- Nausea
- Dry mouth

- Headaches
- Tiredness
- Tics (repetitive movements, e.g. blinking, twitching, jaw clenching)
- Irritability
- Mood swings
- Palpitations

If you have any of these or other side effects, tell your parents and discuss it with your doctor. Maybe you need to try a different dosage of the same medication or change to a different medication that works without causing these side effects.

Medication Response Form

Below is a list of some side effects that may result from taking ADHD medication. Logging this information will help your doctor identify what problems were present before ADHD medication was started and what problems may have developed after the treatment started. If you are experiencing other issues you would like to monitor, you can add them in the blank spaces.

Problem	Time on Medication				
	Before	1st week	2nd week	3rd week	4th week
Reduced appetite					
Weight gain					
Insomnia					
Nausea					
Dry mouth					
Headaches					
Tiredness					
Tics					
Mood swings					
Increased anxiety					
Palpitations					
Irritability					
Chest pain					

Topic 7: Going Solo at the Doctor

By Dr Bennett

Adolescence is a time of increased independence. It's also a time when health professionals assume that you can make decisions about your health. This includes seeing a general practitioner (GP) on your own, confidentially. This is often a gradual process, and you need to feel confident that you have the skills to manage your own health. Your parents can guide you as you slowly gain confidence to assume responsibility for your health and general well-being.

The age at which a young person can consent to simple health care treatments without a parent or guardian present differs from country to country. In some countries, it can be as young as 14 years of age.

Did You Know? It is always important to have open communication with your parents, especially about health-related concerns. However, at times you may find it difficult to speak to your parents about specific health issues and this is when having the confidence to see your GP alone can be helpful. The concerns that teens discuss with their GP the most include general worry, bullying at school, relationships and substance abuse. The GP can offer guidance on things like sexual health, sleep, hygiene, fitness, healthy eating habits and overall mental well-being. If you are not comfortable about going to the same GP as your family, you have the right to see a different GP. Speak to your parents about your concerns.

Reasons reported by teens for wanting a different GP include:

- no longer feeling comfortable with their family GP
- wanting to see a GP who does not know their parents
- wanting to talk more openly about issues like relationships, including sexual matters and substance abuse
- wanting to manage their own health and start a new doctor-patient relationship
- not trusting the family GP with confidential information.

If you do decide to change GPs, make sure that you know important aspects of your family history (e.g. information about conditions such as allergies, mental health issues, asthma or diabetes) for your new file.

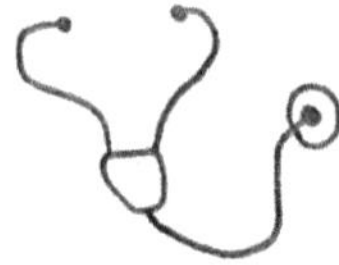

Be strong enough to stand alone, smart enough to know when you need help, and brave enough to ask for it.

Did You Know? Seeking and accepting help from others, such as a psychologist, a mentor, a coach or tutor, is very important. Often parents and friends can become your ADHD coach or mentor, or you might be lucky enough to find a counsellor or tutor who can help you. Unfortunately for some children, seeking and accepting help from family members is a hard thing to do. You can always make a deal with your parents about what and how much input you would like from them. In this way, you can still feel supported without feeling that you have no control. What you need to understand is that no person is an island, and we all need support at some point in our lives. As we know, ADHD struggles cut across many areas of your life. This means that you're probably going to need help t some stage. Accept support so that you can do better at school and maintain good relationships. Many studies support the finding that school performance and mood are related – the better you perform, the happier you are and vice versa. Often, as you learn skills to compensate for your attention deficit, your need for support decreases.

Does your family value seeking help?

____

____

____

Are there situations where you find it easier to ask for help?

____

____

____

Describe a situation where you asked for help. What was the outcome?

____

____

____

Do you believe that needing help is a sign of strength or weakness?

____

____

____

Do you sometimes wish that someone else would make the first move and offer you help?

____

____

____

Topic 8: Circle of Support

Don't be afraid to ask questions. Don't be afraid to ask for help when you need it. I do that every day. Asking for help isn't a sign of weakness, it's a sign of strength. It shows you have the courage to admit when you don't know something, and to learn something new.
~Barack Obama

Did You Know? A Circle of Support is based on an understanding of the importance of relationships in our life and the need for strong support networks. This is especially important for someone who might be vulnerable because of a mental health illness. Many of us have friends or informal networks that we rely on when we need advice, when we are in a crisis and when we want to celebrate successes. These relationships are important. At times it can be useful to include professionals that help you in your Circle of Support.

Example: Circle of Support

These are the people in Tristan's Circle of Support: the people he can go to when he has a problem or wants to share his successes.

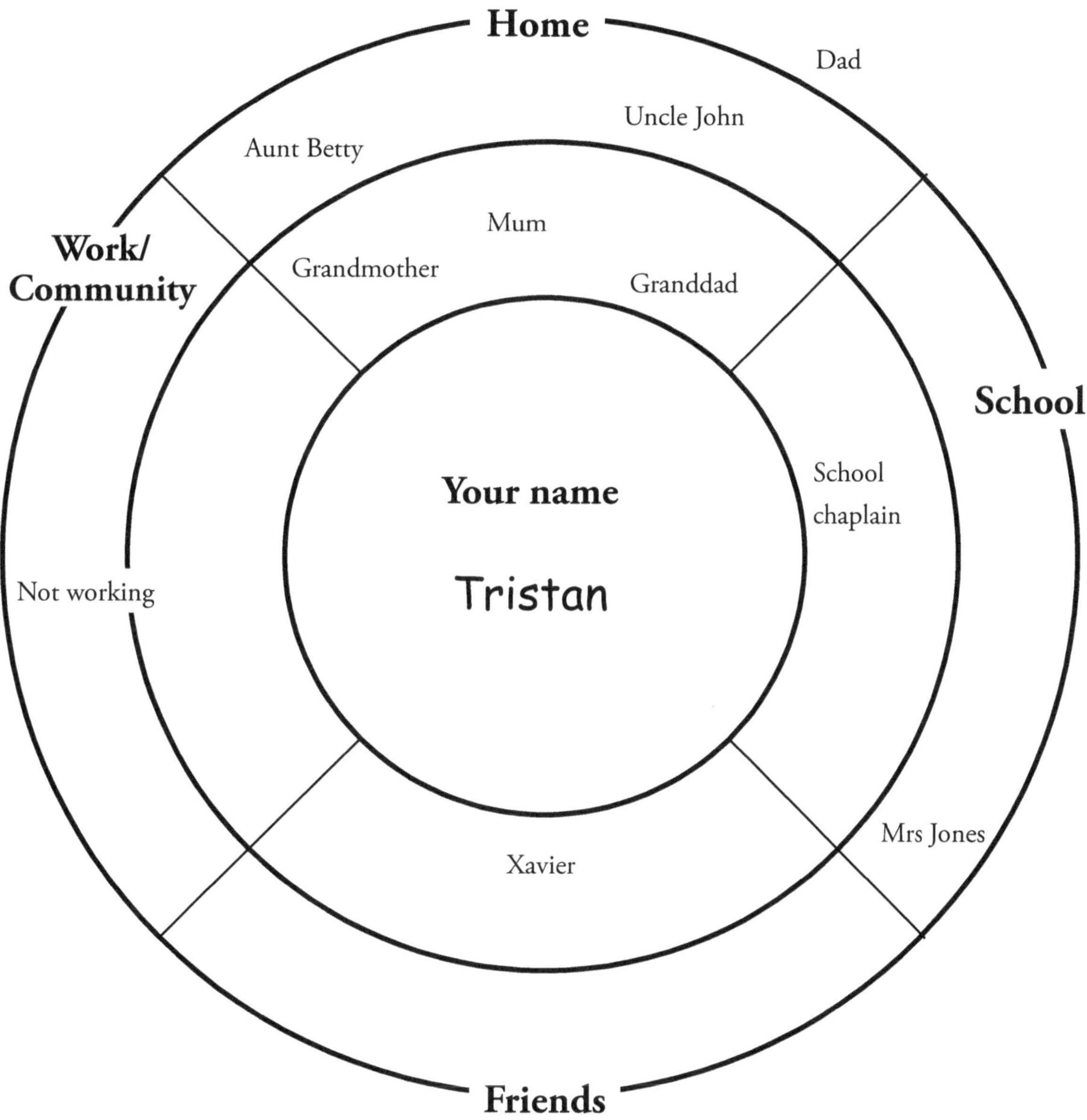

Adapted from https://cosam.org.au/

Who Is in Your Circle of Support?

Look back at Tristan's Circle of Support. Use it as a guide to complete the diagram below, indicating your own Circle of Support. Put the people who you go to for support often in the inner ring. Put the people you go to less often in the outer ring.

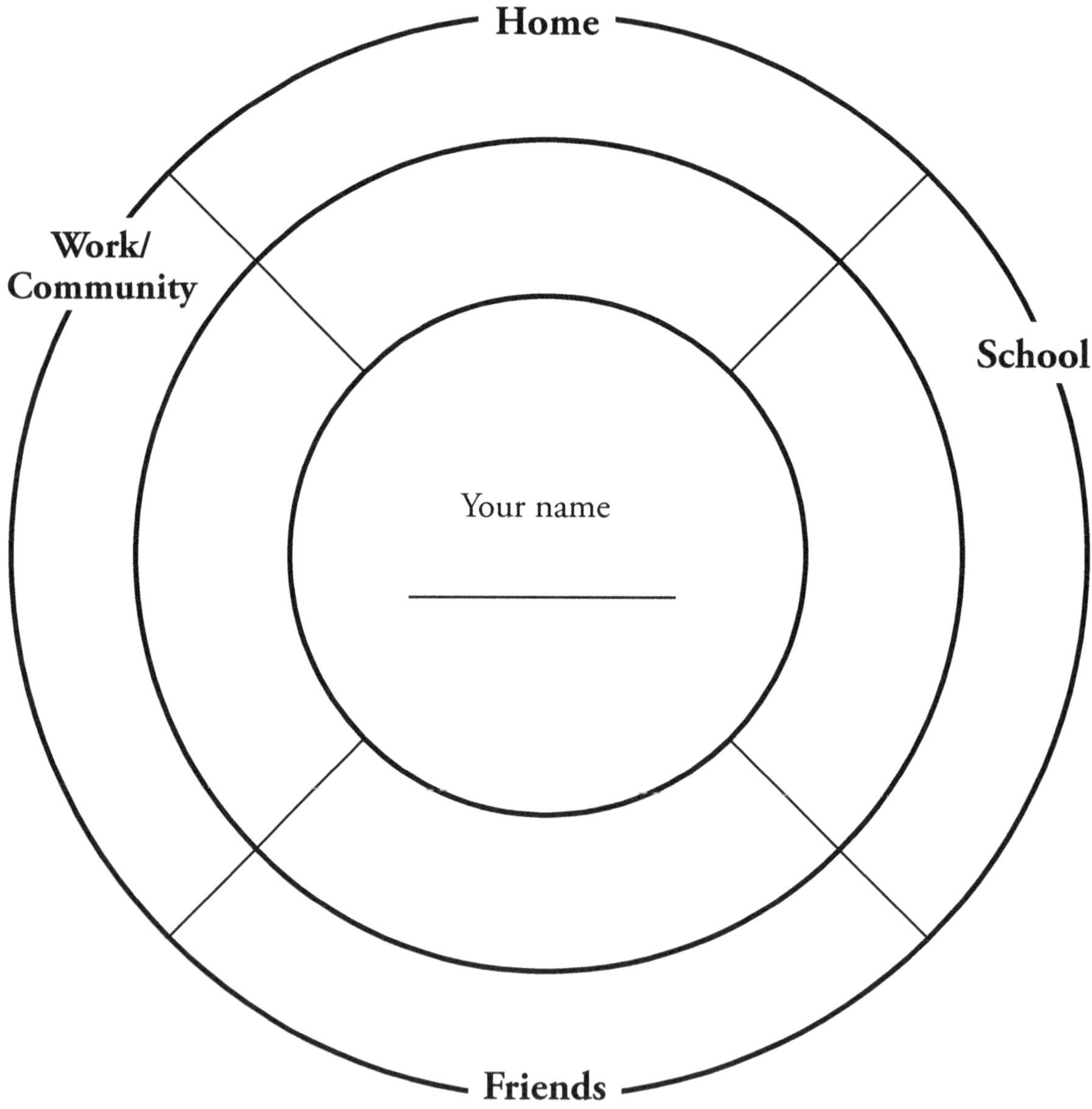

Topic 9: Telling People That You Have ADHD

Having ADHD is nothing to be ashamed of. That being said, many people worry about telling someone they have ADHD. This is understandable, as even the people that love you the most may not understand when you tell them.

Before telling someone that you have ADHD, ask yourself whether you really want this person to know and how it will make a difference. You have the choice to tell people if you want to, if it would help them understand you better, but don't feel obliged.

If you decide to tell someone, rather than simply saying 'I have ADHD', try this method:

Ask the person a question to find out how much they know about ADHD. For example, 'What do you know about ADHD?' or 'How much do you know about ADHD?' Listen carefully to their reply.

Asking an open question like this will let you know two things: their attitude towards ADHD and their factual knowledge about it.

Attitude Towards ADHD

Attitude is everything! As they are replying to your question, you will quickly know if they are anti-ADHD or open-minded and compassionate about it. There are still a lot of people who don't believe it exists or that it's something people use as an excuse for being lazy (I know!).

Factual Knowledge About ADHD

There are still many misconceptions about ADHD. For example, some people still think that ADHD is a childhood disorder and that adults don't have it. Others know about hyperactive ADHD and not inattentive ADHD.

Some people know a person with ADHD, so they base their knowledge on how it affects that person without realising it is different for everyone.

Once you know the person's attitude, you can decide if you want to tell them you have ADHD. Remember, you don't have to!

When you know their knowledge base, you can fill in the blanks and explain how ADHD shows up in your life. Even if a person knows about ADHD, they don't know how it affects you personally.

This method does take a little more time; however, it is worth it as it results in a positive experience for both of you.

Have you had to explain your diagnosis to anyone?

____

____

____

What was that like for you?

____

____

____

Topic 10: Introducing Yourself

> ***True education is a kind of never-ending story – a matter of continual beginnings, of habitual fresh starts, of persistent newness.***
> ***-J. R. R. Tolkien***

Did You Know? When you are struggling with your ADHD challenges, you may find yourself thinking that everyone else in your grade has it easy compared to you. However, the reality is that life is a mix of good and bad, and we all have challenges and opportunities in our lives. Each day you have the choice to define yourself by your strengths or by your weaknesses. It is important to remember that teachers are there to help, and they can do this better if they know a little bit about the challenges you are facing.

At the beginning of your school year, you might want to introduce yourself to your new teacher in writing. Ideally do this within the first two weeks of the school term.

Here are some ideas to help you decide what to include:

- Name (and what you prefer to be called)
- What you like doing in your spare time
- Activities that you enjoy
- The subjects that you enjoy the most
- Subjects you find most challenging
- What you want to be when you grow up

Situations when you are most productive and study the best:

- When?
- Alone or with someone?
- Where (e.g. floor, desk?)

- Conditions – (e.g. kneeling at your desk, in a quiet area, wearing headphones?)
- When you need a study breaks – (e.g. every 20 minutes)
- Where you work better sitting – (in the front, at the back of the classroom etc.)

Strategies that help you to stay organised and complete your work:

- Use a homework diary
- Take a picture of the information on the board regarding homework assignments
- Write assignments
- Email assignments to your parents
- Keep an extra textbook at home
- Work with a buddy to stay organised
- Estimate how long an assignment will take
- Colour-code subjects
- Break down assignments into chunks with different due dates
- Send home a reminder of due dates for the final project

What helps you learn and remember information?

- Write things down
- Use mind maps
- Use a computer for writing
- Read out loud
- Make or build something
- Use songs and rhymes
- Use flash cards
- Listen to a recording of the lesson
- Talk about the information with a buddy

- Use associations and mnemonics
- Fidget
- Doodling

What else would you like your teacher to know?

____

____

____

____

____

____

DISCOVER YOUR HIDDEN STRENGTHS

Re-frame your thinking about ADHD

Easily distracted
Forgetful
Can't stay on point
Hyperactive
Impulsive
Disorganised
Stubborn
Inconsistent

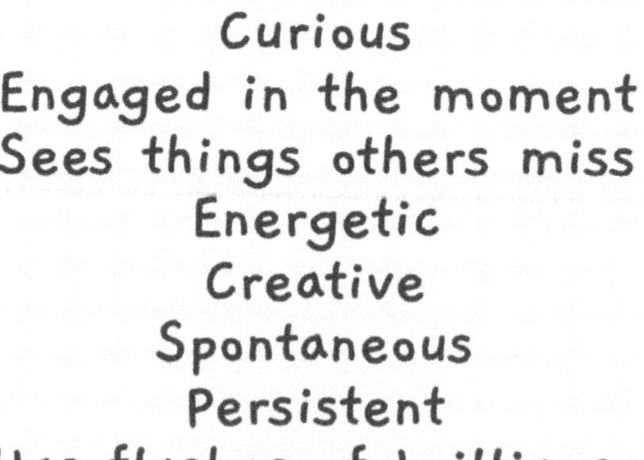

Curious
Engaged in the moment
Sees things others miss
Energetic
Creative
Spontaneous
Persistent
Has flashes of brilliance

Topic 11: Discover Your Passion

Strength does not come from winning. Your struggles develop your strengths. When you go through hardships and decide not to surrender, that is strength.
~Arnold Schwarzenegger

Did You Know? People with ADHD, just like those without it, have unique sets of interests and skills that they are passionate about. Remember that you are unique with many good qualities; you are a one-of-a-kind personality. You can begin to discover your passion and purpose by exploring two things:

What you love to do

What comes easily to you

For example, JP did work experience in the fitness industry in Year 10. During this time, he discovered his true passion for this industry. He decided that he wanted to become a personal trainer and work towards owning his own gym one day. He was so excited by this idea that he started researching alternative ways of following his passion and opted to go to college at the end of Year 11 to pursue his fitness certification.

Below are some jobs that have been identified as suitable for individuals with ADHD. Write three qualities that would help people do well in the following jobs:

Personal trainer (fitness)

1. ______________________________

2. ______________________________

3. ______________________________

Teacher

1. ____

2. ____

3. ____

Journalist

1. ____

2. ____

3. ____

Small business owner

1. ____

2. ____

3. ____

Emergency first responder

1. ____

2. ____

3. ____

Now:

Write two things that you love to do and that you are good at.

1.____

2.____

List two jobs that match one (or both) of the things you listed above.

1.____

2.____

Ask someone in your Circle of Support if they know anyone who works in one of the areas you've identified, then set up a time to meet with that person. During the meeting, ask questions and take notes. Possible questions:

- What do I need to do to prepare for a career in this field?
- What sort of volunteering would help me determine if this career is a good fit for me?
- What specific interests and talents would I need to succeed in this field?

Notes:

Quiz 1 (see Appendix E for answers)

Circle the correct answers.

1. **What does ADHD stand for?**

   A. Aggressive daring hyperactive disorder

   B. Attention deficit hyperactivity disorder

   C. Adventurous daring hypersensitive dude

2. **JP was diagnosed with ADHD. Which of the following is true about JP?**

   A. His body is sick and will never get better

   B. His brain has a virus and he can't learn

   C. Some brain differences make JP impulsive, hyperactive and inattentive

3. **What is the best thing for JP to do about his ADHD?**

   A. Learn as much as he can about ADHD, so that he can manage it better

   B. Refuse medication because ADHD does not exist

   C. Blame his parents for his ADHD

4. **Tristan tells you that he got a raw deal in life and that others do not understand or care about his struggles. How would you help Tristan?**

   A. Agree with him that the world is a terrible place

   B. Tell him not to expect any better in the future

   C. Tell him that we all have struggles in life and highlight his strengths, like his sense of humour and ability to 'think outside the box'

5. **Xavier wants to become a peer mentor so that he can help other children with their problems. What can Xavier do?**

   A. Dream about being a mentor

   B. Find out what skills are needed to be a mentor and enrol in a course

   C. Accept that, because of his ADHD, he will never be able to be a mentor

6. **JP confides in you that he is ashamed about having ADHD. How can you help him?**

   A. Ask JP to imagine that you, his friend, is the one who has ADHD. What advice would he give you if you had the same concern?

   B. Agree with him that he should keep it a secret (and so will you)

   C. Go behind his back and tell your friends about it

7. **JP often gets into trouble for showing aggression and for being disruptive in the classroom. How can you help JP?**

   A. Tell him that it is okay to get angry because he has ADHD

   B. Help him understand what is triggering the frustration and anger, so that he can learn skills to cope better

   C. Agree with him that the teacher does not like him and that's why she always picks on him

8. **Tristan tells you that having a Circle of Support is dumb because you can just share stuff with anyone. How do you respond?**

   A. You agree that it is a dumb idea

   B. You tell Tristan that he needs one, but that only family members should be in the Circle of Support

   C. You disagree with Tristan and tell him that it is important to have people of different ages and backgrounds, family and not family, that you trust and who have your back

9. **Tristan tells you that medication for ADHD is addictive and it should not be given to children. What will you tell Tristan?**

   A. You agree and feel that no child should be given stimulants

   B. You disagree and explain that at times medication may be needed in a treatment plan. And if it helps the child to achieve at school, it should be used

   C. You tell him that medication is the only treatment for ADHD

Module 2:

Adaptive Thinking

Section 1:

Learning to Cope Inside Out

Topic 1: Adaptive Thinking

Stop being afraid of what could go wrong and start being positive about what could go right.
-Zig Ziglar

An important aim of this module is to help you think more adaptively and learn to cope inside out. This involves learning to observe your thoughts, name them and develop alternative thoughts to replace the negative and unhelpful ones. This is achieved by using Cognitive Behavioural Therapy (CBT) principles to help you understand that it is not what happens to you, but rather how you interpret it, that determines how you react.

Learning to think adaptively can help you be more aware of negative thoughts, find strategies to keep your thoughts in check and find ways to reduce your symptoms.

The diagram below can help you understand how the relationship between thoughts, feelings and behaviours works.

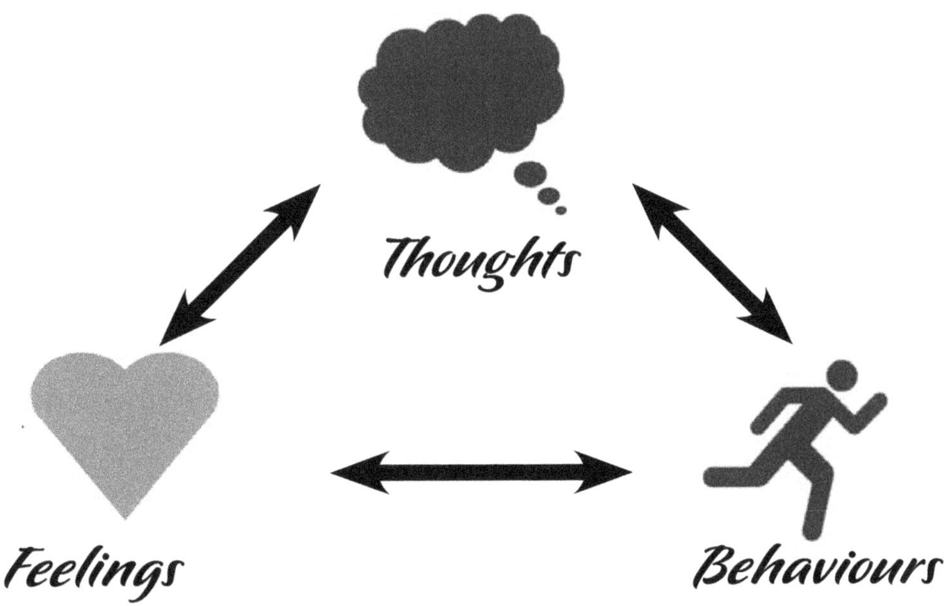

The following example shows how CBT might play out when two different people experience the same situation:

Situation: Emily and Olivia have ADHD. They both fail a science test.	
Emily	**Olivia**
Thought: If I didn't have ADHD, I would be smarter and would have passed the test. I'm so stupid.	**Thought:** I must've underestimated this test. I didn't study hard enough.
Emotion/Feeling: Depressed and negative about her ability to do well in future tests	**Emotion/Feeling:** Disappointed, but confident about the next test
Behaviour: Emily develops a negative opinion of herself and doesn't adjust her test preparation, because she believes she is the problem.	**Behaviour:** Olivia isn't happy about her test score, but it doesn't affect her self-esteem. She plans on using different strategies and being better prepared.

Let's understand each of the components of CBT, starting with thoughts.

Thoughts are the messages that our mind gives us every moment of the day. They are the many things that you tell yourself about what is going on in your world. When we see, hear, smell, feel and taste something, our thoughts tell us what it all means. Without thoughts we would be in big trouble. We are constantly bombarded with so much information that we can only pay attention to a small percentage of our thoughts at any given time. Because of this, many of our thoughts occur outside of our awareness – these are called automatic thoughts. Irrational negative thoughts can increase stress levels and worsen your mood, and this can interfere with starting and completing tasks.

Emotions/feelings come and go as a result of our thoughts. You may experience a range of feelings all in one day, or even a mix of feelings at the same time. Look at the example on the next page and see how people can feel very differently about the same situation, because of their thoughts:

What feelings do each of these thoughts lead to?

Cute... a dog!
It looks a little feisty. I bet he just wants to play.

Oh no
... a dog!
It looks aggressive!
I bet he wants to jump on me or bite me!

Feeling:________

Feeling: __________

It is important to understand that, just like thoughts, feelings can occur outside of your awareness, yet still impact your behaviour.

Behaviours are the reactions we have when we interpret a situation with our thoughts and experience an emotion. This process happens constantly and is often not noteworthy. Other times, the process does not work quite as well, and we start behaving in ways that are counterproductive and hurtful to us.

Consider this situation, as experienced by two different people:

Situation: Dean and Nicholas have ADHD. They call a friend who does not answer the phone.

	Dean	**Nicholas**
Thought	He must be busy or just not in the mood to talk right now.	He does not want to talk to me because I'm so boring and weird.
Emotion	Neutral/No change	Sad/Hurt
Behaviour	Dean tries to call his friend again later or the next day.	Nicholas does not try to call his friend back and avoids him the next time he sees him.

Did You Know? Hassles and problems are part of everyday life – parents, teachers, friends, school, work. In fact, almost everything can create problems at one point or another. The way you think about these problems affects how you feel about them, and what behaviours you use to deal with them. Although ADHD is not caused by negative automatic thoughts, living with ADHD, especially if untreated, can cause frustration and underachievement in various aspects of life, such as school, work, and relationships. This can erode away the self-esteem and confidence that we need when we approach everyday tasks. Learning to think adaptively can help you be more aware of negative thoughts, find strategies to keep your thoughts in check, and find ways to reduce your symptoms. Use the thought diary on the next page to monitor your thought process and challenge your negative thinking.

Exercise: Thought Diary Template

Use this template to keep a record of your automatic thoughts.

Situation (Something happens)	**Automatic thoughts** (The meaning we give to the situation)	**Feelings** (How do you feel and where in your body do you feel it?)	**Behaviour** (What did you do in response to your thoughts and feelings)	**Did it work for you?**	**What could you have done differently?**
Mum asking me to do chores as soon as I get home from school.	'She should just let me relax when I get home from school.' 'She always nags me but not my brother.'	Upset, overwhelmed, angry	Talking back. Going to my room and slamming the door	No. I had to do them anyway and got in trouble for talking back.	Ask if I could have some time to relax before starting chores. Stay calm even though I didn't think it was fair

Topic 2: Unhelpful Thinking Styles/Errors

A man is but the product of his thoughts. What he thinks he becomes.
-Mohandas Gandhi

Did You Know? Everyone falls into the trap of unhelpful thinking at some point in their life. However, when you are struggling with a condition like ADHD, extremes in thinking can become the norm. Personalisation, blaming, comparing and jumping to conclusions are just a few of the many unhelpful thinking traps that you can fall into. It is important to exercise self-compassion and see mistakes as opportunities for learning. Even when something has gone wrong, you still have the choice to ask positive questions and look for alternative ways of understanding the situation. For example, 'What really went wrong?' 'What have I learned?' 'What can I do differently next time?' Don't beat yourself up. Use your energy to focus on bringing about positive change.

Unhelpful Thinking Styles/Errors

The only person you need to compare yourself with is who you were yesterday
~Rushton Hurley

The following thinking styles can be subtle yet very powerful in causing us to experience needless emotional distress. Interestingly, the more distressed we become, the more our thinking can become narrowed and focused, making it difficult to think in balanced ways. These thinking traps often creep in unnoticed. If you can identify which thinking styles you are using, it can be very liberating, allowing you to break free from narrowed, unhealthy thinking patterns.

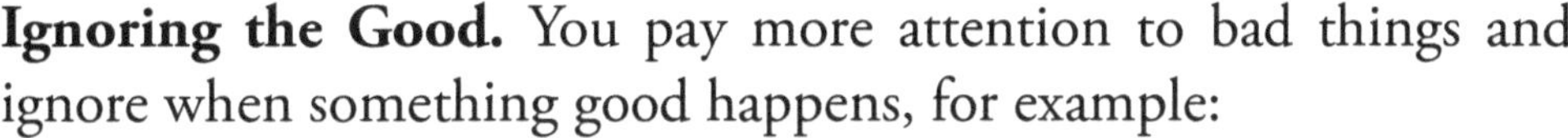

Ignoring the Good. You pay more attention to bad things and ignore when something good happens, for example:

- You score three goals in a footy game, but all you can think about is the kick you missed.
- You get a good grade in a test, but you can't stop thinking about the one question you got wrong.

Blowing Things Up. Making a really big deal out of something small or making something a little bit bad seem like the worst thing ever, for example:

- You get a little stain on your favourite shirt and you think that it's ruined and can't be worn anymore.
- 'I'm not allowed to see my friends this weekend. My life is horrible!'

Fortune Telling. Thinking you know what will happen in the future, and that it will be bad, for example:

- 'I know if I ask her to go out with me, she's going to say no.'
- 'I bet no one will come to my birthday party.'

Mind Reading. Believing you know what others are thinking or why they are doing something, without having enough information, for example:

- 'People are looking at me. They probably think my shirt is ugly.'
- 'Emma didn't invite me to her party. I bet she thinks I'm weird.'

Negative Labelling. Having a negative belief about yourself and thinking it applies to everything you do, for example:

- 'I'm a loser so my artwork stinks.'
- 'I'm so stupid. Everything I say is dumb.'

Setting the Bar too High. Thinking that you must be perfect in everything you do, otherwise you're no good, for example:

- 'If I don't get an A on every test, I'm not smart.'
- 'I have to win every tennis match I play, otherwise I'm worthless.'

Self-blaming. Blaming yourself for anything that goes wrong around you, even if you had nothing to do with it, for example:

- When your basketball team loses a game, you think it's entirely your fault.
- 'Alicia is sad today. I probably did something to upset her.'

Feelings as Facts. Believing that if you feel something, it must be true, for example:

- 'I feel ugly, so I must be ugly.'
- 'I feel like I'm a bad friend, so I must be a bad friend.'

'Should' Statements. Believing things have to be a certain way or setting up expectations that are unrealistic, for example:

- 'People should always be nice to me.'
- 'I should always be happy. I should never feel sad.'

Comparing and Despairing. Seeing only the good and positive aspects in others, and comparing ourselves negatively against them, for example:

- 'I am not as pretty as all the other girls in my class.'
- 'Everyone has more likes than me on their social media.'

Do you identify with any of the thinking styles above? If so, what behaviours do you engage in that show it?

____

____

____

____

How would your life improve if you could escape this thinking trap?

____

____

____

____

Scenario

It was Tom's first day at a new school. As he got out of his mum's car, he could see all the students standing around in groups, laughing and talking together. Were they laughing at him? His heart beat painfully fast and his face burned. He kept his eyes down, watching the ground in front of him so he didn't have to look at any of the new people crowded around. 'I bet they don't like me', he thought. He sat at his desk and kept his eyes on the teacher to avoid making eye contact with the other children. He was sure they were looking at him and whispering mean things to each other. When he got home, he was sad and told his mother that the children were mean and didn't talk to him.

How was Tom's day affected by his thinking?

____

____

____

What thinking traps had Tom fallen into?

____

____

____

Challenge your unhelpful thinking: Replace it with a new thought

Unhelpful thinking | **New thought**

Emily is sad today. I probably did something to upset her.

Maybe she is just not feeling well.

People are looking at me. Maybe they don't like my t-shirt.

Maybe they just recognise me from school.

I'm not smart enough. I might as well give up.

As long as I do my best, I am happy.

Fact or Opinion?

At stressful times, we tend to be driven by our emotions and opinions, which creates a vicious cycle. This leads to impulsive acts and unhelpful longer-term consequences, which help to maintain the overall problem.

Realising that many thoughts are opinion rather than fact makes it less likely that we'll be distressed by them, and more able to make wise and calm decisions about the best action to take.

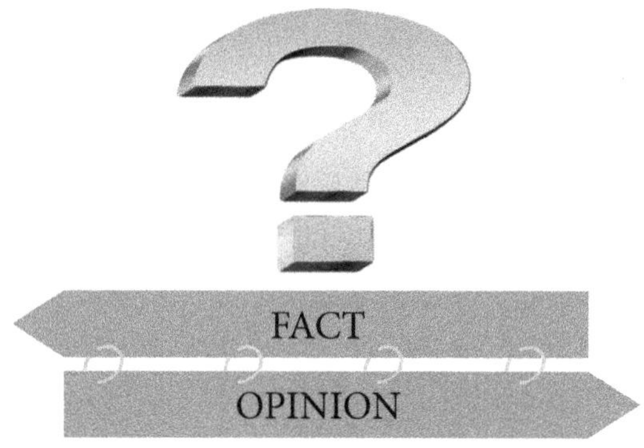

FACT	OPINION
Evidence to support its truth	Based upon a belief or personal view
Indisputable	Arguable
Driven by rational thought	Driven by and reinforced by emotion
Head	Heart

It is helpful to ask ourselves whether our thoughts are **fact** or **opinion**.

- If **opinion**, then we can look at the facts: what we do know about the situation.
- If **fact**, then we can make choices about the best thing to do.

Example:

What words might you use to describe this picture? Different people would use different words to describe it, which might be fact or opinion.

FACT **Evidence-based**	**OPINION** **Varies, personal view**
Rat	Cute
Has whiskers	Scary
Furry	Smart
Eats cheese	Icky
Round ears	Ugly

In the same way, individuals can have many varied opinions about the same event or situation. If someone we know walked past us without saying hello, we might think, 'they deliberately ignored me', 'she's being snooty and rude', 'they didn't want to talk to me because they don't like me' and so on.

This might lead us to feel upset and react in ways that are unhelpful.

The only fact is that the person walked past. Anything else is opinion – our own personal interpretation of the event.

Topic 3: Core Beliefs

We don't see things as they are, we see things as we are.
-Anaïs Nin

Core beliefs are a person's most central ideas about themselves and the world. These beliefs act like a lens through which every situation and experience is seen. People with different core beliefs in the same situation may think, feel and behave very differently. Even if a core belief is inaccurate, it still shapes how a person sees the world. Harmful core beliefs lead to negative thoughts, feelings and behaviours, whereas rational core beliefs lead to balanced reactions.

Many people have negative core beliefs that cause harmful consequences. To begin challenging your negative core beliefs, you first need to identify what they are. Here are some common examples:

I'm unlovable	I'm stupid	I'm boring	I'm a useless person
I'm a failure	I'm broken	I'm worthless	I'm not good enough

What is one of your negative core beliefs?

____

List two pieces of evidence contrary to your negative core belief.

1) ____

____

2) ____

____

Facts About Core Beliefs

- People are not born with core beliefs – they are learned.
- Core beliefs usually develop in childhood or during stressful or traumatic periods in adulthood.

- Information that contradicts core beliefs is often ignored.
- Negative core beliefs are not necessarily true, even if they feel true.
- Core beliefs tend to be rigid and long-standing; however, they can be changed.

Core beliefs stem from a person's unique personal experiences. However, these beliefs aren't always accurate. For example, someone who was mistreated by a parent as a child might develop the belief that they are unlovable, when the problem was their parent's.

Your core beliefs are like a filter that each thought must pass through. Ideas that contradict your core beliefs will be rejected.

Example: If someone has the core belief that they are unlovable, each of their thoughts will have to make sense in the context of that belief. The process might look something like this:

Situation: Emily and Olivia both call a friend to invite her to watch a movie

	Emily	**Olivia**
Core belief	Emily believes that she is unlovable	Olivia believes that she is lovable
Thought	My friend did not answer the call because she does not like me and thinks that I am boring.	My friend did not answer the call because she must be busy or has no battery. If she does not call back, I will call her tomorrow.

Now look at another scenario where the situation is a positive one:

Situation: Emily calls a friend to invite her to watch a movie. Her friend answers the phone and is happy to be invited to watch a movie with Emily.

Core belief: Emily believes that she is unlovable.

Thought: My friend is really nice to put up with me. She probably feels sorry for me and that is why she agreed to watch a movie with me.

Can you relate to Emily's core belief?

____

Topic 4: When Actions Speak Louder Than Words

Understanding the Function of Your Behaviour

Children's actions are often communicating that they are struggling with something they can't explain or don't understand. This behaviour becomes an important form of communication, and it's key for you and your parents to try to understand what is going on. In other words, what is the function of the behaviour?

Behaviours to Watch for

Behaviours at school are sometimes mirrored by behaviours at home. Here are four types of behaviours you might be engaging in, and potential reasons behind them.

1. Escape/avoid: Some students use behaviour to avoid a task, demand, situation or even a person they find difficult. This may be the student who says inappropriate things to the teacher or a parent so they can escape a stressful situation.

Example: JP, who struggles with reading, refuses to take out his book during silent reading time. He eventually throws it to the floor, calls the teacher a name and gets sent to the office. At home he refuses to do his homework and purposely lashes out at his mum, even knowing that he will be sent to his room. What JP is trying to communicate is that he's struggling with reading and would rather get into trouble than be asked to do a task that is challenging for him without the support he needs.

Can you relate to JP? If so, how?

___

___

___

2. Attention: Some people depend on approval and attention from others, especially people like parents and teachers, and go out of their way to seek attention rather than moving forward with a task on their own.

Example: Sarah is what some people might think of as clingy. She really wants to show how hard she worked on her maths. At school, she raises her hand in class over and over. At home, she keeps interrupting her mum to report her progress. When she doesn't get a response, she keeps tapping her mum's arm and pulling on her sleeve. Sarah is trying to tell her mother that she's unsure about her strengths. She's expressing that she needs her mum's approval to be sure she's done a good job on her maths.

Can you relate to Sarah? If so, how?

____

____

____

3. Tangible gains: Some behaviour is aimed at getting what you want, when you want it. This behaviour is very common for children who struggle with impulsivity or flexible thinking.

Example: Peter often talks back and comes off as disrespectful. He misses or ignores cues to lower his voice. He gets agitated when he is told to stop. He argues that he's just trying to get answers to his questions and believes that he should be given a response right away.

Peter is communicating that he needs more information to understand what's happening around him. His behaviour shows a communication skills deficit, providing an opportunity to learn the social skill of waiting.

Can you relate to Peter? If so, how?

____

____

____

4. Sensory needs: Students' brains are constantly taking in information from their senses. For children with ADHD, that stream of input can be challenging. They may underreact or overreact to sensory input, which can be problematic when it is disruptive or interferes with learning. Is this you?

Example: Noah has a problem standing in line at school. He says he feels crowded and pushes other children out of the way – literally moving them out of his personal space.

At home, he may need to find a space to get away and process his sensory input, which may be a larger area than typical for others.

Can you relate to Noah? If so, how?

____

____

____

Power and control are other payoffs of behaviour. Do you relate to these?

____

____

____

Functions/Payoffs of Behaviour

Sometimes, inappropriate behaviours continue even though unpleasant consequences follow. It's important to understand the reason these behaviours are happening, and what the payoff is for each one.

For example, Brad might get up and kick his chair over when the teacher asks the class to take out their homework. The class is disrupted and Brad receives the negative consequence of being sent to the office for punishment. However, he also achieves the payoff of avoiding having to explain why he hasn't done his homework.

Part of understanding your own behaviour is realising when you are engaging in a behaviour, knowing it will have a negative consequence, and working out what your payoff is for that behaviour.

Payoffs can include attention, distraction, escape, power and control, among other things.

Check the functions of your behaviour by checking the ones that are true for you. Identify the long- and short-term benefits and costs of these behaviours.

Functions of Behaviour		Benefits: Short and Long Term	Costs: Short and Long Term
	Escape/Avoid		
	Attention		
	Tangible gains (get material things)		
	Power		
	Control		
	Revenge		

Which of the behaviours that you identified have the most payoffs for you? Give reasons for your answers.

____

____

____

Example of Behaviour Payoffs

Situation	**Thoughts and Feelings** (Judgments and feelings about the situation)	**Behaviour** (A person's action)	**Payoffs** (Outcomes of the behaviour that keep it going)
James is studying for a maths test.	'I don't like maths, this is a waste of time.' Feeling bored and having the urge to play games instead.	Packs books away. Plays computer games online.	Winning games. Feeling happy, socially connected and relaxed.

Given the payoffs of James' behaviour, is he more likely to study or play games next time he has a maths test? Give reasons for your answer.

____

____

____

Topic 5: Let it Go

Losing Control and Gaining Balance

Focusing on things you can't control can send you spiralling into worry. It's more productive to invest energy into controlling the things you can. Even with all the things we can't control – like what other people think of us, the weather, losing a loved one or how others behave or what they say – there are many things we can control.

Some days, it doesn't feel like it. It feels like everything is falling apart and we're caught in a tsunami. But it's empowering to remind ourselves that there are actions we can take, even in difficult times.

Below is a list of what people can control. Tick the ones that apply to you.

- ☐ How I talk to myself.
- ☐ How I react to others.
- ☐ How I use technology.
- ☐ How I structure my day.
- ☐ Whether I seek help, and the people I turn to for help.
- ☐ When and how I say yes or no.
- ☐ How I practice self-care.
- ☐ How honest I am.
- ☐ How I manage my feelings.
- ☐ Whether I step outside my comfort zone.
- ☐ Whether I forgive myself.
- ☐ My social media use.
- ☐ My priorities.
- ☐ The music I listen to.
- ☐ The people I listen to.
- ☐ How much responsibility I take.
- ☐ How hard I work at something.
- ☐ What I do with my racing thoughts.
- ☐ The people I surround myself with.
- ☐ What I wear.
- ☐ The art I create.
- ☐ How kind I am to others.
- ☐ How patient I am.
- ☐ How often I brush and floss my teeth.
- ☐ What inspiration I let into my life.
- ☐ How I respond to my needs.
- ☐ The boundaries I set.
- ☐ How I treat my body.
- ☐ What I do with my self-doubt.
- ☐ How grateful I am.
- ☐ How much time I spend with my parents and family.
- ☐ How I respond to distractions.
- ☐ What I learn from my mistakes.
- ☐ When I get out and enjoy the fresh air.

What Can I Control?

Think about the things you can control and the things that are out of your control. Write them in the circles.

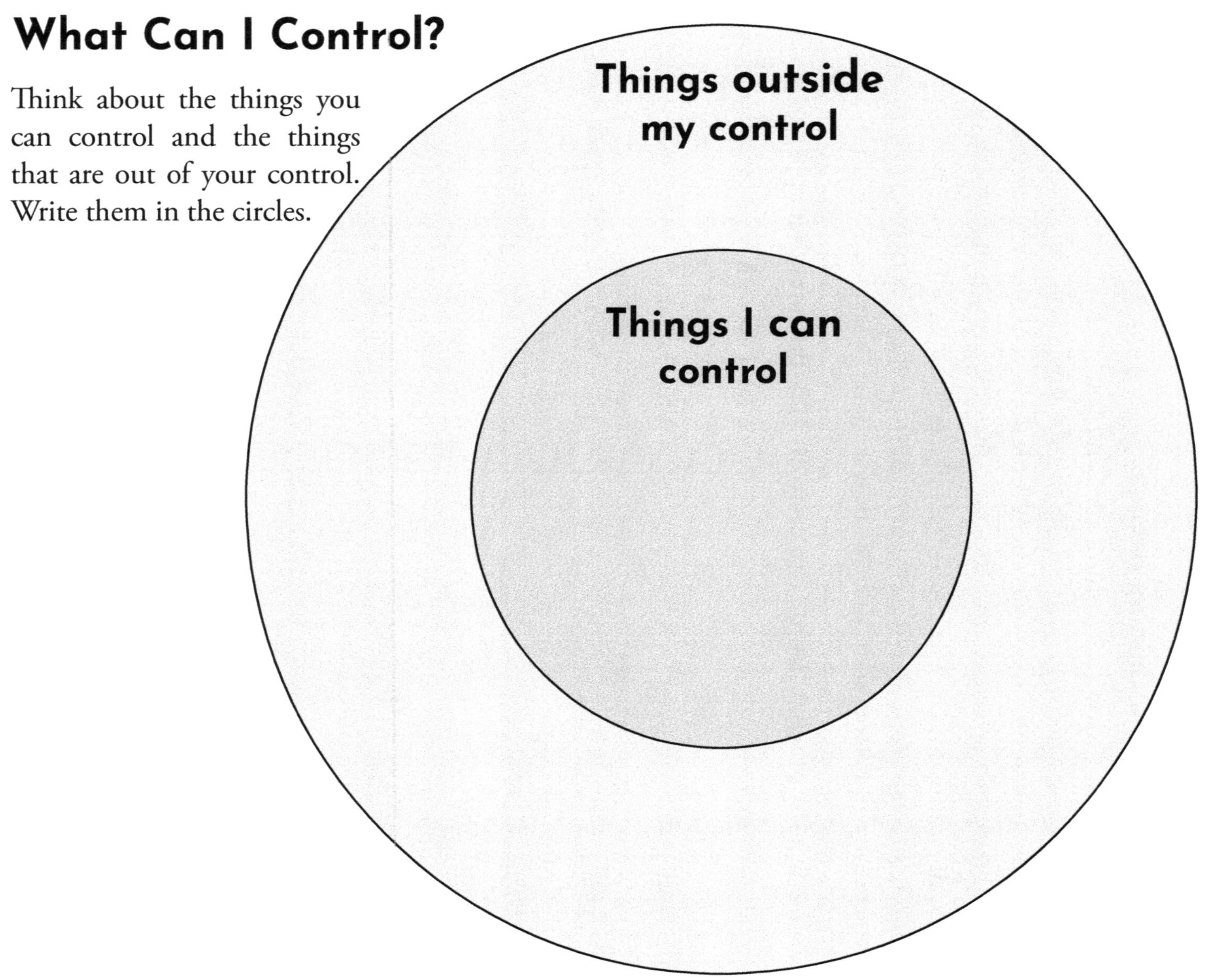

Module 2:

Adaptive Thinking

Section 2:

Mindfulness: Mind and Body

Topic 1: Mindfulness

Children must be taught how to think, not what to think.
~Relax children

Did You Know? The quickest way to change your mood is to practise mindfulness. This includes being aware of your thoughts, feelings and senses. The aim is not to distract, clear or stop your thinking – it's about noticing and namingyour feelings in a non-judgmental manner.

For example, if you are feeling anxious, simply tell yourself, 'I notice that I am feeling anxious'. Accept it for what it is – just a thought or a feeling – don't fight it. The more you fight it, the bigger the struggle. Mindfulness breathing can stop a cascade of inner events that cause anxiety and stress – states that challenge your ability to concentrate and pay attention. Anytime you're feeling stressed, angry or sad, try doing breathing or muscle relaxation exercises. This will help you calm down and be more rational in the way that you respond.

The way we breathe is strongly linked to the way we feel. When we are relaxed, we breathe slowly, and when we are anxious, we breathe more quickly. Let's look at different patterns of breathing:

Normal breathing: When we breathe, we take in oxygen that is used by the body. This process creates carbon dioxide, a waste product that we breathe out. When our breathing is relaxed, the levels of carbon dioxide and oxygen are balanced, allowing our body to function efficiently.

Exercise Breathing: When we exercise, our body uses more oxygen to fuel our muscles and, therefore, produces more carbon dioxide. Since our breathing rate increases during exercise, we breathe in extra oxygen and breathe out the extra carbon dioxide. This means that the balance between oxygen and carbon dioxide levels is maintained.

Anxious breathin: When we are anxious, our breathing rate increases. We take in more oxygen and breathe out more carbon dioxide than usual. Because we are not exercising, our body is not using up the extra oxygen or producing any extra carbon dioxide. Because carbon dioxide is being expelled faster than it is being produced, the levels of carbon dioxide in the blood go down, leading to a temporary change in the pH of the blood. This can lead us to feeling unpleasantly light-headed, tingly in our fingers and toes, and clammy and sweaty.

When our breathing returns to its usual rate, the levels of carbon dioxide return to normal and the symptoms resolve. You can deliberately relax your breathing to feel better by using the 'Take five' breathing exercise on the next page.

Like any new skill, the more you practise, the better you will get at it. But do not wait until the storm hits to secure your belongings. The idea is that we equip ourselves so that when life throws curve balls at us, we know what to do. Do you run and catch it, or duck and dive to avoid it? Be prepared!

Practise the following simple mindfulness exercises:

- 'take five' breathing exercise
- mindfulness meditation
- grounding with your five senses
- guided visualisation.

'Take Five' Breathing Exercise

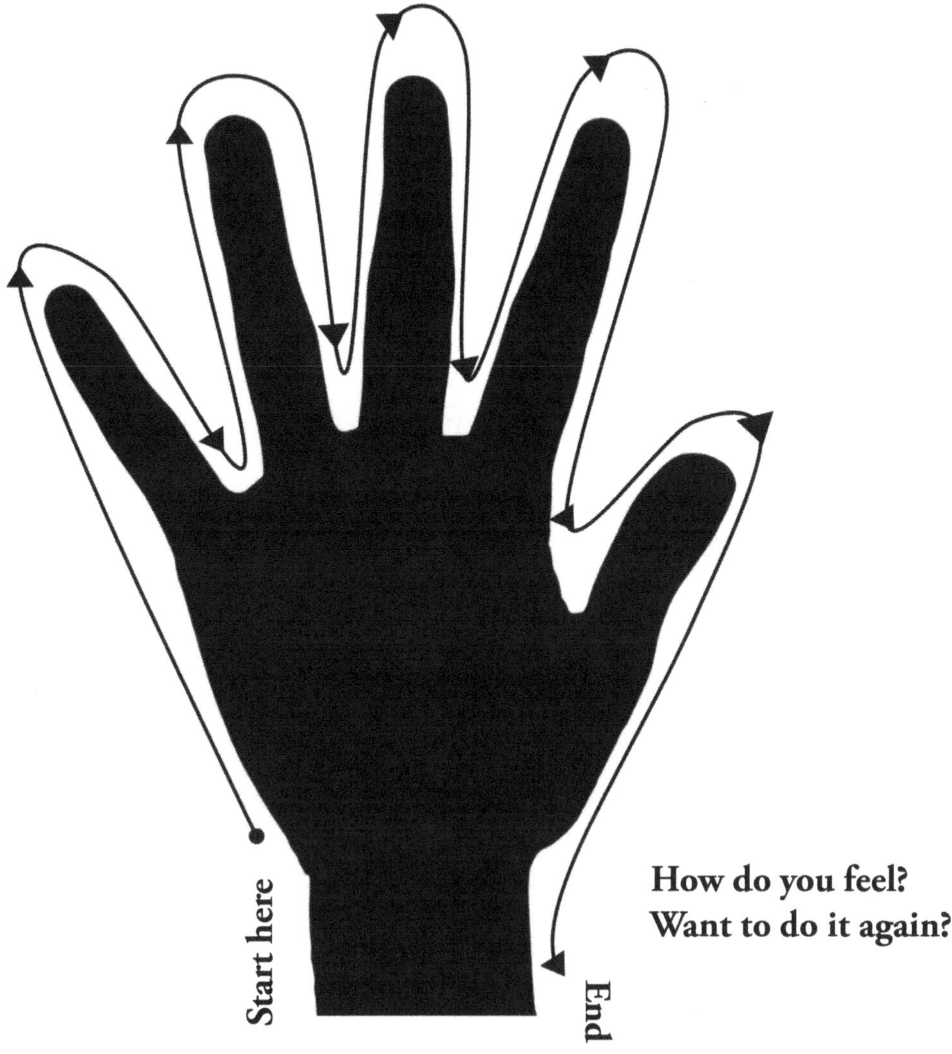

Spread out your hand like a fan. Use the pointer finger of your other hand to trace along your fingers, up and down. As you trace up your finger, inhale through your nose for a count of four. At the top of the finger, hold your breath for a count of four. When tracing down your finger, let the breath out through your mouth as if you are blowing through a straw, again for a count of four.

Repeat with all five fingers. Keep the pace slow and steady.

Continue the breathing process until you feel calm.

Mindfulness Meditation

Breathing

Sit in a comfortable place. Begin by paying attention to your breathing. Notice the physical sensation of air filling your lungs and then slowly leaving it. When your mind wanders, which it will, simply notice your thoughts and turn your attention back to breathing.

Noticing Game

Spend one minute silently looking around the room. Try to notice things in the room that you've never noticed before. Maybe you've not noticed all the elements of a poster that is hanging on the wall, or a spider web on the corner of the ceiling, or the pattern on the carpet. After the minute is up, write down what you noticed or discuss it with your parents.

Sea Waves Crashing

Sit or lie down in a comfortable position. Breathe in through your nose, and then out through pursed lips, as if you are blowing through a straw. The slow and steady breathing may sound like sea waves, gently crashing on shore. Continue breathing and making the ocean sound for two minutes.

The Power of Listening

Ring a bell, or anything else that creates a long trailing sound. Listen until you can no longer hear the sound. After the ringing ends, continue listening to any other sounds in your environment for the next minute. Write down what sounds you heard. If you are doing it with your friends, take turns to discuss what you heard.

Body Squeeze and Hold Exercise

Sit or lie down in a comfortable position. Squeeze and relax each of the muscles in your body, one by one, starting at your toes and working your way up to your face. Hold each squeeze for about five seconds. How do you feel after you release the squeeze? If you want, imagine that you are squeezing particular muscles using imagery, such as picking up a pencil with your toes, tensing your legs while trying to touch a piece of furniture, wiggling your nose as if a fly has landed on it and you are trying to get it off, then scrunching your face to make the fly go away.

Grounding

Hey mate!
Tough one today?

You bet. My mind is racing and just won't stop!

Have you tried grounding? This is when you pay attention to your five senses to slow down your thoughts.

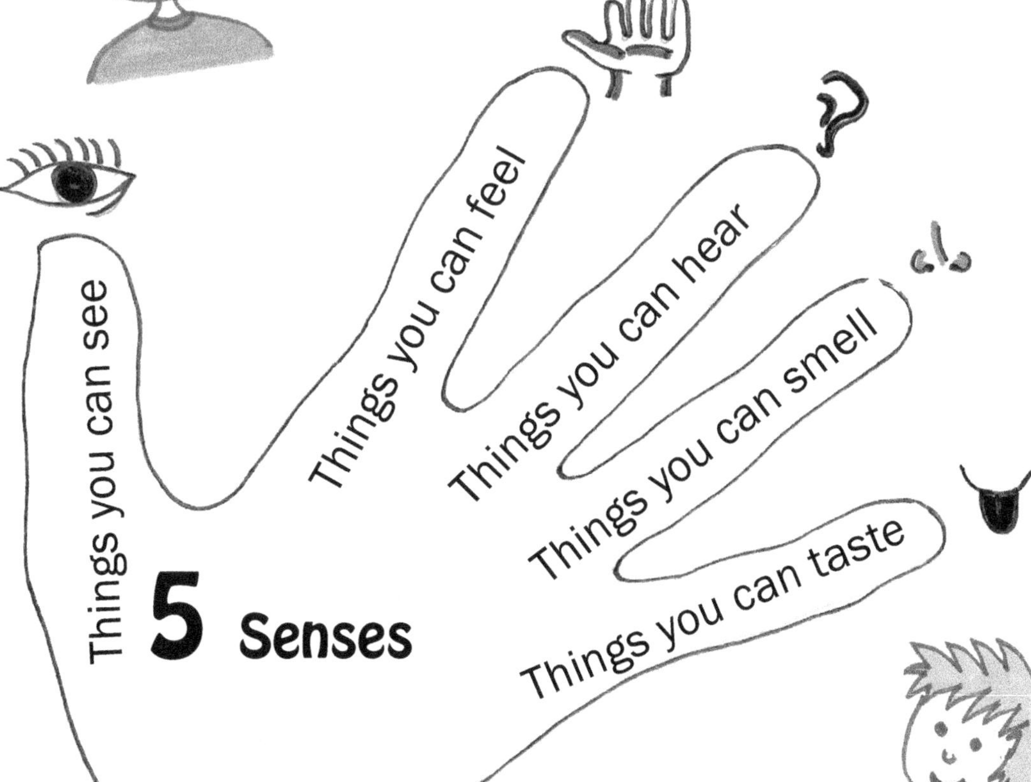

Wow!

Visualisation

This is a guided meditation. Have someone read the passage in a slow, calm voice as you sit or lie in a comfortable position with your eyes closed. Try to see, hear and feel all the sensations described.

You are walking on a beautiful, deserted, pearly-white beach. You feel the warm white sand on your feet as you glide, carefree, along the water's edge. The sounds of the waves are rhythmic and peaceful. You feel free.

The water is turquoise blue and the sand shimmering white. The waves come and go, and you watch as the sand gets pulled backward and forward. In the distance you see the horizon and follow it, noticing how it curves as it touches the clear blue sky. A sailboat appears and slowly moves across the horizon.

Everything you see helps you to let go and become more and more relaxed. You smell the fresh, salty scent of the ocean and taste the salty mist on your lips. You feel increasingly relaxed and refreshed. Seagulls fly gracefully on the wing and you imagine how it would be to experience the freedom to fly. You are completely relaxed as you continue to walk along the beach. In front of you, you see a lounge chair under a palm tree. Slowly you walk towards it, sit down and relax in it. You lie back and feel a total sense of relaxation and tranquility come over you. Your eyes close and the only sound that you pay attention to is the waves coming and going. The rhythmic sound of the waves takes you into a deep state of relaxation, of peace and calmness.

Take three deep breaths. In through your nose – hold – and out through your mouth as if you are blowing through a straw.

As I count down from five to one, you will begin to come back to the room. When I finish you can open your eyes and sit up, alert and refreshed.

***Five:** gradually starting to come back*

***Four:** you're becoming more and more aware*

***Three:** start to move your hands and legs a little while you awaken*

***Two:** you're almost completely awake*

***One:** open your eyes; you're alert and refreshed*

Reflect on the following after the visualisation:

- What did you notice?
- How did you visualise your thoughts (i.e. words, images or something else)?
- Did your mind get hooked by thoughts? If so, were you able to unhook yourself and come back to the present?
- Did any negative or painful thoughts show up? Were you able to allow the thoughts to come and go?
- How do you feel now?

Have you tried any of these mindfulness strategies in the past? Did they help?

____

____

____

____

Which ones do you think will be helpful?

____

____

____

____

Keep practising. The more you practise, the better you'll get at mindfulness.

Building happiness and well-being

Roll a dice to move your counter around the board, exploring strategies to build your happiness and well-being.

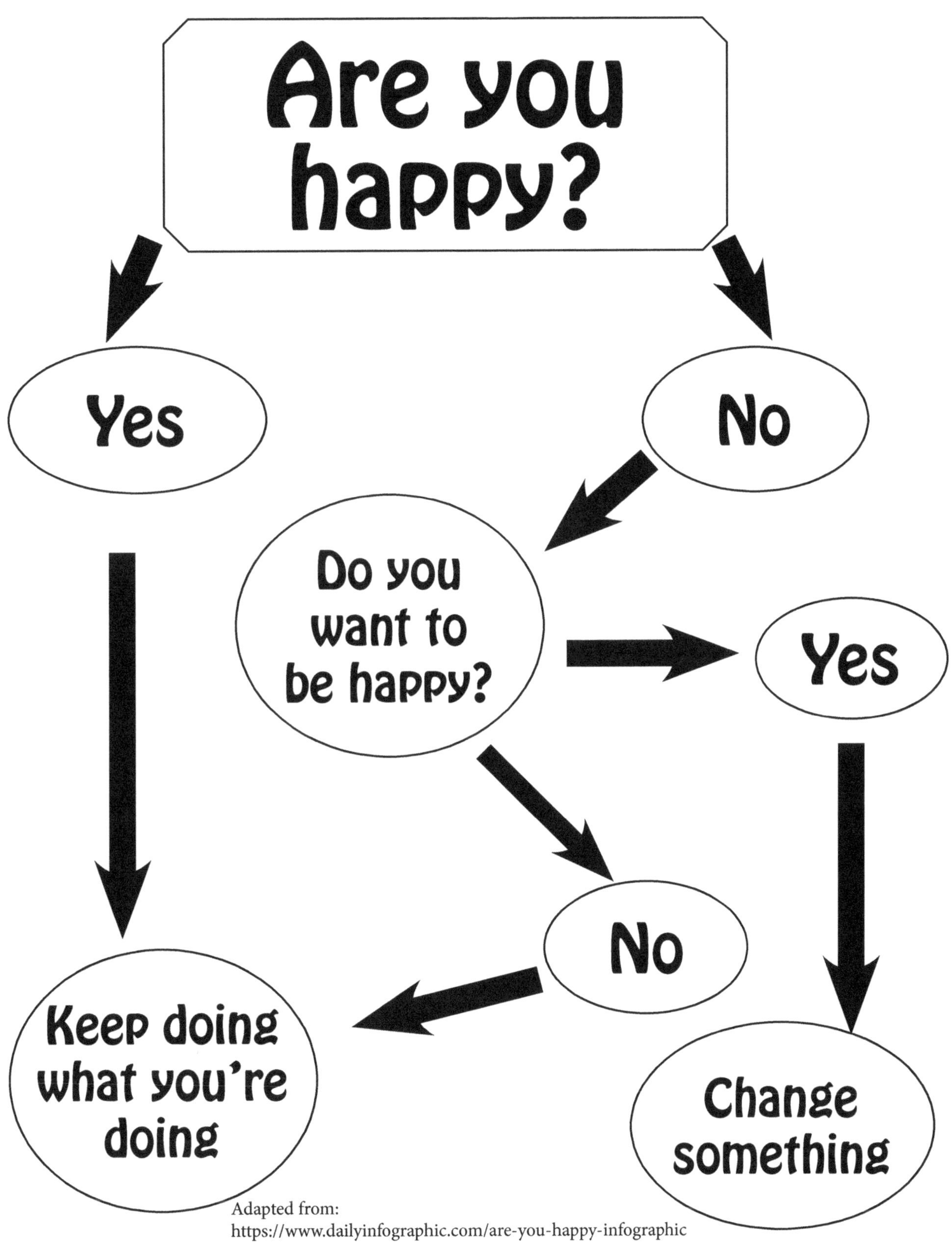

Adapted from:
https://www.dailyinfographic.com/are-you-happy-infographic

Topic 2: Physical Activity

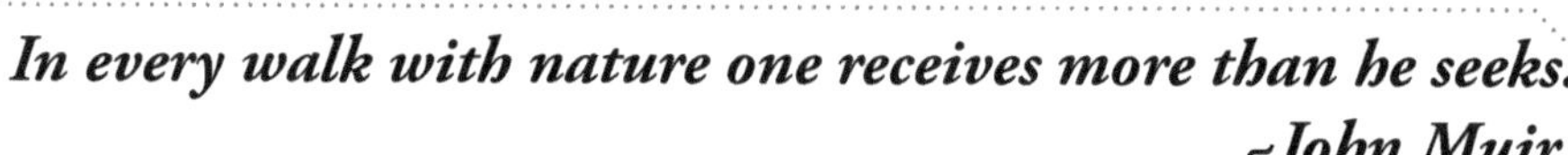

In every walk with nature one receives more than he seeks.
~John Muir

There are many activities that you can do in nature. Add your own ideas to the ones below:

- Walking in the park
- Hiking
- Walking in the rain
- Bird-watching
- Swimming outdoors
- Climbing a mountain
- Lying on the ground and watching the shapes of the clouds
- Walking your dog
- Biking on a nature trail
- Sleeping outdoors
- Fishing
- Camping
- Photography

Others:

____

____

____

After you've engaged in outdoor activities, do you notice any changes in your mood or in your ability to focus and concentrate?

____

____

____

Exercise and Mental Health

> ***The best six doctors anywhere, and no one can deny it, are sunshine, water, rest, air, exercise and diet.***
> ***~ Wayne Fields***

Did You Know? Exercise helps manage ADHD symptoms. Exercise is often said to be the body's natural antidepressant. Physiologically, it contributes to better sleep; increases the release of chemicals, such as serotonin and endorphins in the brain; and increases blood flow, which improves neural functioning. Psychological benefits are many, and include heightened self-esteem, interruption to negative thoughts and an increase in social contact. Recent studies have also shown that as little as 30 minutes of exercise per day can increase your ability to concentrate, and improve general executive functioning. The key is to make exercise part of your lifestyle and of an ADHD management plan.

Exercise also helps with conditions that can co-exist with ADHD, such as:

- Depression
- Substance Abuse
- Sleep Difficulties
- Low Energy
- Anxiety
- Oppositional Defiant Disorder
- Stress
- Low Self-esteem

Benefits of Physical Exercise

Physical health: The more you move, the better your movement skills will be. Physical activity helps build healthy bones, muscles, heart and lungs. For maximum benefit, aim for activity that gets you breathing a bit harder and sweating a bit!

Brain functioning: Being active develops the brain and improves mental functions. Exercise leads to improved motor skills, better thinking and problem-solving, stronger attention skills and increased learning. Even the simple act of playing outside with friends can help you do better on tests and assignments.

Emotional and mental health: If you're feeling depressed or anxious, or just having an off day, exercise might seem too hard. But if you can get started, physical activity releases 'feel-good' chemicals (endorphins) in the brain. These help to improve mood, energy levels and even sleep. These positive effects will flow on into things like self-confidence, resilience and learning.

Reduced anxiety: By focusing on the demands of physical activity, an anxious person can pull their attention away from anxiety-inducing issues, developing new skills and achieving a sense of accomplishment.

Improved relationships: Exercising and playing sports together can give you a sense of belonging and companionship. Focusing on the sport can help relieve social anxiety over being in a group situation. Positive effects of shared experiences, developing rapport and working towards common goals help develop confidence and foster friendships in school if the activities are school-based.

Improved body image (self-esteem, self-worth and self-confidence): When you see how much fun it is to be able to dance, jump, walk, run, stretch and play, you are more likely to want to continue enjoying being active throughout your life. Seeing and appreciating what your body can do, rather than how it looks, is a great way for you to build a positive body image and self-esteem. As you develop this awareness it becomes part of your lifestyle.

My ABC exercise chart

Name a feeling and spell it out. Do the exercises that correspond to each letter.

A	5 push-ups	N	20 second plank
B	10 star jumps	O	10 squats
C	10 arm circles	P	10 push-ups
D	10 basketball bounces	Q	20 arm circles
E	10 second plank	R	5 frog jumps
F	20 high knees	S	5 burpees
G	10 hops on one leg	T	10 ab cycles
H	10 squats	U	10 second plank
I	5 frog jumps	V	20 high knees
J	10 jump squats	W	20 jumps on the spot
K	5 burpees	X	10 star jumps
L	5 sit-ups	Y	10 second wall sit
M	10 ab cycles	Z	20 high knees

Created by: Anne-Marie Douse

Topic 3: ADHD and Nutrition

Brooke Penny, Paediatric Dietitian, APD

What is a balanced diet?

A balanced diet includes foods from all five food groups. The food groups are:

1. Fruit
2. Vegetables
3. Dairy
4. Meat and meat alternatives
5. Grains and cereals

We should also be having a small amount of healthy fats (avocado, olive oil, nuts, margarines) every day, and limiting our intake of junk foods and highly processed foods.

Which foods help with ADHD?

Having foods from all five food groups is important for everybody. Each food group provides us with different nutrients to help with bone growth, immunity, muscle building, energy levels, brain function and the prevention of diseases, just to name a few! There are no particular nutrients or foods that people with ADHD need more of; however, if someone with ADHD does not get enough of some nutrients, this may make their ADHD symptoms worse. Iron, magnesium, zinc and Omega-3s are particularly important for this. If you are following a balanced diet, it is easy to get enough of these!

There might be a food group, or multiple food groups, that you do not eat or eat very little of. This may be because you are following a certain style of eating (e.g. vegetarian), you may have an allergy or intolerance, or it might just be a personal preference. If this is the case and you are worried about whether your diet is balanced, chat to your GP or a paediatric dietitian.

Nutrition and Behaviour

Does sugar cause hyperactivity?

Research has shown us that reducing sugar in the diet has no effect on hyperactivity. However, limiting sugar is still an important part of a healthy diet. This is because sugary treats provide us with very little of the good stuff: vitamins, mineral and fibre. Consuming sugary foods also gives us a very short burst of energy. After eating something sugary, our energy levels rise up quickly, then drop back down quickly – you might have heard of a 'sugar crash'. This makes it more difficult for us to focus and complete tasks to the best of our ability, you might even feel more irritable and short tempered when having a sugar crash.

Do food additives have any effect on behaviour?

In children with and without ADHD, food additives have been shown to affect behaviour. So, should we eliminate them from our diet? There is not a straightforward answer. We don't have enough evidence for us to recommend an elimination diet as a treatment strategy for everyone with ADHD. The research shows us that not all children will improve with the removal of these additive-containing foods, and if it does work, the effect it has can also be relatively small. Eliminating these types of foods is difficult; you and your family need to discuss whether this is something that will be achievable and worth the hard work. What we know for sure is that many foods that contain food additives also tend to be higher in sugar, therefore, not consuming too much of these foods is beneficial either way for someone with ADHD.

Is breakfast essential?

Breakfast itself may not be essential, but having something to eat in the morning is important for the brain to function properly. If we do not have regular meals, the brain is running on empty and does not work as well as it could. This can cause issues when we are having to concentrate for long periods, like at school! Eating regular meals helps us to function at our best.

An ideal breakfast will include a high-fibre carbohydrate (e.g. multigrain toast, weetbix, muesli, porridge, fruit) and a source of protein (e.g. baked beans, smoked salmon, sardines, yoghurt, nuts, seeds). The combination of protein and carbohydrate will give you a good boost of long-lasting energy to start your day.

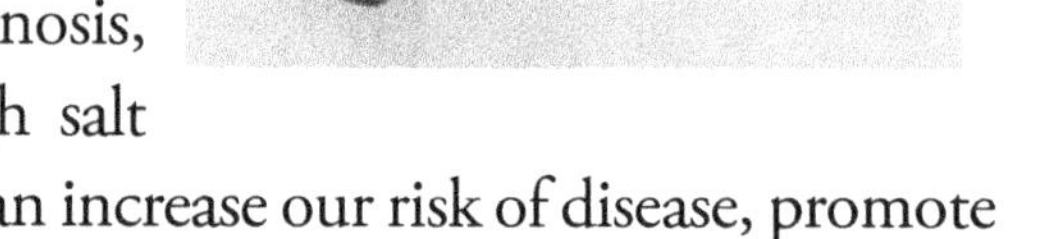

Are there any foods that I should avoid?

Regardless of whether we have an ADHD diagnosis, everyone should enjoy sugary, high fat and high salt foods in moderation, as too much of these foods can increase our risk of disease, promote weight gain and negatively influence our concentration levels and mood.

Eliminating foods, food groups or nutrients completely (e.g. gluten or dairy) is not recommended unless you have an intolerance or allergy. If you feel you are developing symptoms from any particular foods, chat to your GP or a paediatric dietitian so that they can assess whether an elimination diet would be helpful, and the best way to approach it to ensure your diet remains balanced.

Fill in the food diary on the next page. Record the foods eaten, how many serves from each food group, and calculate the total number of serves across the day. Compare this to the recommendations in the lower table. Is there a food group you need to eat more of or less of?

Remember that this is to be used as a guide only. Everyone's medical background, eating style, activity level, body type and food preferences are different.

What is a 'serve'?

Grains/Cereals: 1 serve = ½ cup pasta/rice, 1 slice of bread, 1 bread roll, 2/3 cup cereals or 3 wholegrain crackers

Meat/meat alternatives: 1 serve = 1 palm size portion of chicken/meat/fish/tofu, 100g tin of tuna/salmon, 1 handful of nuts/seeds or 1 cup of beans/legumes

Dairy: 1 serve = 1 cup cow's milk/fortified plant milk, 2 slices of cheese or ¾ cup of yoghurt.

Vegetables: 1 serve = 1 cup of raw veg, ½ cup of cooked vegetables, or 1 medium potato.

Fruit: 1 serve = 1 whole large fruit (banana, apple), 2 smaller fruits (apricot, kiwi) or 1 cup tinned fruit.

For more detailed information on serving sizes and recommendations for age groups and genders, visit www.eatforhealth.gov.au.

Exercise: Food Diary

Meal	Foods Eaten	How Many Serves
Breakfast	Example:1 slice of toast 1 kiwi fruit 1 small tub of yoghurt	1 x grains 0.5 x fruit 1 x dairy
Snack		
Lunch		
Snack		
Dinner		
Supper		

Recommended number of serves per day by age				
Grains/ cereals	**Meat/meat alternatives**	**Dairy**	**Vegetables**	**Fruit**
9-11 yrs: 5 12-13 yrs: 6 14-18 yrs: 7	9-18 yrs: 2 ½	9-11 yrs: 2 ½ 12-18 yrs: 3 ½	9-18 yrs: 5	9-18 yrs: 2
Your total number of serves per day:				

Topic 4: The Importance of Sleep

I want to sleep but my brain won't stop talking to itself.

Did You Know? Having good sleep hygiene is vital for good functioning, better school performance and general well-being. Although many mechanisms of the brain remain a mystery, there is no doubt that the brain requires a lot of energy to function as the body's management system. In addition to food, water and oxygen, the brain needs sleep. A good night's sleep is exactly what the doctor will order to prepare us for the many things that we have to do in any given day. In essence, no sleep equals no energy in the brain to help us recover from the day and recharge our minds for the adventures of the next day. If, after using the sleeping tips below, you are still struggling to get a good night's rest, speak to your family doctor. Sleeping tablets are an alternative but should be avoided, as these tend to be only effective in the short term. Long-term use may lead to dependence and prolong your sleep difficulties. Generally, tweens and teens need between eight and 12 hours of sleep per night. Use the 'Sleep Diary' on page 151 to monitor your sleep patterns.

Scenario

Jane did not like going to bed at a set time. Her bedtime was 9 o'clock, but she would find as many excuses as possible to stay up, and most nights, her bedroom light was not switched off before 10 o'clock. She would sneak a small torch into her bed and read under the blankets until midnight.

Every morning Jane would sleep through the buzzing of her alarm clock and would not wake up until her mother came in to wake her. Jane would be moody and complain about being tired.

'If you went to sleep on time, you would not be so tired in the morning. Now you have to suffer the consequences of the lack of sleep, and be worn out all day', her mother

told her. 'As of Monday, I will no longer wake you up in the morning. If you are not ready when I need to leave at 8 o'clock for work, you'll have to walk to school; and you know what the school rule is for students who arrive late – detention on Friday afternoons. You have the weekend to think about a solution to this problem. I am available to help to brainstorm some strategies if you want.'

Jane's mother reminded her of the new rules on Sunday night. On Monday morning, Jane was still asleep when her mother left for work and had to walk to school. Not only did she get a detention for Friday afternoon, but she was late for Science (her favourite subject), and didn't have time to finish her test.

Jane decided she had to take control of her sleep and work on getting up on time. It took a few weeks, but she was able to change her sleeping habits until she could get up on time for school every day, feeling rested and ready to face the day.

Guidelines to Enhance Good Sleep

Caffeine: Good sleep hygiene begins in the day, with the consideration of your food and drink intake. Caffeine is a stimulant that prevents sleep. Caffeine is present not only in tea and coffee, but also in cola and energy drinks. If you drink these, try to limit your intake and avoid them altogether after lunchtime.

Food: Eating a large meal before bedtime can affect sleep. Consider the best time to eat your dinner, and talk to your parents about having your dinner earlier on school nights. You can still all have family meals at weekends and during holiday periods. A glass of warm milk can help you fall asleep.

Exercise: You may have difficulty in falling asleep if you have been inactive throughout the day. Where possible, engage in sports and play outside. This will help you to burn off energy and feel tired at the end of the day. Even if you are not very sporty, just going for a walk in the fresh air can be helpful. However, exercise should be avoided directly before bedtime, as the heat created in the muscles by exercise can prevent you from falling asleep.

Environment: Your sleep environment should be a place where you feel safe and secure, and is not associated with play. There are several ways to adjust your sleep environment. For example, do you prefer a night light or total darkness? What about the temperature and noise level of the room? Clear your room of things that distract you from sleeping.

Routine: Have a bedtime routine and a set bedtime. A routine can start well before bedtime and include activities to help you wind down, such as a warm bath or shower, and practising mindfulness. Sticking to a set pattern each night will help you calm down from the stress of the day before sleeping.

Technology: The use of electronic devices (such as televisions, mobile phones and tablet computers) close to bedtime can prevent you from settling to sleep. This is because they produce light that is good at suppressing natural hormones in the brain that cause sleepiness.

Ideally, these devices should not be used in the hours before bed and should not be in your room overnight. If you use these devices to help you fall asleep, consider replacing this routine with reading or playing soothing music.

Use a sleep diary: A sleep diary can be a useful way of making sure you have the right facts about your sleep, rather than making assumptions. Because a diary involves watching the clock, which can lead to increased wakefulness or anxiety, it is a good idea to only use it for two weeks to get an idea of what is going on and then perhaps two months down the track to see how you are progressing.

Sleep Diary

Date	Example 30 March					
What time did you go to bed?	9:00 pm					
Approximately what time did you fall asleep?	11:00pm					
What time did you wake up?	6:00am					
How many times did you wake up during the night?	4 times					
How many hours of sleep did you get during the night?	5 hours					
What was the total time that you were awake during the night?	2 hours					
Reasons for waking up during the night	Mind racing Over tired Worried about not sleeping					
How rested do you feel in the morning? Score from 0-10 (10 most rested)	5					

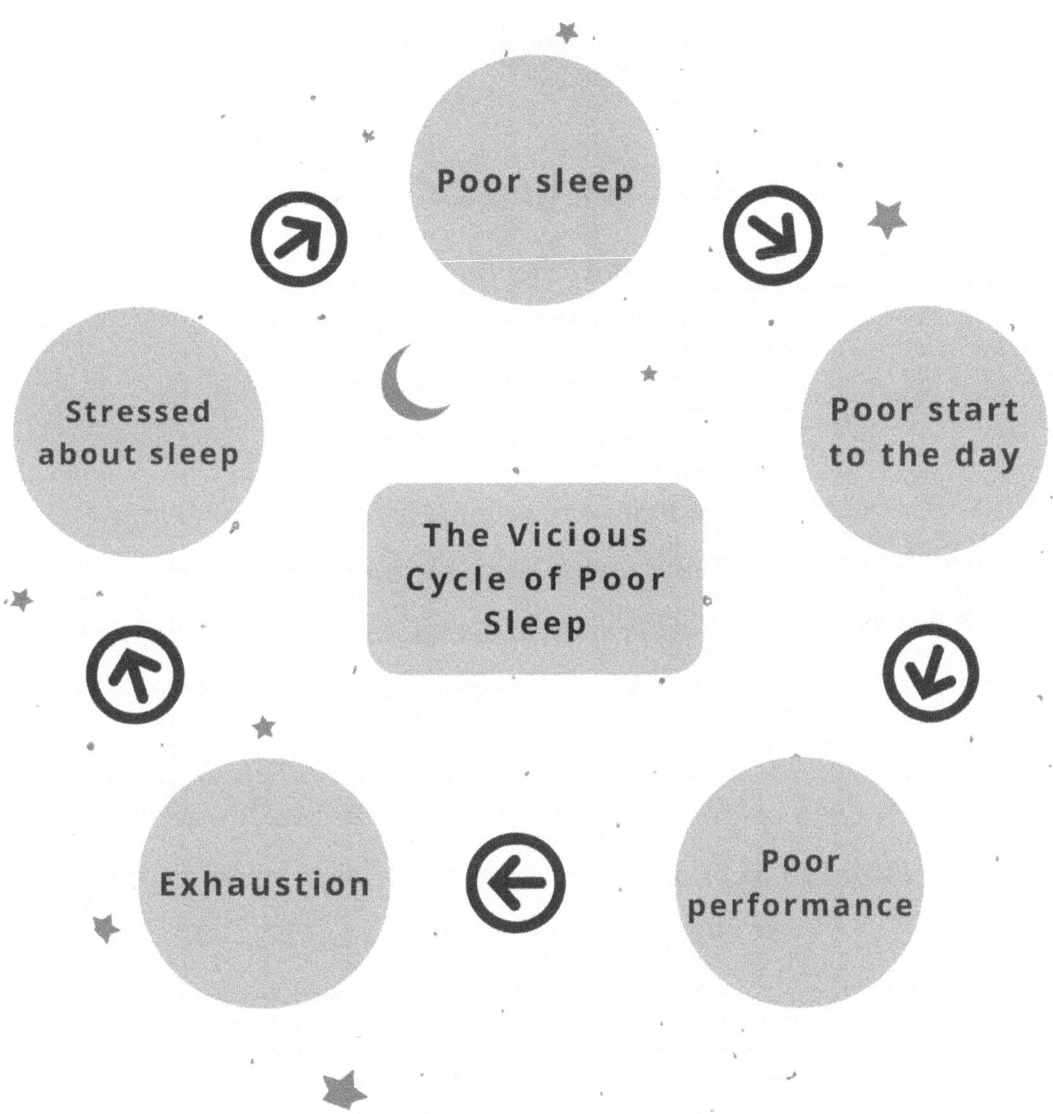
Poor sleep
Poor start to the day
Poor performance
Exhaustion
Stressed about sleep
The Vicious Cycle of Poor Sleep

Sleep Hygiene

Tips for good sleep:

- Build a bedtime routine
- Make after-dinner time relaxing time
- Avoid eating big meals close to bedtime
- Ensure that your bedroom temperature is comfortable
- Make sure that your room is dark and noise free
- Avoid taking naps during the day
- Ensure that you get enough exposure to natural light
- Exercise can promote good sleep
- Associate your bed with sleep
- Try to avoid confrontation or upsetting activities before sleep time
- Avoid all technology for at least two hours before bedtime
- Keep a sleep diary (see page 151)
- Speak to your GP about your sleep patterns and see if there are other alternatives to help you sleep

Module 2:

Adaptive Thinking

Section 3:

Identifying Your Values and Goals

Topic 1: Knowing Your Values

Values are like fingerprints. Nobody's are the same, but you leave them all over everything you do.
-Elvis Presley

Did You Know? Values are those qualities, principles, beliefs and ideas we feel strongly about. The main benefit of knowing your values is that you will gain great clarity and focus about what really matters to you, and you can use this new-found clarity to set goals and take committed action. Values signify what is important and worthwhile in our lives. Different people have different values and that is okay. Values help us prioritise how to best spend our time, right here and right now. Here are two reasons priorities are important.

Firstly, time is our most limited resource – it does not renew itself. Once we spend a day, it's gone forever. If we don't prioritise, and waste that day on actions that don't produce the results we want, that loss is permanent.

Secondly, priorities matter because we humans tend to be inconsistent in how we invest our time and energy. We are easily distracted and fall into the trap of living by different priorities every day. One day we exercise; the next day we slack off. One day we work productively; the next we procrastinate and lack motivation. If we don't consciously use our priorities to stick to a consistent course, we'll naturally shift all over the place. Like a ship without a radar in the middle of the ocean, who knows where it will dock – before you can set a course for your ship, you must first determine the port where you want to dock.

> ***If you don't know where you are going, any road will get you there.***
> ***~Lewis Carrol***

The way a GPS system works is a good analogy of how our values guide us and help us stay on course.

A GPS:

- **requires you to input your destination.** Nothing happens until you decide where you want to go. The same is true of values.
- **gets you to your destination faster with less hassle.** I am not that good with directions. I get lost easily. My navigation system gets me to my destination without the stress of trying to figure it out on my own. The same is true of values.
- **gives you constant feedback on your progress.** I always know the street I am on, how far I must travel to the next turn and how far to my ultimate destination. Values are similar. They tell me where I am in relation to where I want to go. They provide the context and keep me oriented and on the right track.
- **helps you get back on track when you go off track.** The system never scolds me, it simply tells me what I need to do to get back on track. Same with my values. They give me a reference point, so I know how to get to my destination.
- **re-directs you around roadblocks.** It is inevitable that you will encounter obstacles on the way to your destination. A good GPS is able to adjust and recalculate the route. The same is true of values. They provide the flexibility to overcome obstacles and keep moving forward.
- **is not always accurate.** This is not surprising. It's a challenge for GPS databases to keep up

with all the changes: new roads, closed roads, road works, traffic accidents, etc. The same is true of your values: you won't always get it right. You will have to adjust to changing situations. Values give you a structure/framework for doing that.

- **requires an investment.** Values are similar. They do require an upfront investment of time. But the rewards are well worth it.

Did You Know? Living your values means listening to what is important to you and choosing to act accordingly. When you have a value, it usually shows up in every aspect of your life. For example, if you value 'kindness' and 'knowledge', you don't just talk about it – you spend time and energy practising being kind and being open to learning new things. During childhood, you may hold similar values to those of your parents. However, during your teen years, and as you transition into adulthood, you may start to question your parents' views on religion, politics and other social issues, and decide that you no longer hold the same views as them. This should be appreciated as a sign of maturity, when done with respect. Another point to make here is that some individuals confuse goals and values. Listening and living your values is different from achieving goals. Values are your compass; they tell you which direction you want to travel. Goals are the concrete actions that you take, in service of your values.

Name two values that are important to your family and give an example of how your family's actions show that these values are important to them.

____

____

____

Give an example of an education value that you have been taught.

____

____

____

How does it feel to stand up for your values when family members disagree with your position?

____

____

____

What happens when your behaviour is not aligned with your parents' values?

____

____

____

If your values and behaviours are inconsistent with each other, what should you change – your values or your behaviour? Give a reason for your answer.

____

____

____

Clarifying Your Values

The following table shows some of the most common values that young people say are important to them. Using a scale of 0–10, where 0 is not important at all, and 10 is very important, rate how important each one of these values is to you right now. Add your own in the blank spaces.

0	**1**	**2**	**3**	**4**	**5**	**6**	**7**	**8**	**9**	**10**
Not important					Moderately important				Very important	

Value	Rate	Value	Rate
Honesty – being truthful and sincere		**Personal safety** – feeling safe from harm or danger	
Courage – willingness to do difficult or scary things		**Wealth** – having a great deal of money or resources	
Fairness – acting in a just way, sharing appropriately		**Kindness** – being considerate and treating others well	
Sincerity – openness, honesty, being true		**Family** – supporting and respecting family members	
Knowledge – lifelong learning		**Career** – occupation or work life	
Stability – a calm, settled life, without wild ups and downs		**Freedom** – the right to act, speak or think as one wants	
Education – gaining knowledge, skills and qualifications		**Independence** – being in control of your own life	
Integrity – sticking to your moral and ethical principles and values		**Spirituality** – being concerned with the human spirit or soul	
Justice – being just or fair; showing respect for others		**Status** – having social or professional standing	
Approval – the good opinions of others		**Achievement** – reaching goals or objectives	

Trustworthiness – able to be relied on as honest or truthful, being true to your word		**Perseverance** – sticking with something, despite difficulties, until it is done	
Appearance – the way you or things look		**Power** – control of oneself or others	
Love – intense feeling for someone or something		**Adventure** – undertaking exciting activities	
Learning – acquiring new knowledge and skills		**Success** – accomplishing something	
Health – looking after your physical and mental condition		**Happiness** – a satisfied way of being	
Resilience – the ability to endure and recover from difficulties		**Respect** – due regard for the feelings, wishes or rights of others	

Once you have identified your values, choose your top five and list them in order of importance. Then complete the bull's eye exercise on the next page. Choose an area of your life you want to work on. For each value that affects that area of your life, make a cross in the bull's eye to show how consistently you are living at vthe chosen value. The further away from the bull's eye you place the cross, the more inconsistently you are living your values.

The aim of this exercise is to help you reflect and understand the importance of living a value-guided life.

1) ____________________

2) ____________________

3) ____________________

4) ____________________

5) ____________________

Exercise: Bull's Eye

The closer you are to the bull's eye, the more consistently you are living your values.

The further you are from the bull's eye, the more inconsistently you are living your values.

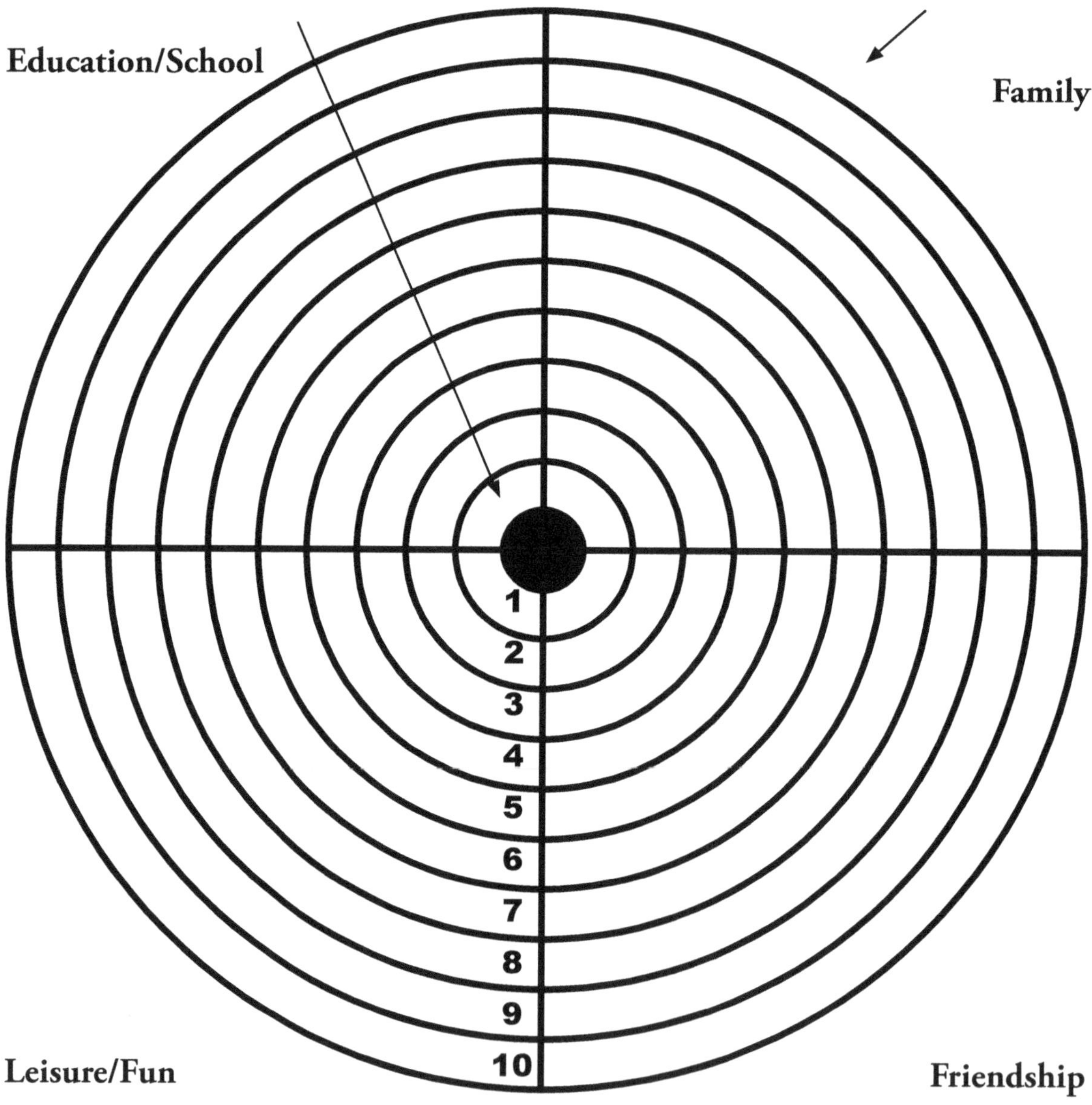

Adapted from: Tobias Lundgren- Swedish ACT therapist

How close are you to your bull's eye in relation to your chosen values?

____

____

____

Are you happy with how your bull's eye looks?

____

____

____

If not, what changes would you like to make?

____

____

____

What can you start doing today?

____

____

____

Topic 2: Goal-setting

When it is obvious that the goals cannot be reached, don't drop the goal – adjust the action steps.
~Confucius

Did You Know? Most of us do not spend much time thinking about how we set goals. In fact, many of us do not even think of goal-setting as a skill; rather, it's just something we do without reflecting on it much.

However, goal-setting is a practice that operates on a set of specific skills. Luckily, these skills are relatively easy to teach. As with most skills, it's best to learn goal-setting early – but it's never too late to improve.

Setting goals is a vital practice that can benefit anyone with a dream or a vision for their future. Young people who are just starting out on the grand journey of life are at a particularly opportune time to start building their goal-setting skills – not only will these skills serve them throughout their lives, but building them now will help them mould their future into one that they desire.

Every time you go after something you want, be it better grades, making friends, getting a place in the sports team or getting your driver's licence, you will face obstacles. An obstacle should not be a reason to give up, but rather motivation to figure out how to get past it. See an obstacle as a stepping-stone to growth, rather than a stumbling block to hold you back. If you see obstacles as the world being against you, you are likely to be overwhelmed with negative thoughts; but if you think ahead about the possible obstacles that you may encounter in each situation, you can better prepare yourself to face them when they show up, and feel more in control.

Exercise: Set a Goal

Write a goal you want to accomplish and two obstacles you might encounter along your way. Then write three steps you could take to overcome those obstacles. Where possible, identify the values underpinning this goal.

Example:

Goal: To get better grades

Values: Education/Learning/Success/Knowledge

Obstacle: I don't like doing homework

To overcome this obstacle, I can:

- ask myself, 'In service of what value am I willing to do my homework despite not liking it?'
- use my diary to allocate blocks of time for homework.
- reward myself after completing each block.

Now, write your own:

Goal: ______________________________

Values: ______________________________

Obstacles: ______________________________

To overcome this obstacle, I can

____

____

____

Skills/strategies I will need to achieve my goals

____

____

____

What can I start doing today to work toward my goals?

___

___

___

Who can help me and how?

___

___

___

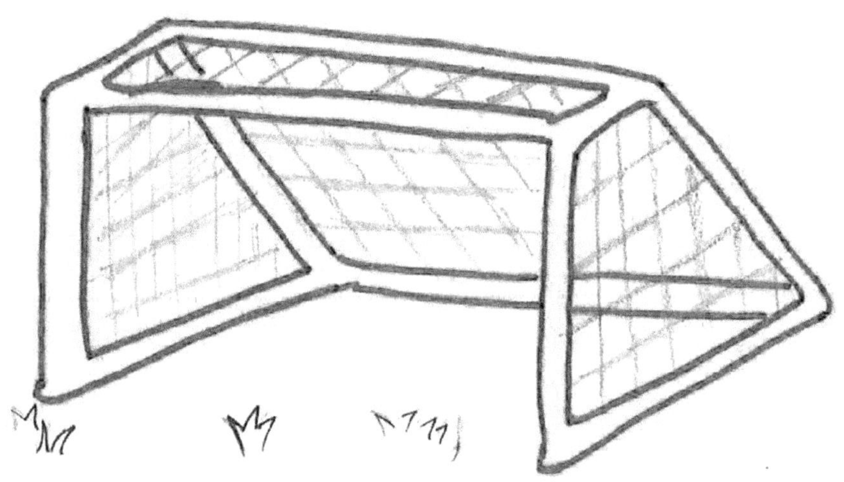

Benefits of Goal Setting?

SMART goal setting benefits children in many ways; for example, it:

- provides direction, which most youths are either seeking or trying to nail down
- helps children clarify their values, understand what is important to them and then focus on it
- facilitates more effective decision-making through better self-knowledge, self-esteem and direction
- allows children to take a more active role in building their own future
- acts as a powerful motivator by giving children something to hope for and aspire towards
- gives children a positive experience of achievement and personal satisfaction when they reach a goal
- assists children in finding a sense of purpose in their lives.

When you want to give up on your goal:

- Remember the value underpinning your goal.
- Review your action plan.
- Take small steps.
- Talk to someone in your Circle of Support about their own struggles when they were your age.
- Focus on how you can continue improving.
- Reward your effort, determination and persistence.
- Practice positive self-talk.

Tips on Setting Goals

1. **Always write down your goals**. Research suggests you are much more likely to achieve your goals if you write them down.
2. **Write your goals in the first person (I).** Make them truly motivating. Visualise yourself accomplishing your goals. Example: *After I graduate, I see myself on the way to Africa to work on the Save the Rhino project. I will be working with people with the same interests as me and doing what I really love.*
3. **Create a specific action plan for each goal using a graded/step approach.**
4. **Be clear on the relevance/why of your goal.** Keep the focus on the value underpinning the goal. This will motivate and energise you with the necessary fuel to keep going despite possible obstacles.
5. **Reflect on your progress to see if you are on target**. Achieving your goal is a process. You don't always know where your path might lead you, so reflect on what is happening and be prepared to brainstorm new pathways.
6. **Revise your action plans if needed.**
7. **Celebrate and reward your accomplishments.**

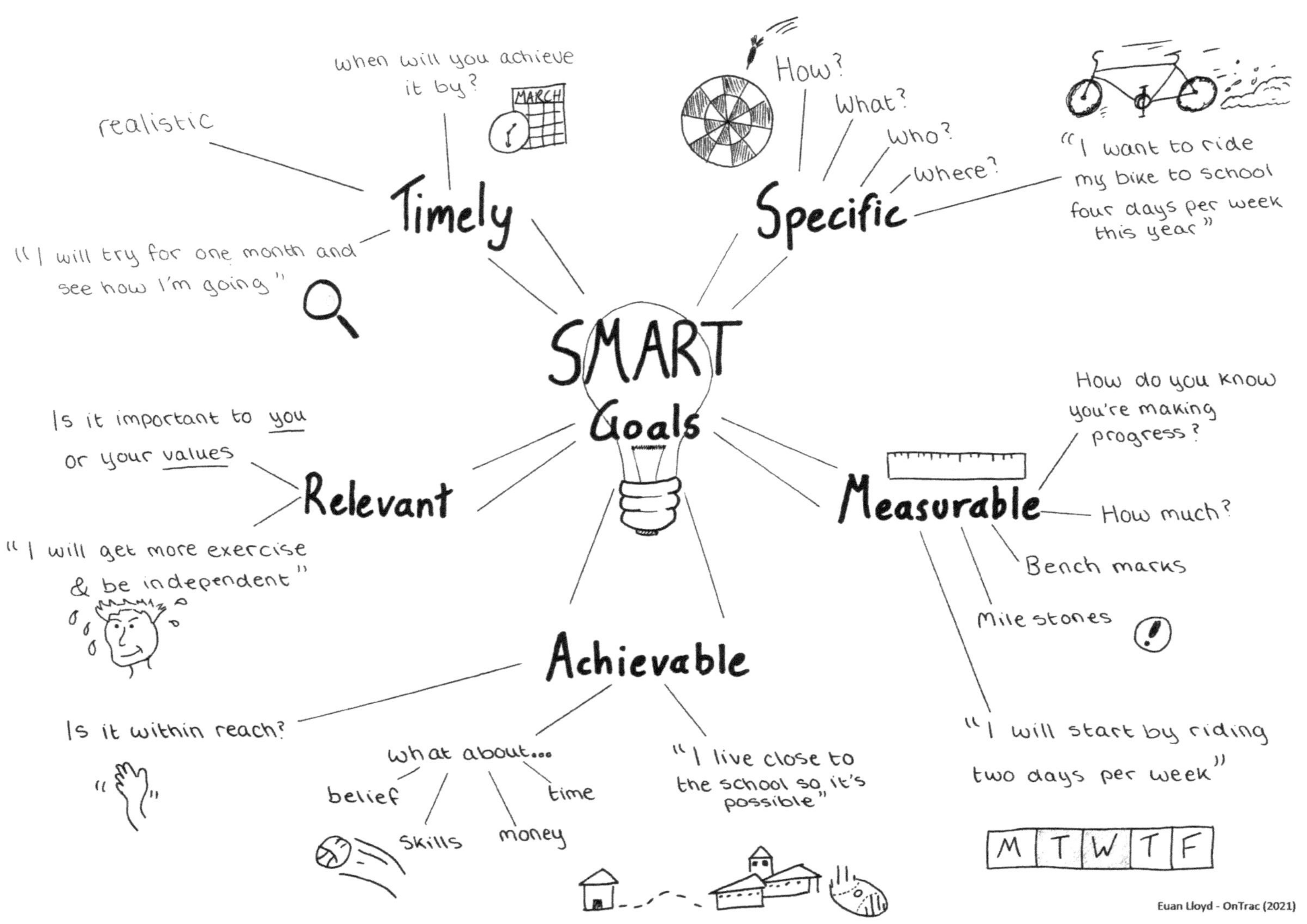
SMART
Goals
Timely
when will you achieve it by?
MARCH
realistic
"I will try for one month and see how I'm going"
Specific
How?
What?
Who?
Where?
"I want to ride my bike to school four days per week this year"
Relevant
Is it important to you or your values
"I will get more exercise & be independent"
Measurable
How do you know you're making progress?
How much?
Bench marks
Mile stones
"I will start by riding two days per week"
M T W T F
Achievable
Is it within reach?
what about...
belief
skills
money
time
"I live close to the school so it's possible"
Euan Lloyd - OnTrac (2021)

SMART Goal Planning

Set your goals high enough to inspire you and low enough to encourage you

Identify a goal that you would like to accomplish and develop a plan using the SMART approach.

My goal is: ______________________________

S Specific ______________________________

____

____

M Measurable ______________________________

____

____

A Achievable ______________________________

____

____

R Relevant ______________________________

____

____

T Timely ______________________________

____

Topic 3: Problem-solving

We cannot solve our problems with the same thinking we used when we created them.
~Albert Einstein

Scenario

Day one: *Tristan slogged home, barely aware of his surroundings. Mrs Jones had picked on him again about his messy work. It wasn't his fault she couldn't read his writing; maybe she needed better glasses! He'd been late to Science because he hadn't heard the bell ring, and then in Maths he got in trouble for talking too much. He hadn't meant to keep talking, but Maths was so boring, he didn't understand it at all. The numbers just moved around and didn't make sense.*

No one was home, so he made a quick snack and headed to his bedroom. He just needed a few minutes on the iPad to calm down after the bad day, then he'd get started on his homework.

Mum burst through the bedroom door, furious, just as he was getting close to the end of a difficult level. Oh no! He'd been on the computer for two hours, where had the time gone? Mum was mad about so many things – the mess he'd left in the kitchen making his snack, his school bag in the middle of the floor and he hadn't taken out the rubbish bin. And now he had chores to do before dinner, and he wouldn't get his homework done before tomorrow. Another bad day coming up.

Day two: *Tristan came home after another bad day. He felt like the whole world was against him, with everyone picking on him and saying mean things. He knew he had lots of things to do, but he really needed to just chill for a while. He went to his bedroom and flicked on the computer, then set a timer for 15 minutes.*

He lost himself in his electronic world, feeling calmer almost immediately. When the timer went off, it felt like he'd only been playing for a minute, but he did feel better. The sick feeling in his stomach had gone, and his heart rate and breathing were back to normal. Reluctantly he pushed himself away from the computer and went back to the kitchen.

Tristan looked at the list on the whiteboard. Bag to bedroom – yes, he'd done that. Empty dishwasher – that would be next. Pretty soon he'd done everything on the list, except the dreaded homework. He set his books out on the kitchen table, away from the computer, and got to work on his Maths. He set the timer again, and after half an hour he got up and made a snack, remembering to clean up after himself. The Maths was still tricky, but with practice and organisation it was making more sense.

When Mum came home, Tristan was back on his computer. She opened his bedroom door and smiled at him. 'Had a good day, love? I see you've done all your chores and homework, well done!'

What did Tristan do differently on day two?

____

____

____

Did Tristan still have time to have fun despite having done his chores?

____

____

____

Did You Know? As you get older, it will seem as though you have many more decisions to make and more problems to deal with. Using clear steps will help solve any type of problem, whether it's school, family or friend related. When a problem occurs, refrain from action, slow down and think about the situation. Ask yourself, 'What exactly is the problem?' Be specific.

- Brainstorm solutions. Think of as many solutions as possible to reach the desired goal.
- Analyse the pros and cons of each solution.
- Select a course of action.
- Implement your chosen action.
- Evaluate. If that plan doesn't work, try another solution.

Overcoming Obstacles

A problem well defined is half solved.
-John Dewey

Problem-solving is something we do every day. Some problems are small or are easily solved. Some problems are more complicated and can seem overwhelming. One way of tackling problems is to use a specific and systematic problem-solving procedure. If you have tried to solve certain problems without much success, try these steps out and see if they help. Learning to solve problems effectively will help you to minimise the level of stress in your life and improve your overall sense of well-being. Try it out and see! Remember, you can always talk to your parents, someone in your Circle of Support or a professional and ask for help.

Having ADHD can make it difficult to get on task and reach your goals, which can cause stress. Problem-solving is a technique you can use when you are overwhelmed and under stress.

Follow the following steps:

Step 1: Identify the Problem (Obstacles)

The first step is to identify what the obstacle is. It's important to be specific and clear.

Step 2: Think of Solutions to the Problem

The following study was conducted with several classrooms of school children. Some of the children were shown a picture of a young man in a wheelchair and asked if the young man could drive. The answer was overwhelmingly 'no'. In other classrooms, they asked the children **how** the man could drive. Those children came up with many ideas. The moral of the story is that we should ask ourselves how we can do something and not whether we can.

In this step, just brainstorm all the possible solutions. Do not overthink whether a solution is good or not. The table below lists possible solutions to different obstacles:

Obstacles	Possible Solutions
I have no time	Learn to plan, organise and prioritise. Use a diary.
Tried the activity and did not like it	Try it one more time, reward yourself. Chunk the activity so it's not so overwhelming.
I have no energy do anything	How is your sleep and diet? What time of day are you most productive? Be mindful of your thoughts.
Too much schoolwork and sport commitments	Speak to your parents and your teacher. The rule of thumb is to spend around 10 minutes on schoolwork per grade per day, i.e., Grade 6 = 60 minutes
Intrusive thoughts	Practice mindful breathing and relaxation exercises
Negative self-talk	Challenge your negative self-talk, exercise self-compassion
Planned a lot of activities and felt overwhelmed	Learn to be assertive and how to say 'no' assertively
Don't think that I'll enjoy a new activity	Try it anyway; you might surprise yourself

No transport	Ride your bicycle to school, get a ride with a friend, ride the bus. Use your problem-solving skills
My teacher does not like me	Keep the lines of communication open, tell your teacher what you are struggling with, learn to manage your anger so that you don't become aggressive or disruptive in class. Use 'I' statements when stating your feelings, needs and wants.
My parents are always on my case	See things from your parents' perspective, keep lines of communication open, keep your cool and remain respectful. Excuse yourself from the table if you start feeling angry. Show your parents that you are responsible by your actions. Use 'I' statements when stating your feelings, needs and wants.
I don't like being told what to do	Have a to-do list so that you remember what needs to be done. Don't wait to be reminded.
I have no friends	Learn social skills and try to identify things that you might be doing that are contributing to not having friends. Are you bossy? Or very talkative? How much do you talk during a conversation?
I am very forgetful	Use reminders and a diary every day. Keep your routine, even on weekends, if possible

Step 3. Choose the Solution that Makes the Most Sense

Now that you have identified the problem and brainstormed all the possible solutions, it is time to choose one or two solutions and try them. Work on one problem at a time.

Step 4. Try the Solution and See if it Works

Implement the solution that you feel will give you the best outcome.

Step 5. If the Solution Does Not Work, Try a Different Solution

Sometimes multiple solutions may look equally workable; however, you have to make a choice. The good thing about this process is that if the option that you chose is not giving you the result that you expected or wanted, you can always go back and try another option. Don't give up!

Problem-solving Questions You Can Reflect on:

- What can I do differently from now on, so that I don't lose my books?
- How can I ensure that I don't leave my homework at home again?
- What can I do to remind me to take my dishes up to the sink when I've finished eating?
- Whoops! What can I do about the spilled milk?
- What can I do to help me get out of bed on time to get ready for school?
- What's a good strategy to make sure sports stuff gets put away in the shed when I'm finished with it?
- What can I do to ensure that I stop gaming when the time agreed upon is over?
- What can I do to stop me from losing my cool when Mum asks me to do a chore?
- What can I do next time to make sure that I get home before the agreed-upon curfew time?
- What can I do to make sure that my room remains neat and organised?
- What can I do to remember to wash my footy gear in time for the next game?

Problem-Solving Sheet

Identify the problem ______________________________

____

Possible Solutions:

1.____

2.____

3.____

4.____

5.____

Solutions	Pros	Cons
1		
2		
3		
4		
5		
Best Solution:		
Implement:		
Evaluate:		

Euan Lloyd - OnTrac (2021)

STEPS TO HELP YOU

Problem Solve

STEP 1

IDENTIFY THE PROBLEM

- what is the problem?
- be specific and clear

STEP 2

BRAINSTORM SOLUTION

- as many as you can think of
- absolutely any solution
- doesn't matter if it is good or bad

STEP 3

CONSIDER THE PROS AND CONS

- what is good and bad about each solution

STEP 4

PICK THE BEST SOLUTION AND TRY IT OUT

- take action!

STEP 5

CHECK IF IT'S WORKING

- if not, try another solution
- what can I try instead?

Quiz 2 (see Appendix E for answers)

1. Xavier finds it very difficult to name his values. What would you suggest he do?

A. Ignore his values and do what he wants.

B. Think about what's most important to him, the actions that make him happy; for example, helping the elderly and helping around the house.

C. Just have the same values as his parents.

2. Xavier always agreed with his parents' beliefs, but now that he is 17, he feels that he has better values than his parents. What would you tell Xavier?

A. Not everyone has the same values, and it should not be a competition to see who has the 'correct' ones.

B. It is important for Xavier's values to be the same as his family's values.

C. Once Xavier achieves his values, he can 'cross it off' and set himself new ones.

3. Tristan values being kind and not using bad language. When he goes to his friend's house, he hears his friend's dad swear and his friend also swears when they play games. What should Tristan do?

A. Swear, so that his friend likes him even more.

B. Tell his friend that he does not want to be his friend anymore and call his mum to fetch him.

C. Live his values of being kind and polite. Don't swear, and hope that he can be a good role model for his friend.

4. **Tristan tells you that when he is with other people, he feels pressured to act in ways that are different from when he is with his family or alone. What would you tell Tristan?**

   A. That it is okay to act against your values when you are with other people.

   B. That he needs to behave the same as the other people in the group if he wants to be liked.

   C. To know his values, respect himself and make his own choices. Don't just go along with the crowd.

5. **Tristan tells you that setting goals is a waste of time because he never achieves the goals that he sets. How will you respond?**

   A. Tell him that you also don't set goals.

   B. Tell Tristan that only grown ups set goals.

   C. Explain to Tristan the S.M.A.R.T acronym and tell him that goals need to be Specific, Measurable, Achievable, Realistic and have a Time-frame.

Module 2:

Adaptive Thinking

Section 4:

ADHD and Relationships

Topic 1: Importance of Family

> ***ADHD is a neurological and behavioural disorder that affects not only the person with it, but the entire family, including parents and the extended family of parental siblings and grandparents. It tests the limits of the family's ability to be supportive, understanding and loving.***
> ***~Dresher Larry***

Did You Know? Families are an important part of our lives. In many ways they are our 'social learning laboratory'. We learn from them, play with them, and receive help and support from them. Take advantage of the different qualities that your different family members have. If Dad is good at maths, ask him to help you with your maths homework. If your Nanna is a good listener, speak to her when you have a problem and are not sure how to solve it. If a family member does not want to help and that lack of support hurts your feelings, losing your cool and blaming them for your problems can make things more difficult. Instead, focus on how you are contributing to the problem and change what you can. You may not have control over the other person's actions, behaviours and choices, but you have control over how you respond.

Can you change other people's behaviour? Give a reason for your answer.

____

____

____

If you change your behaviour, what do you think will happen?

____

____

____

The following exercise will help you think about relationships within your family and how they influence your behaviour.

Exercise: Family Relationships

Write your name in the middle circle.

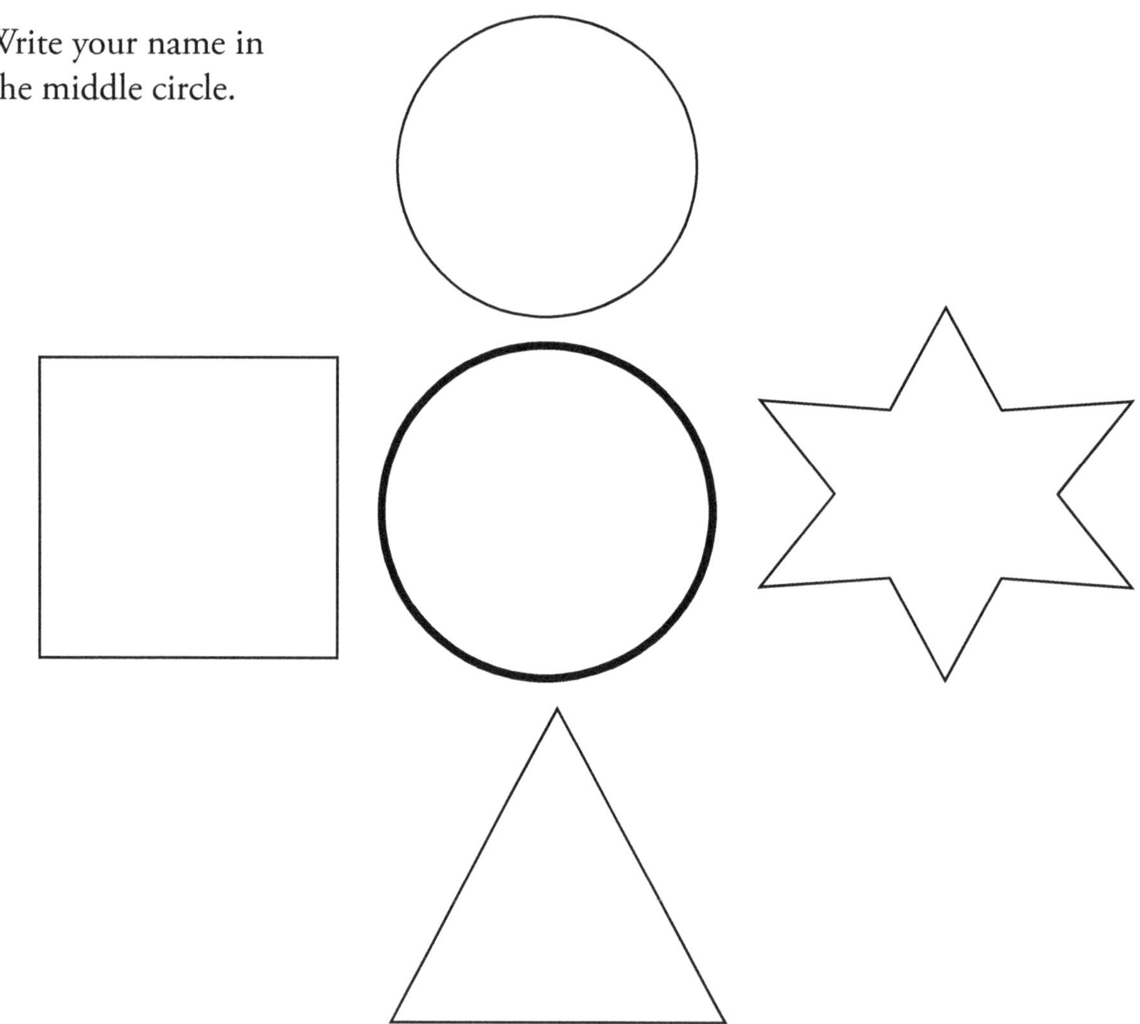

Now, write the name of the family member that you feel the closest to in the top circle.

What does this person do that makes you feel close to them?

____

____

Next, write the name of the family member you have the most conflict with in the square. What is the conflict usually about? Is it ADHD-related?

In the triangle, write the name of the family member you admire the most.

What does this person do that you admire?

____

____

____

Lastly, write the name of the person that you respect the most in the star.

What does this person do that warrants your respect?

____

____

____

Think of one thing that you can change that will improve the relationship with the person whom you named in the square above.

____

____

____

Scenario

It seemed to JP that there was a lot of conflict in his family. JP's father would yell at him for always fidgeting and forgetting to wipe his feet before entering the house. He would yell at JP's brother for being cheeky and loud. His parents would often scream at each other too. JP did not understand why so much screaming was happening. It surely did not improve the home environment!

When JP's mum threatened to leave, his dad agreed that they should all go and see a family counsellor.

The counsellor was understanding and did not take sides. He said that he could see that there was lots of love in the family but that no one was getting enough. 'You need to learn to communicate better with each other. Yelling is not bringing about change and is keeping you from feeling that your home is a happy place', he said.

The counsellor spoke to the family about the benefit of having weekly meetings and gave them a list of suggestions for successful family meetings.

The Benefits of Family Meetings

Family meetings have several benefits. They enable family members to discuss problems before they escalate. They also teach children how to take perspective, negotiate, compromise and express themselves.

Because everyone's voice is heard and valued, confidence and self-esteem often improve. Furthermore, during times of change, family meetings are an effective way to check in and see how family members are doing.

It is important that everyone is given a chance to speak and feel heard.

Family meetings will be ineffective if they are used to argue, blame and point out mistakes. If you feel that chores are unevenly distributed, you can say something like, 'I understand the need to contribute to the family by doing chores, however, at times I feel that I am the only one doing chores. Can we do something about it?'

Suggestions for family meetings:

- Agree on a day and time that suits all family members.
- Parents lead the meetings (or rotate the responsibility to lead the meeting among family members) and it should not be longer than 30-45 minutes.
- Each person writes something to talk about and presents to the family; it can be something positive.
- Everyone has the right to say something about the problem, but respect is essential, so no yelling, blaming or name-calling.
- Always aim to end the discussion with more than one possible solution.
- End the meeting by having family members say one thing that they appreciate about everyone in the family.

Do you have or have you had family meetings?

____

____

____

If you had family meetings in the past, why did it stop?

____

____

____

If you've never had a family meeting, and it sounds like something that could work for your family, how could you introduce them?

____

____

____

Transitioning

Your life is a story of transition. You are always leaving one chapter behind while moving on to the next.
~Linda Seidler

Did You Know? ADHD can affect all aspects of your life. Often the impact is not only on the person who has ADHD but on the whole family (e.g. parents and siblings alike). The adverse effects of ADHD on an individual and their family change from the preschool years through primary school and into adolescence. This is often because the environments that you transition into, such as high school, college or the workplace, are not as supervised as previous ones – it's not necessarily because your medication has stopped working or that your ADHD is getting worse. You may need to develop additional compensatory skills to manage these new chapters more effectively.

Transitioning to high school: how did you handle it or how do you think you will handle it?

____

____

____

What was most challenging for you or what do you think will present the greatest challenge?

____

____

____

Who or what could have made the transition easier or who or what do you think will help with your transition?

____

____

____

How I Handle Conflict

Tick the column that best describes how you typically handle conflict with friends and family.

My Response	Usually	Sometimes	Never
Raise my voice or yell			
Ignore			
Walk away			
Apologise			
Suggest solutions			
Complain			
Forgive			
Threaten			
Look for a win-win			
Call people names			
Understand all points of view			
Get upset			
Ask for help from an adult			
Use humour			
Cry			
Let others have their way			
Assign blame			
Work toward agreement			
Make a deal (compromise)			
Work it out fairly			

Are you happy with the way you handle conflict? If yes, carry on doing what you are doing. If not, what can you start doing today to bring about change?

____

____

____

Exercise: Stop and Think

1. What rule did I break?

____

____

____

2. What are the consequences of my actions?

____

____

____

3. Why did I break this rule?

____

____

____

4. What could I have done differently?

____

____

____

Child: ____

Parent: _______________________________________

Behaviour Contract

I, ______________________________ ,agree to make the following changes:

____

____

____

When I successfully complete this contract, I will be rewarded by:

____

____

If I don't follow through with this contract, the consequence will be:

____

____

This contract will be reviewed on this date: ____________________

Outcome: ____

____

Child's name: ______________________________ Date: ______________

Signature: ____

Parent's name: _____________________________ Date: ______________

Signature ____

Witness name: _____________________________ Date: ______________

Signature ____

Topic 2: Stop Blaming and Take Responsibility

You are free to choose but you are not free from the consequences of your choices.

'It wasn't my fault' and 'he made me do it' are phrases that children often repeat. Learning to take responsibility and stop shifting blame for your actions in childhood is very important, both because it's right and because it helps you learn cause and effect. This lesson will serve you well for life.

Essentially, blame shifting happens when you blame others or external circumstances for your behaviour. Whether you did something wrong, failed to do something right or feel a certain way, you may be reluctant to own up to your own part or responsibility. You shift the burden of blame and/or action to others.

- 'He started it!'
- 'I can't help it, I have ADHD.'

Although it's human nature to test boundaries and try new things, even if those are forbidden, it's also human nature to not want to get into trouble and to take the path of less resistance. However, a sign of growing up is the ability to own up to your mistakes and be the master of your own responses and not shift blame.

One of the greatest life lessons to understand in childhood and beyond is **cause and effect.**

Example: If one child takes something off another child and the response is a kick, there are two things happening. One, a child took a possession. Two, a child responded with a kick. Both have a level of responsibility and it's important that both parties shoulder the responsibility for their choices. Excusing bad behaviour (in response to another bad behaviour) just says, 'Sure you can hit/slap/scream if someone does something unpleasant to you.'

Blame shifting also:

- encourages passivity
- discourages ownership
- increases arrogance
- decreases the capacity for humility.

How to Stop Blame Shifting

- Be accountable for your actions, regardless of who 'started it'.
- Notice when you are not taking responsibility for your actions and gently remind yourself where the responsibility lies.
- Ensure that you follow through with what you start.
- Take ownership of your chores and accept the consequences if they go undone.
- Learn to problem-solve and ask questions when you feel powerless.
- Don't engage in self-pity. Think outside of yourself.

Why do you think it's easier to blame others for your problems, rather than to accept responsibility?

____

____

____

____

Next time you find yourself either blaming or being blamed, what can you do to manage your emotions?

____

____

____

____

Saying Sorry

> ***The weak can never forgive. Forgiveness is the attribute of the strong.***
> ***~Mahatma Gandhi***

Did You Know? Saying sorry is an important aspect of relationships. Saying you are sorry is not about who is right or wrong, but more about acknowledging when a wrongdoing needs to be addressed. Essentially, it is about reflecting on what you did wrong, why it was wrong, and the impact that the behaviour had on the other person as well as repairing the damage/hurt caused.

A genuine sorry might sound something like this:

'I'm sorry that I shouted at you when you asked me about my day at school. I overreacted. I should have just told you that I was not in a mood to talk. I will make sure that this does not happen again. I know that you might still be upset, but I just want you to know that I am really sorry.'

You can use the word 'SORRY' to make it easy to structure an apology.

Stand up by reflecting and admitting to your wrongdoing.

Own it by accepting responsibility.

Respond differently than the first time.

Repair/restore the damage by fixing it or making it better.

Yield to their feelings by letting them be upset.

(adapted from understood.org)

Exercise: How Responsible Are You?

The only way to measure responsibility is by your behaviour. Use the template below to monitor your responsible actions.

Responsible Action	Mon	Tues	Wed	Thu	Fri	Sat	Sun	Total
I did my chores without being asked								
I did my homework before gaming								
I kept my room clean								
I followed the established rules about screen time								
I set out my school clothes for the next day								
I ate nutritious meals								
I cared for the family pet/s								
I followed all rules at school								
I told the truth								
I played games by the rules								
I was respectful to adults								
I was on time for school								
I packed my own lunch								
I did not flip my lid								
I took my medication without nagging								
I advocated for myself respectfully								
I lived by my values today								

Of the above responsibilities, which ones do you find most challenging to do? Why do you think they are difficult?

____

____

Exercise: Responsibility Pie

Name a problem that you are currently dealing with:

____

____

1. Make a list of the people or events you think caused the problem.
2. Think of the amount of responsibility each person or event has.
3. Fill in the pie chart by figuring out how many pieces of the pie each person or event gets. Fill in the whole pie.

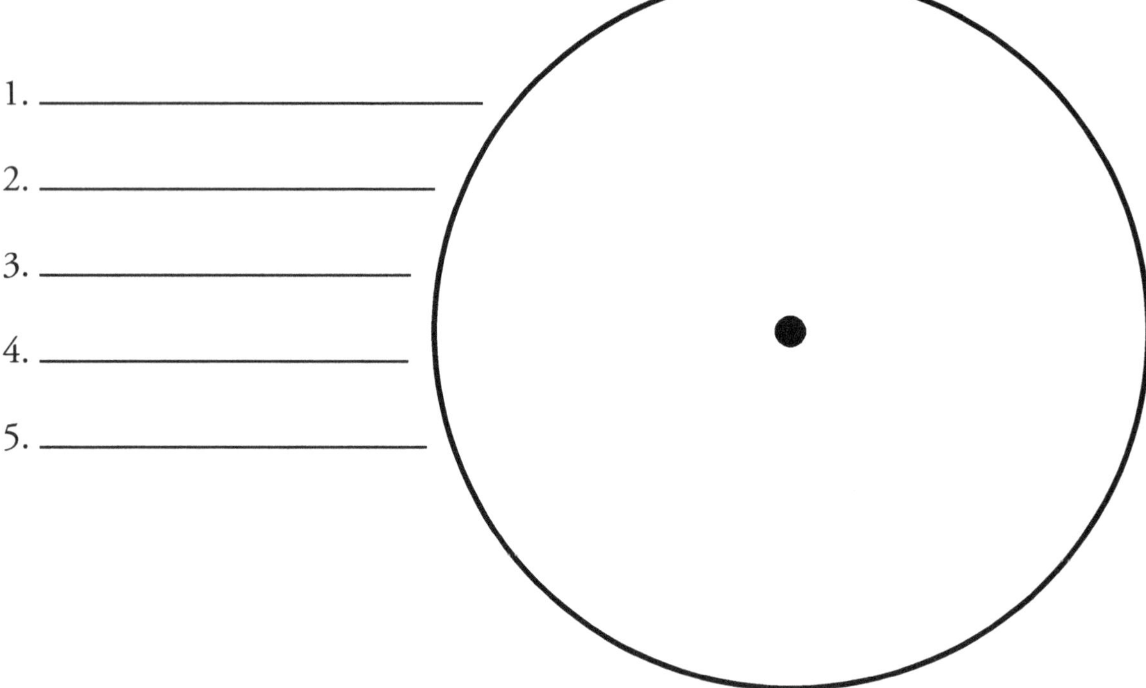

What did you learn from this exercise?

____

____

____

How Many Personas Do You Have?

A persona is an image you show the outside world. It is a mask you wear to fit the situation. If we didn't have personas, we would act the same way all the time. A teacher would go home from school and act like a teacher with their family. Or a teacher would go to school and act like a parent with their students. Most people have at least two personas: a private one and a public one. The persona they use depends on where and who they are with. Some of your personas may be friend, student, sister, brother, son etc. Each of your personas is made up of your real qualities, but it also hides some qualities you don't want other people to see. The persona you show your teacher may not have a temper. The persona you show your footy team may never cry.

Read the list of behaviours below. Check the ones you sometimes do. Then look at the list of people in your life on the next page. Next to each behaviour, write the name/s of the people who would be very surprised to see you do that particular thing.

- ☐ Become very quiet ____________________
- ☐ Start an argument ____________________
- ☐ Brag about your grades ____________________
- ☐ Break up a fight ____________________
- ☐ Show your temper ____________________
- ☐ Cry about something ____________________
- ☐ Talk a lot ____________________
- ☐ Finish your schoolwork or chores on time ____________________
- ☐ Act really silly ____________________
- ☐ Give in to someone ____________________
- ☐ Use bad language ____________________
- ☐ Offer your help ____________________

People in your life

- Mother
- Father
- Brother
- Sister
- Friends
- Teachers
- Grandparents
- Coaches
- Aunts
- Uncles
- Cousins

Others: ____

____

____

____

How many of the behaviours did you check? ____________________

How many people did you list? ______________________________

- If you listed lots of people, chances are you have many personas.
- If you listed few people, you probably tend to show more people the 'real you'.

A persona may be positive: a good student, a singer, a loving daughter or son etc. Or a persona may be negative: a bully, a know-it-all, a troublemaker etc. Sometimes people hide behind a persona because they are afraid others won't like their 'real self'. Their masks keep people from getting to know them.

It's important to note that having different personas is different to having multiple personalities. Personas are healthy ways of dealing with a variety of situations in our lives. If you feel that you have too many personas or you think that they are too different from the real you, talk to an adult. Talking to someone you trust may help you to get rid of a mask or two so people can see the real you.

Ask your parents to describe the personas they have. They may wear different 'masks' around you, the people they work with, their friends, siblings and their own parents.

Pick three situations that are common in your life (such as your school, home and a sports club). Do you have different personas for some of these? If yes, describe them.

____

____

____

Imagine a world without personas, where everyone said and did exactly what they felt like all the time. Would you like to live in this kind of world? Why or why not?

____

____

____

Do your personas help you live the life that you want to live or do they sometimes get in your way?

____

____

____

Adapted from: Kincher, J., 2008.

Family and Friends Board Game

As you go around the board, answer each of the questions you land on. If you land on a question mark (?), ask another player a question about family or friendship.

START 1	Relax AND ENJOY! 2	Family is ... 3	How would you define an ideal family? 4	A friend is someone ... 5
HOORAY! Go forward 4 spaces 6	Are friendships important to you? Why? 7	What do you think are the most difficult things that parents have to do? 8	? 9	Who is your best friend? Why? 10
Who do you look like the most in your family? 11	What do you look for in a good friend? 12	Is it better to be male or female? Why? 13	OOPS! Go back 4 spaces 14	Is it important for friends to have much in common? Why? 15
Is having siblings important? Why? 16	HOORAY! Go forward 4 spaces 17	Why is it important to say sorry? 18	How do you show your friends they are important to you? 19	Can boys and girls be good friends? Why? 20
Are you a good friend? Why? 21	OOPS! Go back 4 spaces 22	How important are family celebrations? 23	? 24	YOU WIN! 25

Topic 3: Self-Esteem and Peer Pressure

It's not what you look at that matters, it's what you see.
~Henry David Thoreau

Did You Know? Your self-esteem reflects your beliefs and feelings about yourself. It's important to examine these beliefs, as the way we feel about ourselves affects the way we treat ourselves and others, as well as the choices we make. Positive beliefs make us feel good about ourselves and raise our self-esteem.

Do you ever think that you are weak, stupid, useless, worthless, ugly, unlovable, a loser or a failure? Everyone uses these words to describe themselves at times, usually when they experience a challenging or stressful situation. But if you often think about yourself in these terms, your self-esteem will suffer, causing damage to your confidence and abilities.

People with low self-esteem usually have deep-seated negative beliefs about themselves. These beliefs are often taken as facts or truths about their identity, rather than being recognised as opinions they hold about themselves.

Does ADHD Affect Self-Esteem?

Any mental or psychological condition can have a negative effect on self-esteem. ADHD, in particular, is far more vulnerable than other disorders; one reason being that it cannot be hidden. The overt behaviours displayed by children with ADHD often receive negative feedback from others. Both the inability to hide the disorder and the negative comments/feedback contribute to feelings of low self-worth. Also, unlike other disorders, ADHD seldom elicits sympathy. For example, while a depressed child might be treated with kindness and patience, ADHD provokes frustration and impatience.

Being told repeatedly to stop moving, talking, interrupting, can cause a child to feel as if they always doing something wrong. This leads to low self-esteem.

From as early as pre-school, children are able to make assessments about how they feel about themselves in a number of areas. You can improve your self-esteem by engaging in activities that increase your chance of succeeding. The more activities and experiences you have in which you feel good about yourself, the higher your overall level of self-esteem will be.

How Do I Know if I Have Low Self-Esteem?

Children with low self-esteem often reveal the level of their self-esteem through their words. Do you engage in negative self-talk? Listen to your inner voice: what is it saying? Examples of such statements include:

- I'm useless.
- I'm stupid.
- I'm a loser.
- No one likes me.
- I'm not good at anything.
- I'm ugly.
- Everybody hates me.

You may also reveal your level of self-esteem through your behaviour. Notice how you respond to compliments, criticism and defeat. Children with low self-esteem are uncomfortable with compliments. They do not believe them and feel awkward. Instead, they tend to break eye contact and shy away, either saying nothing or berating themselves.

When criticised, children with low self-esteem have difficulty accepting the negative feedback. Because their self-esteem is so fragile, the slightest indication that they have a fault stimulates a sense of failure to which they react with anger. Handling failure is also very distressing for children with ADHD with low self-esteem. Their frustration tolerance is usually very low and their temper flares rapidly if they do not succeed immediately.

Do All Children With ADHD Have Low Self-Esteem?

Despite all the concerns about low self-esteem, studies show that many boys with ADHD actually have over-inflated self-esteem (less is known about girls).

Almost all very young children overestimate their abilities; however, as they grow, they begin to develop more realistic self-appraisals. Some continue to overestimate their own abilities, perhaps in a self-protective manner to compensate for their inabilities. The more hyperactive and impulsive the child, the more they tend to overestimate their ability.

Can an Inflated Self-esteem Be a Good Thing?

The lack of awareness of one's deficits is a characteristic observed in children with ADHD. They are simply unable to accurately observe themselves. What is not known is whether this inability is the result of a lack of self-awareness or if it is a defence mechanism against the emotional pain that comes from admitting to these weaknesses.

If you exaggerate your abilities and worthiness, speak to someone that you trust so that they can help you strengthen your strengths and accept your weaknesses. Speak to your parents about working with a professional to learn how to manage your tendency to overestimate your abilities and to learn other ways to be more realistic about your true abilities.

Can a Child Have Too Much Self-Esteem?

Unfortunately, thinking too highly of yourself turns out not to be such a good thing. Those who think too highly of themselves are often labelled as narcissistic, conceited and full of themselves. Children who show these tendencies tend to be disliked by others, viewed as a 'know it all', condescending and critical of others. Children with ADHD can fall into these categories.

While a child with normal self-esteem may feel hurt when no one in the playground is interested in their dinosaur collection, the child with ADHD will conclude that no one in their class is smart enough to know anything about dinosaurs and derives self-esteem from this belief. They do not understand that the reason no one is talking to them about dinosaurs is because that is all that they talk about and they need to find more common topics to talk about. Instead, they hold on to their beliefs and fail to make any change to the behaviour.

Abilities Associated With High Self-Esteem

People with high self-esteem have a variety of abilities that help them to remain positive about themselves regardless of the challenges they face, the failure they may experience or the criticism they receive. These are some abilities and actions that you can foster to help increase your self-esteem:

- Try new experiences.
- Use positive self-talk.
- Accept compliments.
- Accept that you cannot be good at everything.
- Persevere in tough times.
- Believe in yourself and keep trying.
- Feel comfortable saying 'I am not good at …'
- Focus on what you are good at.
- Separate areas of weakness from overall worthiness.
- Understand that criticism does not mean that you are a failure.
- Measure your success based on effort, fun and experience rather than the outcome.
- Be realistic about your expectations.
- Remain true to your values.
- Develop an 'I can' attitude.
- Always do what you know is right.
- Make good choices for yourself.
- Learn to communicate assertively.
- Take ownership of your feelings.
- Take responsibility for your actions.

Having a healthy self-esteem means that you value yourself. What are the things that you value about yourself?

____

____

____

Are there things you do that indicate that you don't value yourself?

____

____

____

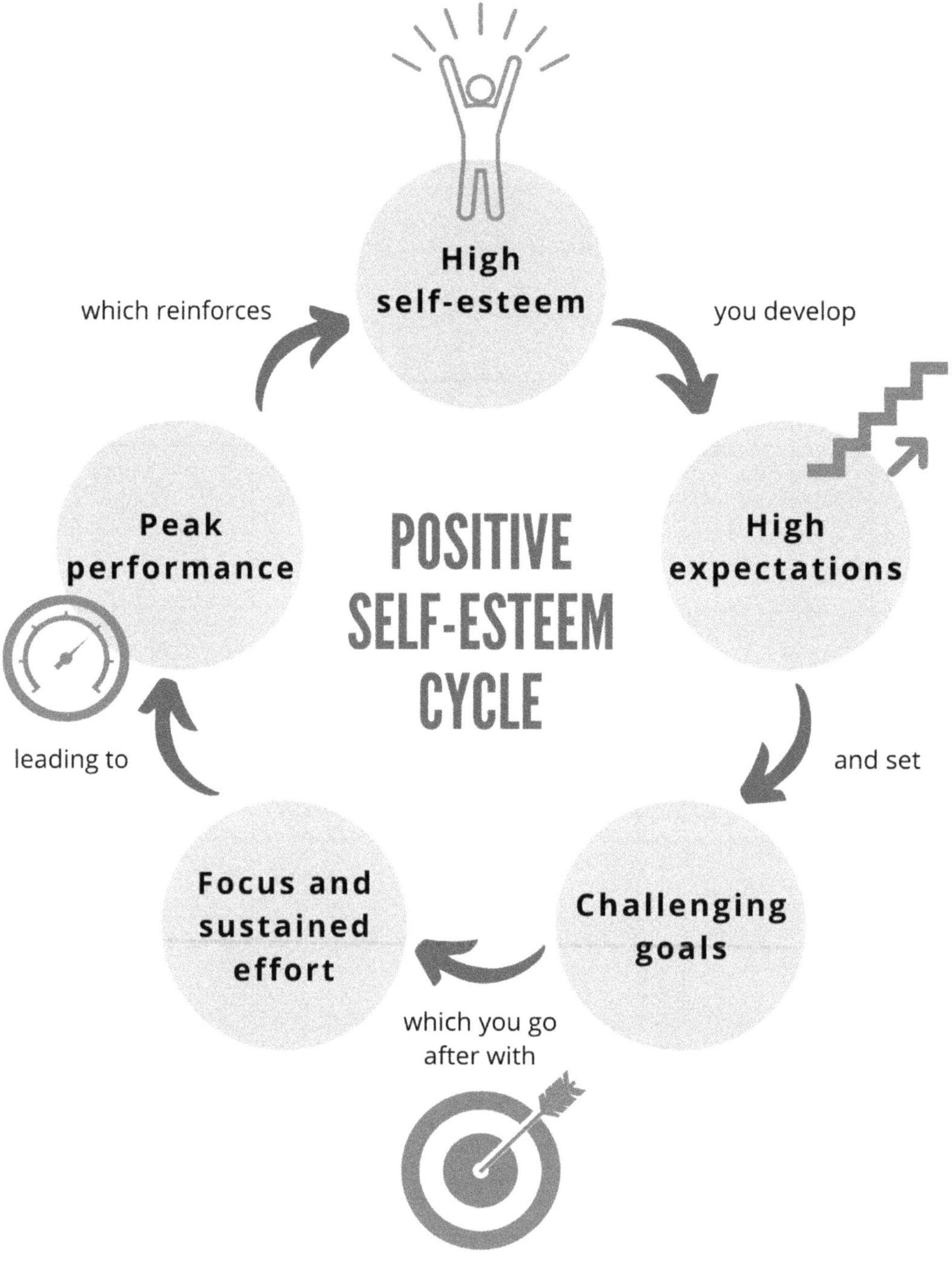
High
self-esteem
you develop
High
expectations
and set
Challenging
goals
which you go
after with
Focus and
sustained
effort
leading to
Peak
performance
which reinforces
POSITIVE
SELF-ESTEEM
CYCLE

Did You Know? You can create confidence by building your self-esteem. Think of confidence as a muscle. When you work it, it gets stronger and more defined. Define yourself by your talents, rather than your failings. Make a practice of noticing what you like about yourself and give yourself credit for handling difficult situations rather than being ashamed of your personal struggles. This does not mean you can't grow, change and learn new ways of being in the world, like learning to be mindful, problem-solving and assertivenes; it means that you don't have to become someone else to 'be enough'. No one is perfect. Those who claim to be perfect are more than likely covering up insecurity and a lack of confidence.

Write three things you think you handled well this week.

____

____

____

Describe a personal struggle that has been bothering you the last week.

____

____

How did your mind beat you up/criticise you regarding this struggle?

____

____

What did you do well in the face of this personal challenge?

____

____

What can you do differently in similar situations in the future?

____

____

Envy is the art of counting the other person's blessings instead of your own.
~Harold Coffin

Did You Know? Although comparisons may help some children decide what they want to achieve and how to do it, for others, this process leads to low self-esteem and disappointment. If you are driven by envy of someone else, you are letting your thoughts about that person control your emotional state. People who are constantly comparing themselves to others, have a diminished sense of self and, ultimately, come to believe that they are worthless. Remind yourself that comparisons are always unfair, as we typically compare the worst of ourselves to the best we presume about others. The chances of reaching your goals improve if you remain in charge of your own emotional state.

How would your life be different if you let go of comparing yourself to others?

____

____

____

When you find yourself feeling envious of someone else, make it a habit to ask yourself, 'Do I really want person X to have control over my emotions?'

How has envy caused you emotional stress?

____

____

____

Peer Pressure

> ***Just because so many conforming children wake up every morning asking, 'What is everybody else going to wear today?' doesn't mean that they don't wish it were different. Peer pressure is just that – pressure.***
> ***~Jerry Spinelli***

Did You Know? Coping with peer pressure is about getting the balance right between being yourself and fitting in with your peer group. Children who have poor self-esteem, who feel they have few friends and who have special needs are more likely to be influenced by their peers. Some ADHD qualities can make some children more easily swayed and, therefore, at risk of giving in to peer pressure. Being aware of this can help you prepare in advance to stand firm against peer pressure.

If your friends are doing something you know is risky, what do they say to urge you to follow along?

____

____

____

Describe a situation where you resisted peer pressure.

____

____

____

What are the positive consequences of resisting peer pressure?

____

____

____

Read the examples below and identify the ones that describe peer pressure. Circle the correct choice and explain why.

1. Sam tells Noah to steal an extra dessert when they're in line at lunch. He says, 'Come on, everyone else does it'. **Is this peer pressure? YES NO**

Why or why not? ______________________________

____

2. Emily asks Olivia to help her with her English homework. She says, 'Can you please help me? I'll owe you!' **Is this peer pressure? YES NO**

Why or why not? ______________________________

____

3. Louis encourages Daniel to make fun of a new student in their class. He says, 'You better do it or I'll tell everyone that you're gay!'

Is this peer pressure? YES NO

Why or why not? ______________________________

____

4. Josh misses the bus home. Emily tells him, 'You can ride home with me and my mum if you want to'. **Is this peer pressure? YES NO**

Why or why not? ______________________________

____

5. Noah and Sam are playing cricket. Sam tells Noah to allow him to win the next game. He threatens to punch him in the back if he doesn't do it.

Is this peer pressure? YES NO

Why or why not? ______________________________

____

Where you have identified peer pressure in the above scenarios, how could each person respond to this pressure?

Positive (Good) Vs. Negative (Bad) Peer Pressure

Positive peer pressure is in your best interest and encourages you to do the right thing. Negative peer pressure, on the other hand, is not in your best interest. It can be dangerous and may break rules at school, at home and in the community.

Positive Peer Pressure	Negative Peer Pressure
• Studying • Telling the truth • Standing up for what you believe in • Being kind • Respecting others • Helping others to make better choices • Volunteering Add your own:	• Bullying • Lying • Stealing • Disrespecting others • Making bad choices to drink or use drugs • Skipping school • Spreading rumors • Cheating in tests Add your own:

Peer Pressure: Rewards vs Risks

Instructions: Place yourself in a scenario in which you might experience face-to-face peer pressure – make it as realistic as possible. Then follow the prompts to assess risks and benefits of saying 'yes' and saying 'no'.

Scenario:

Saying Yes	Saying No
Risks	**Risks**
Benefits	**Benefits**

Do the risks outweigh the benefits? Are they worth it?

Is this a scenario showing positive or negative peer pressure. Why?

At any given point you can release your greatest self. Don't let anyone hold you back. Don't let anyone dilute you. Don't be peer pressured into being less than you are.
~Steve Maraboli

Did You Know? Most teens are more influenced by their friends than by their parents. It's often said that the summary of your three best friends is a good indicator of where you are heading. When you think that your future depends on what your friends are like, you may want to reflect on your friendships. Build friendships where differences are accepted and there is no pressure to fit in. Look for good friends who won't force you to do things that you really don't want to do. Unfortunately, at times, children (out of fear of being alone) just want to find someone to hang out with, without asking themselves if these people can be trusted to be caring, honest, reliable and supportive.

Name three of your best friends, and write a paragraph describing each.

1. ______________________________

____

____

____

2. ______________________________

____

____

____

3. ______________________________

____

____

____

What qualities do these friends have in common?

____

____

Write a paragraph describing the future you imagine for each of these friends.

1. ______________________________________

____

____

____

2. ______________________________________

____

____

____

3. ______________________________________

____

____

____

Write a description of the future you imagine for yourself.

____

____

____

____

____

Did You Know? Developing an independent identity is part of a teenager's development. It is normal for teens to challenge parents as part of defining who they are and how they are different from their parents. You can stay connected to your family even during times when you challenge their values, beliefs or interests. You can even use your differences to gain greater intimacy and support. Keep lines of communication open and agree to disagree in a respectful manner.

Describe a conflict that you have with your parents about independence:

____

____

Describe the conflict from your parents' perspective.

____

____

What do your parents need to know about you in order to see the conflict from your side?

____

____

Describe a family problem that makes it difficult for you to focus on your schoolwork.

____

____

____

Write three things you could do differently to help you separate yourself from the troubling situation.

1. ____________________________________
2. ____________________________________
3. ____________________________________

How different would your life be if the problems that you cannot control were solved?

____

____

____

You know that your parents love and appreciate you, however, you may wish that they would demonstrate their support a little more.

Tick the ways you would like your parents to show their support and add your own.

- [ ] Give you a hug sometimes
- [ ] Understand your point of view
- [ ] Remind you that you are doing well
- [ ] Stay in control so that you can feel safe
- [ ] Be more consistent with rules
- [ ] Be a role model
- [ ] Be on the same page about rules

Others:

____

____

____

Quiz 3 (see Appendix E for answers)

1. **Tristan does not like doing chores around the house. This leads to lots of conflict in the family. What advice would you give Tristan to help improve his family life?**

   A. Tristan should not do chores because he is still at school.

   B. Ask him what he finds most difficult about doing the chores and suggest that he talks to his mum about changing his chores to ones that he likes doing.

   C. Tell Tristan to bribe his younger brother to do his chores.

2. **Xavier's younger brother is bothering him while he tries to concentrate on his homework. What should Xavier do?**

   A. Wish that his brother would disappear.

   B. Lock his brother outside.

   C. Tell his brother how he feels and offer him suggestions of things he could do instead of bothering him.

3. **Xavier wants to improve his relationship with his dad. What could he do?**

   A. Re-organise his dad's toolbox without asking his permission.

   B. Buy him a carton of cigarettes with his pocket money.

   C. Use polite words around the house and help his dad rake and mow the lawn.

4. **Tristan knows that he caused embarrassment and hurt to his mother by calling her stupid in front of the other mums during a school outing. What should Tristan do to make his mother feel better?**

   A. Try to justify his actions.

   B. Apologise to his mother and ask her how he can repair the hurt that he caused.

   C. Blame his mother for his actions.

Module 3:

Practical Coping Skills

Section 1:

Time and Task Management

Topic 1: Time Management

Ordinary people think merely of spending time. Great people think of using it.

Did You Know? Time is our greatest asset. If you spend or lose money you can always make more money. But once you've spent your time, it's gone forever! This is why it's important to use your time wisely. For someone with ADHD, time management can be a real challenge that impacts many areas of their life. ADHD symptoms create a distorted sense of time – you may be unable to accurately judge how much time a task will take. For example, you have one more task to complete and judge that it will only take you 15 minutes – and an hour later you are still in the thick of it. Without estimating time accurately, you will consistently run late and not complete tasks. Some children with ADHD report that they feel overwhelmed by a homework task because they cannot estimate time and have no sense of how long the task will take. They also struggle to plan ahead and, instead, put off projects until the night before the due date. In relation to time, the most important thing that you can do to help yourself is to accept that time is a real challenge for you. Doing so will make you more open to using strategies in your environment that make time more visible.

Remember: 'Time is the most valuable resource that we have, because it is the only thing that we never get back. It is also the one resource that is extremely well distributed: young or old, rich or poor, we all have 24 hours in a day.'

While some people complain about not having any time because of a full-time job, others manage to have a full-time job, study and engage in sporting activities and more.

We all have the time; we just need to manage it effectively. It means changing our habits and using tools that will help us make better use of the time that is available to us.

Tristan needs to leave for school by 7:45 am. Help him avoid distractions and get to school on time!

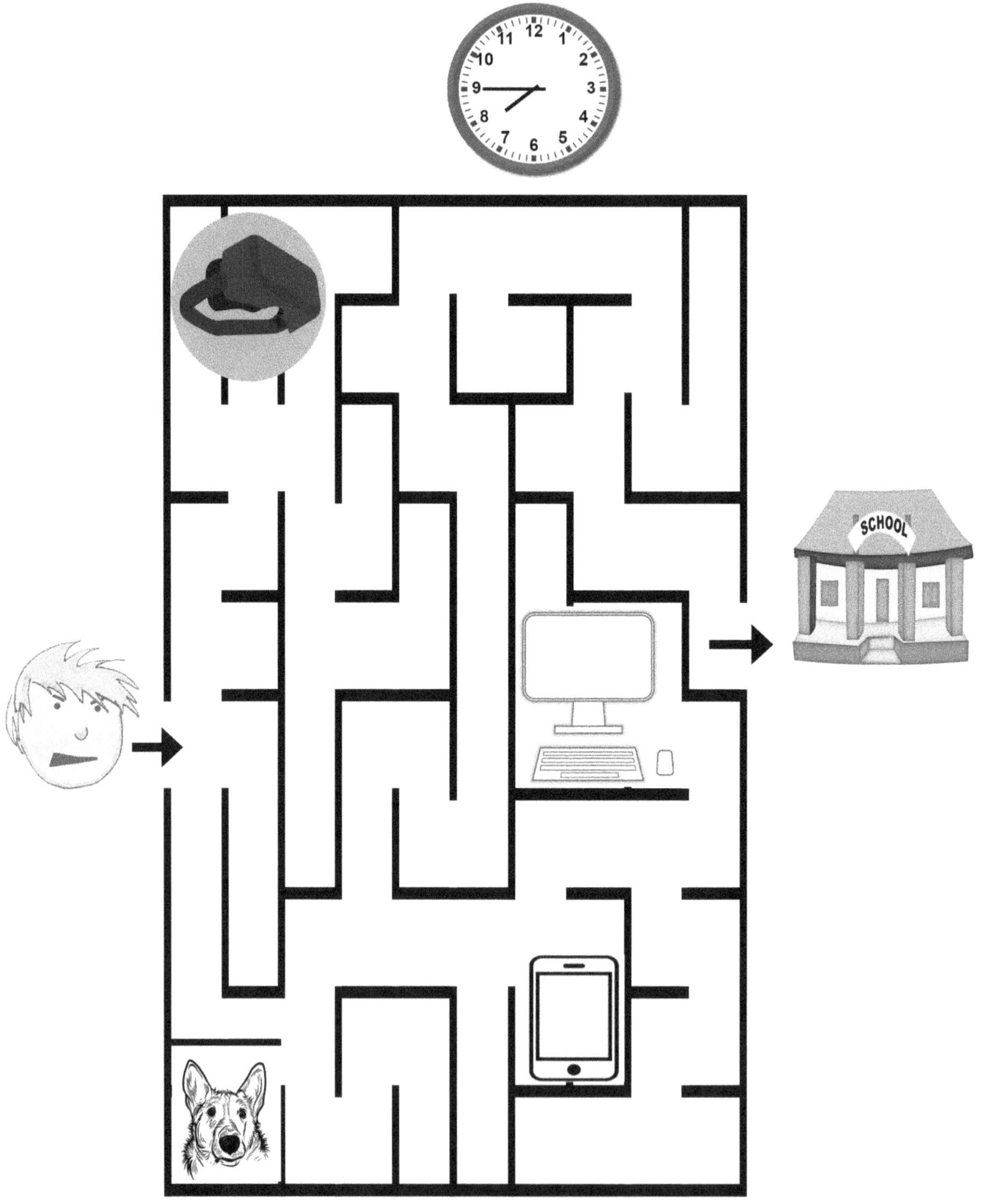

Time Management

When the school year picks up steam, it can sometimes feel near impossible to stay organised. It's important to note that when your schedule gets crazy, keeping your space clean and organised and maintaining a good routine is what will keep you sane and on track. Try the following tips.

- **Get a planner, preferably a paper one.** First create a to-do list; list your commitments for the day. Then go back and fill in time for each of your commitments, starting with the most important, (e.g. homework, studying, eating, sleeping, chores, relaxing and socialising). Stick to the plan as much as possible. Set alarms if you tend to forget to look at your planner.
- **Know when and where you're most productive.** Some people feel most productive in the morning, and others, later in the day. Some need to be in a quiet place to get things done. For others, some background noise, like music, helps. Note that 'background noise' like TV or music with distracting lyrics can take away your focus. Turn off all distracting technology.
- **Study with a buddy or sibling.** If the presence of someone keeps you more on track, study with a buddy, or study alone if the presence of someone else is too distracting.
- **Prioritise your tasks.** If you tend to miss deadlines and have trouble finishing important things, start with the tasks that are most important and due soonest, then work on less-important stuff or things that have a longer deadline (apply the 'pebble jar' rationale on the next page). If, instead, you have trouble getting started, begin with easier tasks, then move on to harder ones once your brain is warmed up.
- **Set realistic day-to-day goals.** Work on one thing at a time and follow it through to completion. Break larger tasks (such as learning a few spelling words each day for the spelling test on Friday) into smaller chunks.
- **Be honest with yourself about how you spend your time.** Look at ways of cutting back on time-wasters. If you spend hours online before starting your homework, try to stick to a plan of starting your homework first, then using online time as a reward for finishing tasks.

- **Break up blocks of study time with short breaks to limit fatigue.** If you study solidly for a couple hours, make sure you give yourself 15 to 20 minutes as a break before you start up again. Get away from the computer or books to stretch or take a short walk. Eat an energy-building, protein-rich snack like yoghurt or almonds.
- **Studies show that rewards are usually more motivating than punishment.** Use this to your advantage by giving yourself a reward when you finish a task; for example, allow yourself to watch a favourite 30-minute TV show as a study break or give yourself some positive feedback. Self-criticism (a form of punishment) is usually not super effective for motivation, so work on recognising and limiting these sorts of thoughts. Easier said than done, but good to work on.
- **Watch your thoughts and work on thinking more positively.** Challenge the negative thoughts that creep into your mind and cause you unnecessary stress. Put more focus on what is going well. That doesn't mean denying or repressing unpleasant thoughts or feelings, but you don't have to dwell on them. If you have a long-standing pattern of negative thoughts, learning a new way of thinking is a necessary process.
- **Consider asking a supportive friend or relative from your Circle of Support to be your mentor.** Agree to text or email the person a list of what you accomplished each day or form a study group to keep each other on track. Studies show that being accountable to someone else can help keep you more focused.
- **Ask for help.** Don't wait until things are completely messed up!
- **There are many apps out there that are useful for students.** One warning though – there is no perfect system. The best thing you can do is to get started and keep going – that is the only way that work gets done.
- **Remember the pebble jar metaphor for time.** The principle of this metaphor is that your day has a finite amount of time in it, just like a jar has finite capacity. Hence, it's important you start your day doing the things that matter the most. Generally, the smaller and easier it is to pour into the jar, the less it matters. The trouble is these are exactly the types of things we end up filling our time with. The antidote, of course, is to set goals.

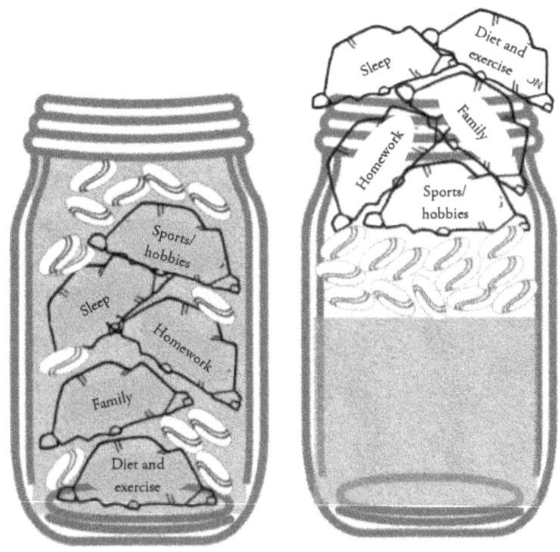

What will

you

fill your jar with

today?

Tips for Creating a to-do List

- **Write down everything you need to do.** Select all the tasks, however big or small, that will need to be accomplished and list them out.
- **Categorise the things you need to do.** It may be helpful to break everything up into separate categories. For example, before school, after school, sports and social commitments, weekend plans etc. Prioritise in order of importance.
- **Create a daily or weekly to-do list.** This may include things from many different categories. You might have several things you need to finish for school by the end of the day/week, as well as other personal and social commitments.
- **Allocate time slots in your planner in order of importance.** Identify the most important or urgent activities on the to-do list and allocate a time to do them. It's all relative to you and the topics on your list, so you might decide that school activities trump social commitments, or vice versa.
- **Break down Long-term goals.** These may include tasks that need to be broken down into multiple steps that you need to prioritise. You might be working on an assignment to be handed in at the end of the school term, which will involve many different smaller activities. The simple act of breaking it down will simplify and reduce overwhelm.

- **Tick things off the list.** Actively crossing out or checking off the items as you complete them can ease some of your stress about getting things done, as well as provide a sense of accomplishment.

Tips on Prioritising Your Time

- **Keep the list visible.** Check your to-do list several times a day to make sure that you are on track. Remember that you can have the best diary system in the world, but if you forget to check it, it will be of no use to you in the long run.
- **Keep it together.** Rather than using sticky notes or other random pieces of paper for your to-do list, you can create one by making a column down the right-hand margin of your diary/planner.
- **Rank the importance of each task.** What are the most important things on your list? You might decide that school tasks will outweigh social activities and household chores, though certain outliers may exist. You've got to eat and bathe, for example, but gaming might be able to wait another day while you finish an important school assignment.
- **Rank the different tasks on your to-do list.** High, medium- and low-importance tasks might be the simplest way to start ranking the importance of things on your list. You can also use colours to rank the items on your list; for example, you could use red to identify important or high priority items on your list, orange for items of medium importance and yellow for items that are not pressing at all. You can also ask the question, 'Is this a rock, pebble or sand task?'
- **Rank the urgency of each important task.** Consider upcoming deadlines and your ability to work within those deadlines. What needs to be done the soonest? What needs to be done by the end of the day? What might you be able to buy a bit more time on?
- **Consider the length of time.** It's important to estimate the length of time that it takes to accomplish each of the tasks, maybe even assigning a set time to certain tasks. If you find it hard to estimate how long each task will take, ask a parent or a supportive friend to help make some best guesses, and adjust the times as you go if you need to.

- **Rank the effort required for each task.** Rank everything on your list in terms of its difficulty. You may decide to pair a difficult task with an easier one, or use the ranking to adjust how long you think a task will take.

Why Time Management Matters

Effective time management allows students to complete more in less time, because their attention is focused and they're not wasting time on distractions such as social media. Efficient use of time also reduces stress, as students tick off items from their to-do list. It can also provide a sense of achievement through fulfilling goals; for example, you might plan to complete an assignment by Friday so you can see friends on the weekend.

Furthermore, by using time efficiently, students can complete their work on time, stay engaged with their learning, and have more free time for pursuing activities that are important to them, such as sports, hobbies and spending time with friends and family.

Other benefits reported included:

- increased independence
- increased self-control
- increased responsibility and discipline
- improved grades
- increased self-esteem and confidence
- decreased anxiety, stress and worry.

Complete the 'After School Daily Routine', on the next page, for four consecutive weeks and monitor your use of time. Ask yourself, 'Am I happy about the way I'm using my time?'

After School Daily Routine

This tool will help you recognise how much time you are spending doing what matters.

Instructions:

1. Colour in the time blocks that you spend on **homework** or doing **school-related activities** in **RED.**
2. Colour in the time blocks that you spend **outdoors** (playing, exercising, gardening, creating etc) in **GREEN.**
3. Colour in the time blocks that you spend **doing chores** at home in **BLUE.**
4. Colour in the time blocks that you spend on **extra activities** (sports, scouts, music lessons, church, community services etc.) in **ORANGE.**
5. Colour in the time blocks that you spend doing **family-enriching** activities (chatting, sharing, helping, contributing, having meals etc) in **YELLOW.**
6. Colour in the time blocks that you spend on **technology** (like gaming, texting, social media etc.) in **BROWN.**
7. Colour in the time block that you **go to bed** in **BLACK.**

Time	Monday	Tuesday	Wednesday	Thursday	Friday
4:00-4:30					
4:30-5:00					
5:00-5:30					
5:30-6:00					
6:00-6:30					
6:30-7:00					
7:00-7:30					
7:30-8:00					
8:00-8:30					
8:30-9:00					
9:00-9:30					
9:30-10:00					
Rate your mood 1-10					
Evaluate:					

How much time do you spend on school-related work per day?

____

____

____

Are you achieving your academic goals? If not, how many more blocks would you have to put in per day?

____

____

____

Are you using your to-do list and diary/calendar to its full potential?

____

____

____

Do you need to work harder or smarter?

____

____

____

Horizontal or Vertical Time?

Did You Know? When you have a task to complete, you can plan the completion time vertically or horizontally.

For example, suppose you are asked to complete a task that will take you 32 hours. There are two ways you can approach this, as illustrated below. Using vertical time, the task is completed quickly, in just two days; however, this leaves little time for other activities. If you focus on vertical time, then you are trying to get the task done in as short a time as possible. On the other hand, if you utilise horizontal time, you can go slowly and, over time, accomplish your goal. Even ordinary effort over time can yield extraordinary results. The latter, however, requires planning, organising and prioritising – skills that you may be struggling with, but that can be learned.

Vertical Time					
Horizontal Time					
	Monday	Tuesday	Wednesday	Thursday	Friday
Morning 8 hours					
Afternoon 8 hours					
Evening 8 hours					

Have you tried to finish a big task with vertical time? How well did it work for you?

____

____

What difference do you think using horizontal time will make for future tasks?

____

____

The Use of a Diary/Planner

By failing to prepare, you are preparing to fail.
~Benjamin Franklin

Did You Know? For some students, a diary/planner represents good self-management in relation to time and an opportunity for better planning, self-management and less stress.

Unfortunately for children with ADHD, maintaining a diary looks like a lot of painful work. But a well-organised planner is perhaps the most useful tool for students with ADHD.

For some time-challenged teens, it can mean the difference between success and failure, both before and after graduation, so it's definitely worth the effort. If you can't see how using a diary is going to help you, despite your parents nagging, you may decide to give it a go for an agreed period (e.g. one month or one school term). If it does not give you the outcome that you want, you can always go back to doing what you were doing. Speak to someone in your Circle of Support, such as a mentor, about the time management challenges that you face, and discuss together how using a planner might help. For example, if you frequently miss deadlines for assignments because you forget to write them down or struggle with procrastination, you can use the planner to break down bigger tasks and make smaller deadlines to reduce stress and last-minute panic. You won't know if it works until you give it a fair go.

Some Ideas on How to Set Up a Planner

We all have a unique brain and time management needs, and this must be taken into account when sourcing a diary/planner. Those of us who are 'left brain dominant' are typically more analytical, logical and objective. 'Right-brain dominant' people on the other hand, are more creative, intuitive and subjective.

The following strategies have proven successful for many who are 'right-brain dominant' individuals:

- **Use colour.** Make the planner visually attractive to help a creative brain stay interested and easily recognise what needs to be done.
- **Personalised language.** Develop an easy-to-remember shorthand – like 'T' for 'test' or 'WS' for 'worksheet' – to keep track of assignments without getting stressed or overwhelmed. Your shorthand can include symbols or stickers – a useful tool for visual learners.
- **Routines.** If using a planner feels unnatural to you, begin by establishing a daily routine to get in the habit of working with a planner. Set a time every day for reviewing and updating your planner – right before homework time works for most. A daily review of assignments will help you determine your most urgent priorities and plan what you need to work on tonight, tomorrow and further down the road.

Things to consider:

- Where will the diary be kept?
- How will you remember to use it every day?
- How will you remember to look at the task list every day?

One good tip is to pick an activity that already occurs every day to link with looking at your diary and your to-do list, for example, before breakfast or before brushing your teeth.

A planner should include more than just homework assignments. Make sure you schedule extracurricular activities, social events and other important information. Once a planner is used to track all your commitments, you will turn to it regularly and begin to see time more clearly – helping you complete your assignments, feel more in control of your time and improve your self-confidence.

Important: It is important to remember that learning any new skill or forming new healthy habits takes practice and time. You may not be used to writing down what you need to do on a daily basis or carrying a diary around. Be aware of thoughts that may sabotage your success. These can include:

- I don't have enough room in my bag for a diary.
- It's a hassle to have to bring a notebook everywhere with me.

- I've never been an organised person, so why start now?
- If I write down my appointments and assignments, I will be responsible for them.

Stay focused on your reasons for wanting to bring about change, the goals you hope to achieve and the accomplishment you will feel for taking positive steps in your life.

Example of a Diary Page with a To-do List

Write down everything you have to do in the to-do list. Rank each one by importance: **A** for the highest priority, **B** for the next most important and so on. Then, allocate time in your diary to complete all of the tasks.

Time	Task	To-do List
6:00	Wake up, take medication	Feed dog Work on shell project (A): 15 minutes Revise presentation (A):15 minutes Other homework (A): 60 minutes FaceTime dad (A) Walk Buddy (B) Pack school bag (A) Pack sports gear (A) In bed by 10 pm (A)
6:30	Get out of bed, get dressed, make my bed	
7:00	Have breakfast, feed dog, brush teeth, wash face, comb hair	
7:30	Pack lunch in school bag Check that I have packed all that I need for school in my schoolbag	
8:00	Walk to the bus stop	
8:30	Travel to school	
9:00 –3:00	School	
3:30	Catch bus home	
4:00	Arrive home, snack and play with Buddy	
5:00	HOMEWORK	
7:00	Dinner, do dishes when it's my turn, FaceTime with dad	
8:00	Screen time of choice, e.g. TV, gaming (as agreed with my parents)	
9:00	Bedtime routine: shower, brush teeth. School clothes ready for the morning Sports gear ready, school bag packed Technology charging in designated area (no technology in bedroom)	
10:00	Lights off	

ADHD Challenges Impact Completion of Homework

Did You Know? The entire process of homework from the time that it is assigned until the time that it is turned in is complex and involves skills and behaviours that are challenging for most children with ADHD.

First, you must listen to the teacher assigning the homework, understand it and write it down correctly. You must decide what items to bring home and put them in your schoolbag to remember to take home.

Resisting the temptation to lie about having homework, you resign yourself to doing it, knowing that you will miss out on fun. Next comes actually doing the work. You must focus and resist distractions. You need to apply effort to boring and tedious tasks, and make yourself slow down and not rush to get it done. When it's done, you need to remember to place it in your schoolbag so that you remember to turn it in.

Each of these steps presents an opportunity for things to go wrong.

What Is the Purpose of Homework?

The answer to this question seems obvious; however, the simple answer – that homework helps children learn – is incomplete and not exactly accurate. Homework serves different purposes, depending on your grade and individual abilities.

Homework for primary school students provides practice of skills taught in class, an opportunity to master and demonstrate knowledge obtained. High school students have the added goal of using homework as a way to apply learned principles to new situations, as well as engage in independent learning at home.

Ultimately, what routine homework teaches in the earlier years is discipline and work ethic. It reinforces and enhances lifelong skills of responsibility, independent learning, time management, organisation, planning, perseverance and self-discipline. A general rule of thumb is 10 minutes per grade level per day, so a child in year six should be doing around 60 minutes of homework per day. Different states have different recommendations about the amount of homework children should be doing, and schools also have individual homework policies.

The majority of children with ADHD can be expected to take at least two to three times as long to complete the same amount of work as their classmates. This can cause much stress and often overshadows the benefits of homework.

How much homework is reasonable for you is best decided with the help of your teacher in consultation with your parents – and with your input, obviously!

Can a Tutor Help?

A tutor can be the best thing for a child with ADHD. Even if you don't need extra help to learn new concepts, a tutor can save your relationship with your parents. The arguing and battle that often happens when doing homework with your parents does not happen with a tutor. Most children with ADHD simply need someone to sit with them and keep them focused. An older or uni student is often all that is needed.

If you feel overwhelmed with the amount of homework expected of you, speak to your parents. They, in turn, can speak to your teacher. Adopt a team approach and listen to what the teacher thinks will work best for you. Whenever possible, contribute some ideas. After all, you are the person experiencing the problem, so you need to be part of the solution.

Accommodations and modifications that you can benefit from in doing your homework include:

- cutting the quantity of homework deemed necessary
- setting a fixed time limit to work on homework
- typing rather than handwrite homework
- having the teacher sign homework when it is turned in
- allowing extra time to complete projects
- having an extra set of textbooks at home
- assigning a study buddy in the classroom
- allowing you to correct errors for full credits
- providing advance warning of long-term projects
- prohibiting incomplete classwork to be sent home as homework
- ensuring neatness has no impact on grades
- allowing for periodic take-home tests.

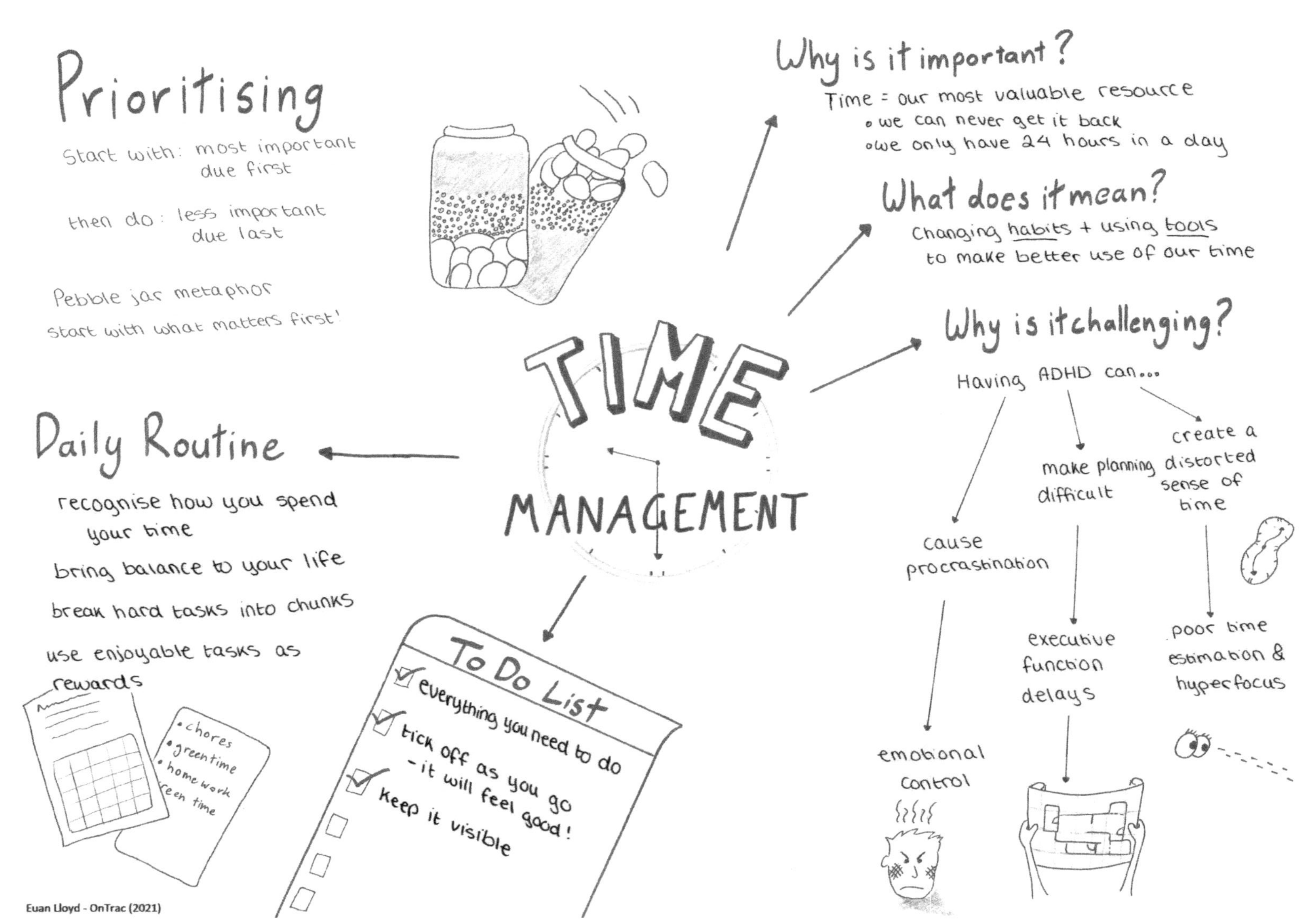
Prioritising
Start with: most important due first
then do: less important due last
Pebble jar metaphor
start with what matters first!
TIME
MANAGEMENT
Why is it important?
Time = our most valuable resource
• we can never get it back
• we only have 24 hours in a day
What does it mean?
Changing habits + using tools
to make better use of our time
Why is it challenging?
Having ADHD can...
cause procrastination
make planning difficult
create a distorted sense of time
emotional control
executive function delays
poor time estimation & hyperfocus
Daily Routine
recognise how you spend your time
bring balance to your life
break hard tasks into chunks
use enjoyable tasks as rewards
• chores
• green time
• homework
reen time
To Do List
everything you need to do
tick off as you go - it will feel good!
keep it visible
Euan Lloyd - OnTrac (2021)

Time Management Snakes and Ladders

Roll the dice to move around the board. Can you relate to these time management challenges and successes?

Topic 2: Organisation, Impulsivity and Distractibility

Being productive and effective when you have ADHD has less to do with your ability and a lot to do with your lack of structure.

Did You Know? Children with ADHD find organisational skills challenging, but organisation is a skill you can build over time. Just like a person who breaks a leg might use crutches as a tool, you can develop organisation tools to help you succeed. As mentioned previously, managing your time, planning and prioritising are key skills to becoming a more organised individual. Learning coping strategies and techniques for dealing with a lack of organisation can make school and home a lot less stressful, because it adds structure and order to your life. Keep a monthly calendar in an area where it is visible (in your locker or above your homework station at home). Mark important dates for school, home or social activities. When you write down your assignments or homework, note all important information, including due dates and any specific instructions from your teacher. Talk with your teacher and ask questions right away to prevent any misunderstandings. Also record any daily or weekly chores or responsibilities that you could forget. For more information on organisation strategies, see **Appendix F.**

Below are some tools and tips to help you organise your workspace, assignments, homework and to save time. I have excluded technology, simply because technology tools can be a source of major distraction for some children with ADHD. Tick the ones you already use. Add in any others you use.

- ☐ Day planner (paper diary)
- ☐ To-do list
- ☐ Wall calendar
- ☐ Homework station
- ☐ Shelving and bookcases

- ☐ Storage bins (ideally see-through ones) for different items
- ☐ Stacking trays
- ☐ A launch pad
- ☐ Colour coding different subjects
- ☐ Wastepaper bin

Others:

____

____

____

Which tools do you use to help manage your disorganisation?

____

____

____

Does your mind give you reasons why you should not try new tools/strategies? Are any of these familiar? Add your own.

- I have tried this before, and it did not work.
- It takes too long to learn how to use a calendar, and it won't work anyway.
- Once I get it started, I'll forget all about it.
- I can't throw things out because I might need them someday.
- I can't throw things out because I need to hold on to the memories in them.
- Getting organised is going to take time away from doing my homework.
- If I get organised, others may expect more of me and I will be overwhelmed.

Other reasons:

____

____

____

Challenge each statement that is limiting your progress in organisation

____

____

____

How to Tidy Up and Organise Your Room

Before

After

Once you have tidied up your room, or any other space for that matter, take a picture and display it on your wall to remind you what tidy and organised looks like.

See **Appendix F** for more tips on organisation.

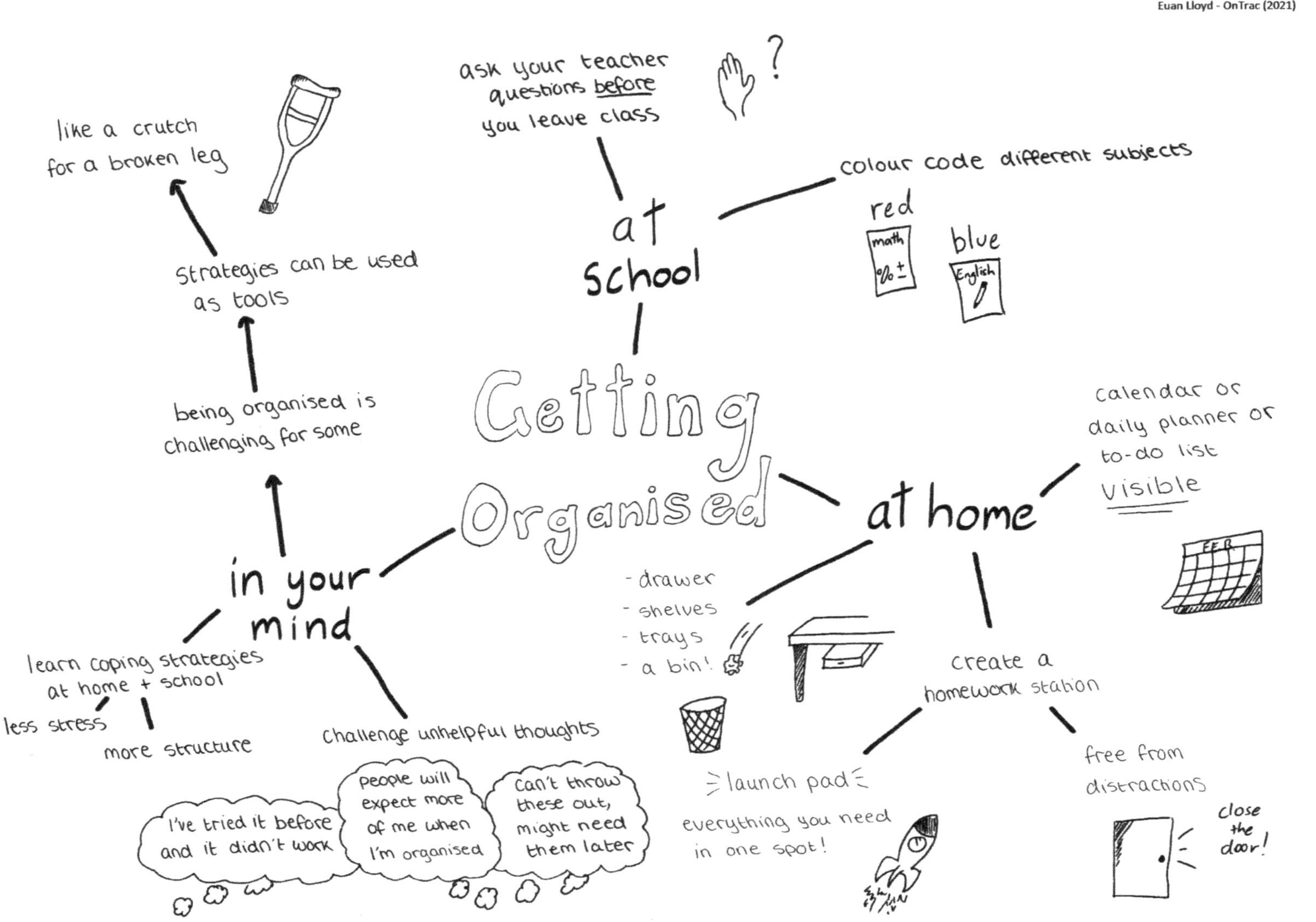
Euan Lloyd - OnTrac (2021)
Getting Organised
at school
ask your teacher questions before you leave class
colour code different subjects
red
math
blue
English
at home
calendar or daily planner or to-do list visible
FEB
- drawer
- shelves
- trays
- a bin!
create a homework station
launch pad
everything you need in one spot!
free from distractions
close the door!
in your mind
being organised is challenging for some
strategies can be used as tools
like a crutch for a broken leg
learn coping strategies at home + school
less stress
more structure
challenge unhelpful thoughts
I've tried it before and it didn't work
people will expect more of me when I'm organised
Can't throw these out, might need them later

Impulsivity

> ***Before you make a decision, ask yourself this question: will you regret the results, or rejoice in them?***
> ***~Rob Liano***

Did You Know? One of the core symptoms of ADHD is impulsivity. Impulsivity means not being able to stop an action before it starts, or to stop or change a behaviour once it's started. The urge to act seems to be independent of reason. Even if the person is aware of the consequences of the behaviour, they still have great difficulty controlling it. Impulsivity can create severe consequences, from school failure to life-threatening situations. The cycle of frustration, acting impulsively, and then feeling more frustration about not controlling your own behaviour, gets replayed over and over.

Write the risky behaviours that you have engaged in and what were/could be their potential consequences, for example shoplifting, drinking alcohol, smoking cigarettes, cheating in a test, spreading rumours, etc. (Maybe you just want to reflect on these things, rather than write them down – it's your choice.)

____

____

____

Of all the risky behaviours that you've engaged in, which were the riskier?

____

____

____

Are you worried about these behaviours?

____

____

____

If you haven't spoken to anybody about these behaviours, who could you speak to in your Circle of Support?

____

____

____

What else can you do to stop these behaviours?

____

____

____

What role does peer pressure play in your involvement in risky behaviour?

____

____

____

Word Finder: Impulsivity Control Strategies

The strategies below can be used to control impulsivity. Find them in the word finder and colour them in.

B	O	I	T	U	Y	T	R	E	W	Q	S	A	D	F	G	H	J	K
W	R	S	A	T	A	C	O	P	I	N	G	S	K	I	L	L	S	M
P	A	D	K	S	S	Q	W	E	R	Y	O	K	Q	Y	E	Y	E	N
T	I	M	E	O	U	T	D	F	J	W	L	F	W	T	T	T	L	B
T	S	A	T	D	J	Z	X	V	B	E	K	O	E	R	G	R	F	V
S	E	S	U	D	H	W	E	T	Y	T	J	R	R	E	O	E	T	C
R	H	D	R	V	G	H	G	F	S	Y	H	H	T	S	R	K	A	X
F	A	F	N	H	D	Q	W	E	R	U	S	E	Y	H	E	A	L	N
D	N	G	S	S	A	F	D	S	A	I	F	L	U	T	A	E	K	Z
K	D	O	N	T	I	N	T	E	R	R	U	P	T	A	S	P	X	M
M	Y	H	Q	Z	X	X	V	V	J	J	F	E	I	E	D	S	Z	L
Z	U	J	W	O	R	T	Y	U	I	O	P	L	U	R	F	O	L	A
S	T	O	P	T	H	I	N	K	A	S	F	H	T	B	L	T	K	C
K	I	K	E	Q	W	E	R	Y	I	O	P	L	R	P	K	T	J	Y
P	O	L	R	T	Y	U	I	O	P	A	S	D	G	E	G	I	H	A
H	Q	E	K	R	T	Y	U	I	O	P	A	S	D	E	F	A	G	T
B	S	L	G	Z	C	A	L	M	D	S	L	O	W	D	O	W	N	S

Ask For Help
Coping skills
Deep Breaths
Don't interrupt
Let Go
Raise Hand
Self-Talk
Slow down
Stay calm
Stop think
Take Turns
Timeout
Wait To Speak

See **Appendix G** for answer key.

Distractibility

I may look like I'm doing nothing ... But in my head I'm quite busy.

Did You Know? Distractions are everywhere and are part of life. Generally, when someone is interrupted in the middle of a task, they will temporarily shift their attention and then move back to the original task. This is not as easy when you have ADHD. It is harder to transition between activities and get back on track. Often, the original task is forgotten and you move on to whatever distracted you. Distractions come in different forms and include inner urges to take breaks, raid the refrigerator or just sharpen your pencil when the task gets boring. Removing distractions from your environment is key to being productive and having good time management – and keep your workplace tidy so that you can work without distraction once you get started.

What tasks make you distracted the most?

____

____

What environments distract you the most?

____

____

Name three activities that you find most boring, and what distractions draw you away when you are bored. For example: homework – gaming, watching TV, etc.

____

____

____

Name three things you love doing, that never make you bored.

____

____

____

Modifying Your Environment

It is important for individuals with ADHD to work in environments that have few distractions. Think about the environment in which you do homework or study and ask yourself, 'What are the things that typically distract me in this environment?'

Some typical distractions include:

- Hearing the telephone ring
- Surfing the internet, chatting online, playing online games
- Replying to messages
- Noticing other things on the desk or table that need attention
- Listening to the radio
- Watching television
- Speaking to a friend or relative who is in the room
- Looking at something going on outside the window
- Internal distractions, such as worry and negative self-talk
- Others: ____

  ____

  ____

What are the types of things that typically get in the way when you are trying to get your schoolwork done? For each item that is distracting to you, try to come up with a strategy that reduces your susceptibility to this distraction.

For example, you can:

- turn off the phone
- shut off notifications
- clear off your desk or homework space
- turn off the radio and television
- ask others not to disturb you because you are working

- place a 'Do Not Disturb' sign on your door
- turn your desk away from the window.

Use the table below to identify and eliminate usual distractions for your school and homework environment.

Strategies for Reducing Distractions	
Distractions	**Reduction Strategies**
Getting notifications on phone	Turn off phone/notifications
Random thoughts	Write them on a piece of paper and think about them later

Did You Know? Distractibility delay is an exercise that you can use for delaying attending to distractions while working on boring or difficult tasks. The first step in this strategy is to gauge the length of time that you can work on a boring or difficult task. The second step is to break down the task into smaller chunks that take that amount of time to complete. This skill involves committing to working on a task for a certain period of time. During that time, write down distractions, but do not act on them. After the agreed-upon period, you can decide if they are tasks that need to be done immediately, tasks that can go into your to-do list, or tasks that are pure distractions and can be discarded.

Do you think that you could use the activities that you love as rewards for completing the boring tasks? If so, how would you do this?

____

____

____

List three strategies that you have tried/used to manage your distractibility

1. ____
2. ____
3. ____

Exercise: Gauging Your Attention Span

Choose a task to work on and have a stopwatch handy. After you start the task, keep track of how long you can work before losing interest and becoming distracted. Record this length of time and repeat this exercise several times. Get an average. Now that you know how long you can concentrate for, break down bigger tasks that you can complete within your attention span.

Do you sometimes feel, given the time you spend studying, that you should be getting better grades? If so, is it possible that you are putting many hours into your studies but not much studying gets done? Can this be changed by modifying your environment?

___

___

___

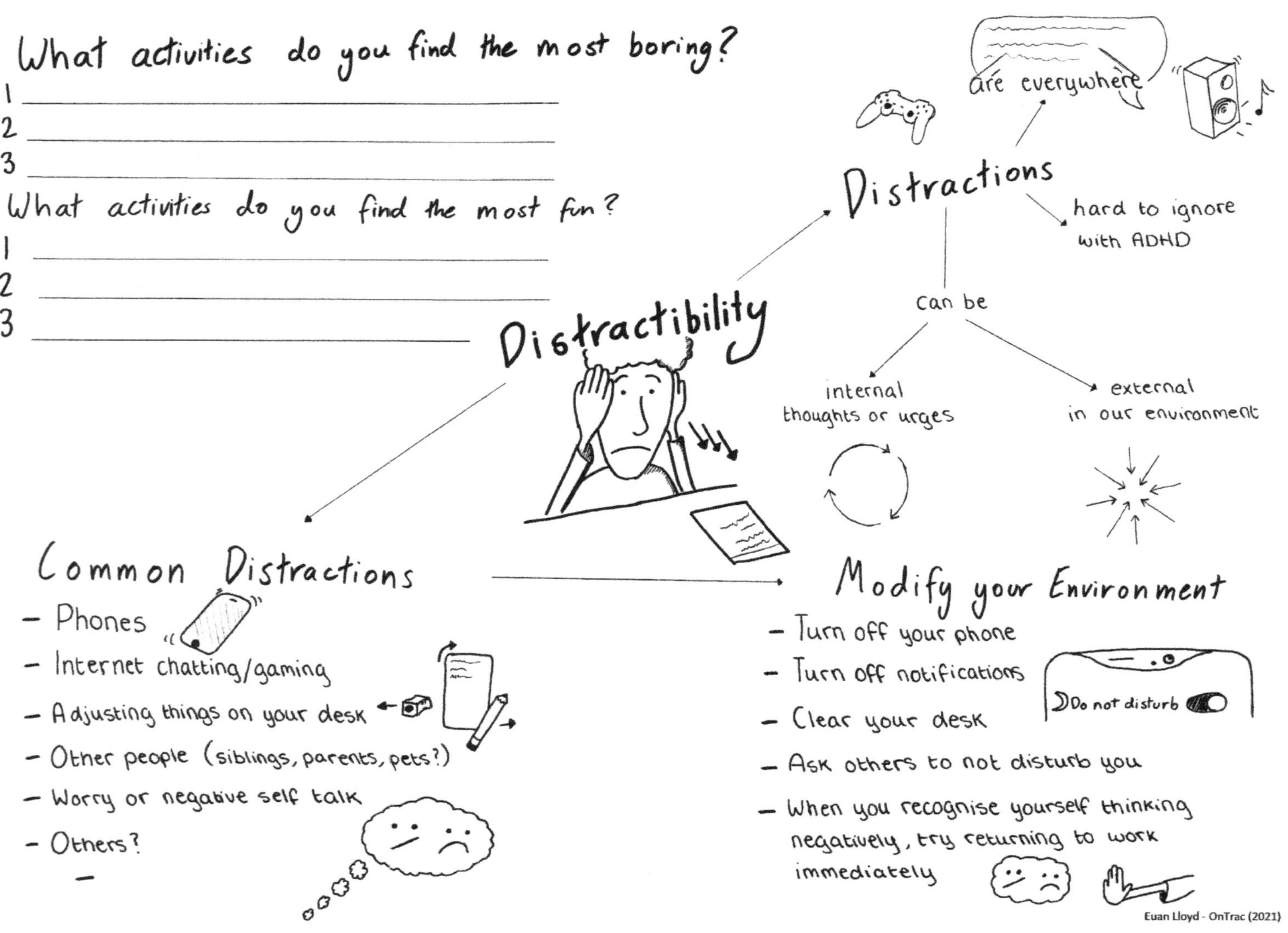
What activities do you find the most boring?
1
2
3
What activities do you find the most fun?
1
2
3
Distractibility
Distractions
are everywhere
hard to ignore with ADHD
can be
internal thoughts or urges
external in our environment
Common Distractions
- Phones
- Internet chatting/gaming
- Adjusting things on your desk
- Other people (siblings, parents, pets?)
- Worry or negative self talk
- Others?
-
Modify your Environment
- Turn off your phone
- Turn off notifications
- Clear your desk
- Ask others to not disturb you
- When you recognise yourself thinking negatively, try returning to work immediately
Do not disturb
Euan Lloyd - OnTrac (2021)

Topic 3: Procrastination

When there is a hill to climb, don't think that waiting will make it smaller.

Reasons why students procrastinate – and what you can do about it.

'You found out about this assignment weeks ago. Why did you wait until tonight to start working on it?' Does this sound familiar?

Did You Know? Procrastination is one of the most common concerns from parents.

Whether it is waiting to start an assignment until the night before the due date, or beginning tomorrow's homework at 10 pm, procrastination is a regular way of life for many children.

For parents, this can be incredibly frustrating, because it seems so easy to avoid. 'If you had just started your homework when you got home, you'd be finished already. Now you're going to be up half the night!'

It is extremely tempting to call teens out for being lazy, lecture them on the costs of procrastination, or point out the bad decisions that got them into this mess. Unfortunately, these responses rarely help.

When tweens and teens don't feel judged or criticised and can let go of their need to justify their behaviour, they admit that they wish they could procrastinate less. They know the damage procrastination does, and that their lives would be easier if they did not do it. They just don't know how to change. So, what works?

The first step is to develop an understanding of **why** you procrastinate. An effective solution depends on understanding the root of the problem. Awareness and self-knowledge are the keys to defeating procrastination. Many students report that understanding the reasons they procrastinate makes it easier to stop.

Common Reasons for Procrastination

Forgetfulness: Some students leave their work until the last minute because they forget or are unaware. Maybe they missed class, were distracted when it was announced, didn't write it down or forgot to check the class app. Until a friend mentions it the day before it's due, or they walk into class on the day, they genuinely have no idea there was work to be done. Technically speaking, leaving things until the last minute would not be classified as 'procrastination' because the student is not resisting their work – they simply do not realise they have any work!

Lack of understanding: When a student doesn't understand what an assignment is about, what is expected of them or where to start, they can become overwhelmed by the apparent enormity of the task. They often put off the assignment in the hope that they will understand it better later. Unfortunately, when they look at it the night before the deadline, they usually have no more information than they did before, and no time left to ask their teacher for clarification or advice on where to start. The inherent difficulty of the project is compounded by the fact that they have run out of time to complete it.

Optimistic time estimates: Optimism is a wonderful quality in most situations. But when it comes to estimating how much time it will take to complete an assignment, unrealistic optimism can create big problems. Students commonly overestimate how much time they have left to complete assignments and underestimate how long it will take to complete them. Consequently, they fail to leave themselves enough time to complete the work.

Overly lenient deadlines: When teachers don't enforce deadlines and allow students to turn in late work without a penalty, students learn that deadlines are not meaningful and stop taking them seriously. Without meaningful consequences, external deadlines can start to feel as arbitrary as internal deadlines, which – while helpful – are not as effective at discouraging procrastination.

Poor study routines: Habitual behaviour can cause students to procrastinate automatically, without even thinking about it. Watching TV after school can lead to procrastination because it is hard to turn the TV off. A pattern of leaving the hardest work until last, when students have the least energy and the smallest amount of willpower, will reduce the chances of the work being done well.

Distractions: Sometimes students set aside time to complete their work, but end up distracted with other things. These distractions can be external (social media, text messages, etc.) or internal (own thoughts and impulses). Either way, this results in them spending time that had been budgeted for their work in other ways.

Perfectionism/fear of failure: When students are overly concerned about doing everything perfectly and not making mistakes, it creates anxiety, which makes it difficult for them to get started. They avoid the project even more as the deadline approaches because they become less and less likely to be able to do a good job on it. Eventually, they are so close to the deadline that producing an ideal assignment is no longer possible, and their only options are to do an imperfect job or turn in nothing at all.

Too many commitments: If a student has so many scheduled activities and so little free time that their life feels like an endless string of obligations and chores, they may use procrastination to artificially create 'free time' for themselves. Unfortunately, this type of free time is usually not very satisfying because it's also accompanied by a sense of guilt for avoiding the things they should be working on.

Resistance: Procrastination can be a form of rebellion. When students view work as something that is being forced on them by an unreasonable teacher or authoritarian parents, procrastination becomes their way of resisting authority, showing teachers and parents, 'You can't make me do it'.

Difficulty regulating emotions: Recent studies suggest that procrastination is less of problem with time management than we had once believed, and more of a difficulty with emotional regulation. Students who feel bored, tired, frustrated or nervous when they work on assignments will often pursue a strategy of trying to make themselves feel better in the short term by downplaying the assignment ('it's no big deal; it won't affect my grade much anyway') and distracting themselves with fun, rewarding activities in order to improve their mood.

Solutions to procrastination: The solutions are different for each of these scenarios, which is why it is so important to identify the root cause of your procrastination before choosing strategies to try. For example, reminders about the consequences of an impending deadline may help a teen who hasn't been taking deadlines seriously but, for a student with a fear of failure or difficulty regulating emotions, it could actually make things worse by increasing their anxiety about the assignment and their desire to do something else in order to avoid these negative emotions.

Which of the reasons for procrastination listed on the previous pages do you identify with?

____

____

____

What type of support or encouragement would help you to get started rather than leaving it until the last minute?

____

____

____

Who in your Circle of Support could provide the support and encouragement that you need?

____

____

____

Reasons for Your Procrastination

Below are some of the most common reasons why students procrastinate. Please check the boxes that you identify as reasons why you procrastinate.

- ☐ Not knowing what needs to be done
- ☐ Not wanting to do something
- ☐ Not caring if it gets done or not
- ☐ Not feeling in the mood to do it
- ☐ Being in the habit of waiting until the last minute
- ☐ Believing that you work better under pressure
- ☐ Thinking that you can finish it at the last minute
- ☐ Lacking the initiative to get started
- ☐ Forgetting
- ☐ Blaming sickness or poor health
- ☐ Waiting for the right moment
- ☐ Needing time to think about the task
- ☐ Delaying one task in favour of working on another
- ☐ Lack of motivation
- ☐ Low self-confidence
- ☐ Fear of failure
- ☐ Trouble concentrating
- ☐ Perfectionism
- ☐ Low energy levels
- ☐ Poor organisation skills

Procrastination Excuses

Below are some of the excuses that people use to justify or make themselves feel better about their procrastination. Check the ones that you have used in the past and add your own.

- ☐ I will do it once this other thing is finished
- ☐ I don't have everything I need; I can't start it now
- ☐ I don't have enough time to do it all, so I will wait until I do
- ☐ It is too late to start it now
- ☐ I won't get much done, so I'll just leave it for now
- ☐ It is better to do it when I am in the mood or feeling inspired
- ☐ I will miss out on the fun happening now; I can do it another time
- ☐ It is too nice a day to spend on this
- ☐ I've got to organise my desk/drawers backpack, etc. first
- ☐ I've got to exercise first
- ☐ I am too busy to do it now
- ☐ I have plenty of time, so I can do it later
- ☐ I work better when I am stressed, so I will leave it to the last minute
- ☐ It might not be good enough, so why bother doing it

Add your own:

____

____

____

Challenging your Procrastination Excuses

The Truth	Unhelpful Conclusion	Helpful Conclusion
I am really tired	I am better off doing it after I have rested	Yes, I am tired, but I can still make a small start now
I will miss out on the fun going on now	I can always wait until nothing fun is happening	If I get some work done, I can reward myself with other fun later
I don't have everything I need	I will wait until I have everything before I start	I can still make a start with what I have
I have other things to do	I will do it once those things are completed	The other things are less important and can be done after this
I have plenty of time	I don't have to start it now	Better to get on top of it now than leave it to the last minute
I work better under pressure	I will leave it to the last minute	It is still worth making a start now
I don't like maths	I am not even going to try	I can try on my own and ask Dad for help if I need.

Procrastination Activities

The more convincing your excuses are, the more likely you will actually procrastinate by engaging in other activities that take your attention away from the task/goal at hand. Below are types of procrastination substitute activities:

- Pleasurable tasks: watch TV, play games, listen to music, read books, surf the net, playing, working on hobbies.
- Lower priority tasks: sorting out things, sort out your toys or games, researching a topic of interest.
- Socialising: phoning or messaging friends or family members, going out.
- Distractions: sleeping, eating, drinking.
- Daydreaming: thinking about the past or future, imagining that the task is already completed, imagining a better life.

It is important to be aware of the things that typically distract you from your tasks and goals. It is not that these activities are in themselves bad and should be stopped. We all need pleasurable things in our lives and we all need a break from tasks by balancing these with things we like to do. We all need social time and distractions in our lives, and a bit of daydreaming can be a nice escape at times.

These activities are only a problem when doing them keeps us from completing really important tasks or goals.

Being a procrastinator, what do I get out of it that is negative? What are the disadvantages? How does it hurt me?

Being a procrastinator, what do I get out of it that is positive? What are the advantages? How does it help me?

If I do change and no longer procrastinate, what will be good about that? How will my life be better? What will be the benefits of change for me?

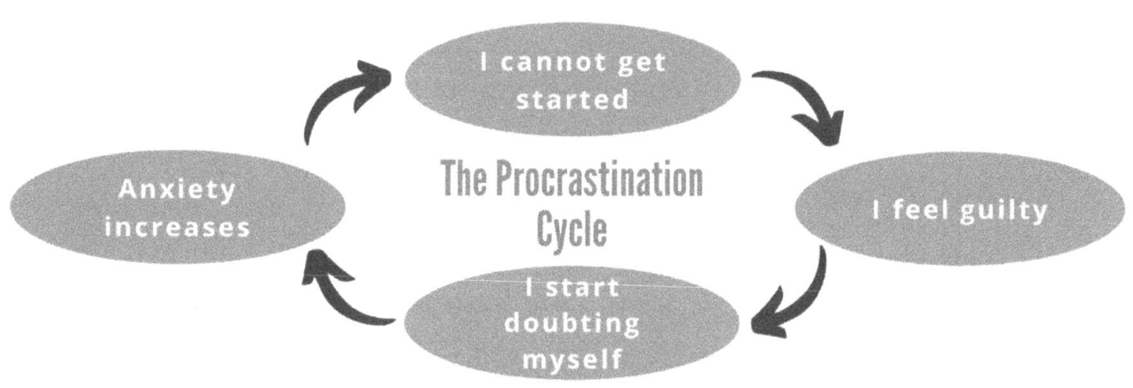

Tips for Managing Procrastination

As we have seen, there are many negative aspects to procrastination: however, it is possible to stop procrastinating and become more productive. In addition to the suggestions already made, we suggest you try the following:

- Be around productive people and emulate the things they do to achieve success, especially in those areas in which you tend to procrastinate.
- Continually clarify your goals, ensuring they align with your values. Remember, you'll never get there if you don't know where you want to go.
- Do not compare yourself or your ability to others. You can always find someone more creative, faster, smarter or better able to complete whatever task you set for yourself.
- Write a plan on how to tackle the task. Break it up into small steps that you can complete within your attention span.
- Take action. Get something done each day – something you can feel good about accomplishing. For time-consuming tasks, take a horizontal time approach and work in steady chunks over time.
- Reward yourself with small rewards for steps completed and with a bigger reward for completion of the entire task.
- Quit making excuses. You may think you have valid reasons for delaying a task, but learn to be honest with yourself when you procrastinate.
- Perfectionism can cause procrastination, so let 'good' be acceptable.
- Use your common distraction as rewards. For example, do you procrastinate on social media? If so, tell yourself that after a chunk of work you will take a five-minute break and check your social media.
- Work with a buddy for added accountability.
- If necessary, see health professional to manage any physical or psychological reasons for your procrastination. Poor health can impede the best efforts.

Do not give up. With time and effort, you can overcome the habit of procrastination and lead a happier, healthier, more successful life.

Overcoming Schoolwork Procrastination

> ***Knowing is not enough, we must apply. Willing is not enough, we must do.***
> ***~Bruce Lee***

- Talk about homework as something you are **choosing** to do, rather than something you **have to** do. For example, tell yourself, 'Tonight I want to do all the preparation work for the project on World War II', rather than 'I have to do the World War II project'. It is a subtle difference, but it can help you feel more ready and in control, which reduces the desire to resist the work through procrastination.
- Show interest in your schoolwork. Be curious, ask questions, get Mum and Dad involved, if possible. Their experiences may help clarify your ideas and define your goals. Also, their interest may help you see the project as more interesting and worthwhile.
- If you are over scheduled and feel overwhelmed, prioritise your commitments and see if there are some things that you can postpone in order to have more time available to complete your schoolwork.
- If you are having difficulty starting a project, it may help to speak to your teacher or parents to identify the first steps to take. This may mean asking questions to help you brainstorm possible essay ideas or type the first few lines of an essay. Usually, once you get started, continuing on your own becomes easier.
- Use language that encourages progress. Reward your efforts, rather than results, and see mistakes as learning opportunities. Celebrating progress, rather than completion, can minimise your anxiety, perfectionism tendencies and fears of failure.
- Do not resist help from your parents; they mean well. However, this is ultimately your problem and not theirs. Do not allow it to cause conflict in your relationship.

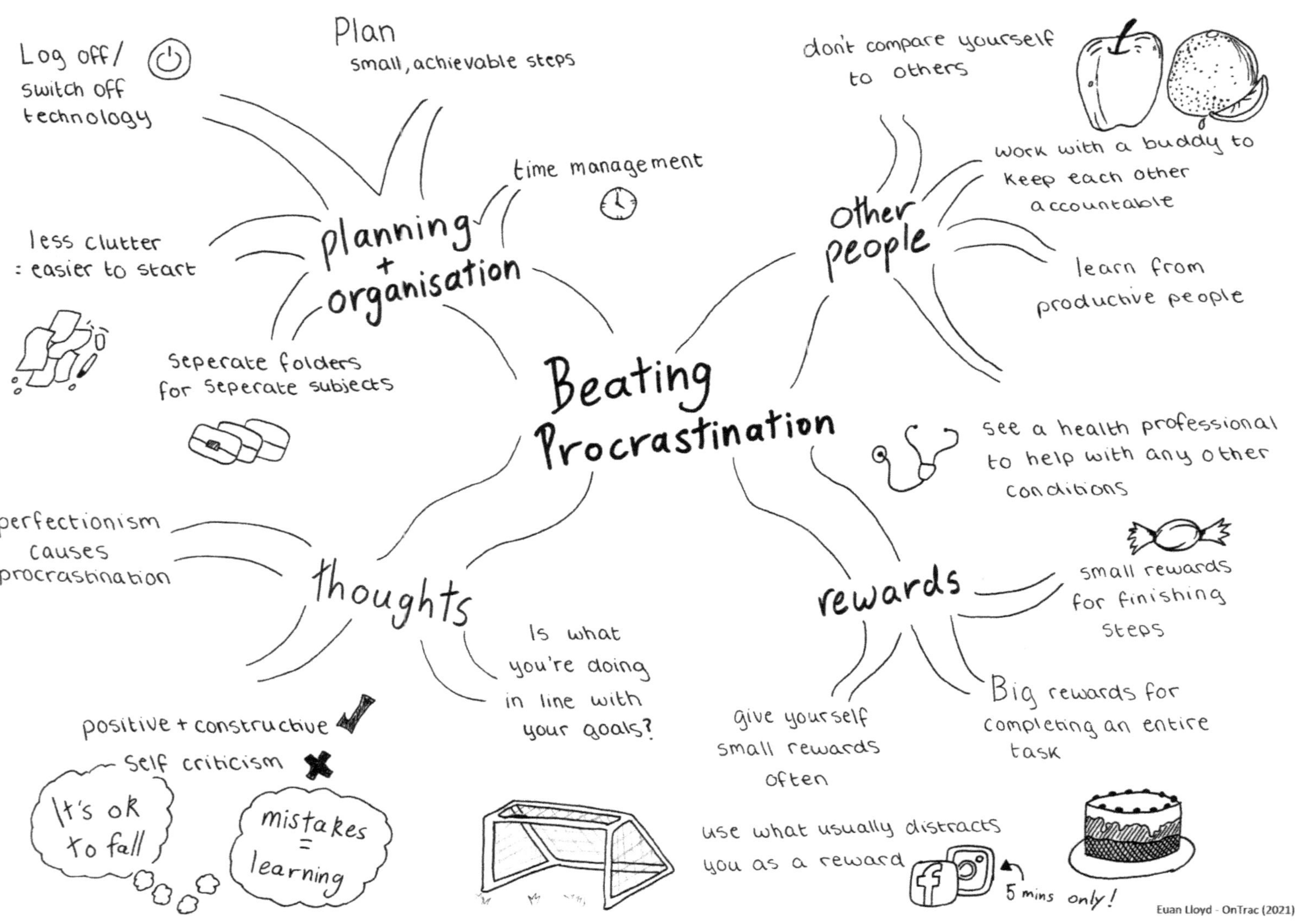
Beating Procrastination
planning + organisation
Plan
small, achievable steps
time management
Log off/ switch off technology
less clutter : easier to start
Seperate folders for Seperate subjects
thoughts
perfectionism causes procrastination
positive + constructive
Self criticism
It's ok to fall
mistakes = learning
Is what you're doing in line with your goals?
other people
don't compare yourself to others
work with a buddy to keep each other accountable
learn from productive people
see a health professional to help with any other conditions
rewards
give yourself small rewards often
small rewards for finishing steps
Big rewards for completing an entire task
use what usually distracts you as a reward
5 mins only!
Euan Lloyd - OnTrac (2021)

Module 3:

Practical Coping Skills

Section 2:

Communication and Social Skills

Topic 1: Communication and ADHD

When we look at something from only our own perspective, we see just one part of the situation. We must see things from different perspectives to understand a situation fully.

Did You Know? Symptoms of ADHD can be barriers to communication. Core symptoms of ADHD like impulsivity can lead to dominating the conversation and interrupting while others are talking. Communication is much more than simply speaking words.

It involves:

- Conveying emotion to another person
- Listening to what someone is saying with words and with their body language
- Being a good listener
- Give and take - listening to another person and waiting your turn to speak

Luckily for us, communication skills can be learned. We need to practise all our skills, and communication is no exception – remember, practice makes perfect.

Are you a Passive, Aggressive or Assertive Communicator?

Every person has a unique communication style, a way in which they interact and exchange information with others. There are several communication styles, but for the purpose of this workbook, we will concentrate on the following three basic styles: passive, assertive and aggressive. It's important to understand each communication style and why individuals use them. In some situations a combination of these styles might be most effective.

Read the list of traits for each style, and tick the ones that relate to you.

Passive Communication

	Speaks softly, if at all		Keeps the peace
	Allows others to take advantage		Does not inspire respect from others
	Does not express their own needs		Lack of confidence
	Poor eye contact		Gives in to others

Aggressive Communication

	Speaks loudly over others		Can lead to shouting or violence
	Will not compromise		Damages others' self-esteem
	Forcefully expresses own needs		Bullies others
	Will not listen to the needs of others		Easily frustrated

Assertive Communication

	Cares for needs of both people		Makes good eye contact
	Stands up for own needs		Listens without interruption
	Respects needs of others		Builds self-esteem
	Willing to compromise		Enhances relationships

It is important to note that learning to communicate assertively doesn't guarantee you will have your needs met, but it makes it more likely; and it can improve your relationships with other people.

What communication style do you use most of the time?

What can you do to improve how you communicate?

Who do you know who is good at assertive communication?

In your opinion, which is your mum's preferred communication style?

In your opinion, which is your dad's preferred communication style?

> ***The only healthy communication style is assertive communication.***
> ***~Jim Rohn***

Communication scenarios:

Scenario	**A friend asks to copy your homework**
Passive	Umm, ok, I guess.
Aggressive	No way! Don't be stupid! Do your own work, lazy.
Assertive	I won't let you copy my work, but I'll help you understand it, or go with you to ask the teacher for help.

Scenario	**Your younger brother is bugging you to play with him, but you want some time to yourself.**
Passive	
Aggressive	
Assertive	

Scenario	**Your parents ask you to do some extra chores around the house today, but you are stressed out about an assignment that is due tomorrow.**
Passive	
Aggressive	
Assertive	

'I' Statements

Taking responsibility for your feelings will help you improve your communication when you feel upset or angry. One way to achieve this is by using 'I' statements. This technique will allow you to communicate what is upsetting you without blaming. If you sound too accusive, the person you are speaking to may become increasingly defensive.

A good 'I' statement explains how you feel, what made you feel that way and what you would like to happen differently.

I felt/feel sad/upset (say how you feel; use the feeling words below)

When you called me names (describe what was said or done)

I would like to be treated with respect (describe what you would like to happen instead; use the ideas on the next page)

Feeling Words				
worried	angry	sad	shy	lonely
afraid	mad	grouchy	jealous	rejected
scared	upset	blue	bored	uncomfortable
fearful	aggressive	down	helpless	sick
disappointed	out of control	insecure	frustrated	overwhelmed
annoyed	enraged	anxious	hyper	weak
irritated	furious	grief	attacked	distressed
silly	bothered	pain	judged	cranky
tired	offended	hurt	antsy	empty
discouraged	shamed	alienated	desperate	devalued
disrespected	agitated	exasperated	defensive	embarrassed

Examples of: **What I would like is…**

- to share and take turns
- to be treated with kindness
- for everyone to follow the rules
- to play together
- to find a solution we agree on
- a second chance
- to be able to focus and work
- to have more say over my life
- to feel included
- to spend time together
- to be in a quiet and calm space
- to feel safe
- to work out the conflict
- some space and privacy
- to make my own decision
- to be heard and listened to

Examples

Regular	'You make me sad because you don't hang around with me anymore'
'I' Statement	'I feel sad when you don't want to hang around with me because I really value your friendship.'

Practice

Scenario	Your friend keeps cancelling plans at the last minute. Last weekend you were waiting for them at a restaurant when they called to tell you they could not make it. You left feeling hurt.
'I' Statement	

Scenario	You are working on a project with a group and one member is not completing their tasks on time. In the past you have lost marks for not meeting the deadline. You don't want the same thing to happen and you feel frustrated.
'I' Statement	

Topic 2: Levels of Domination in Conversation

Communication must be HOT. That's Honest, Open, and Two-Way.
~Dan Oswald

Remember that person who wouldn't stop talking at the last party you went to? Children with ADHD and other conditions can find reciprocal conversation skills particularly difficult. They may say little or nothing on the playground or in class discussions. Or they may dominate in monologue fashion, not noticing the signs that others are becoming impatient. The following exercise will help you become more aware of your level of domination in a group conversation.

Exercise: Conversation Sharing

When people are having a conversation, it should be like sharing a pizza. Each person gets the opportunity to share equally, just like the image here.

This is not fair. Peter is doing all the talking.

Do you relate more to Peter or to the other children in the image above? Why?

____

____

____

Have you ever been in conversations where one person talks much more than others? How did it make you feel?

____

____

Exercise: Think about conversations in group settings – with your friends, your family or in class. Monitor how much time you spend listening and how much time you spend talking in relation to others in the group.

Colour in the portion of the pizza that you spend talking in red and the portion that you spend listening in green.

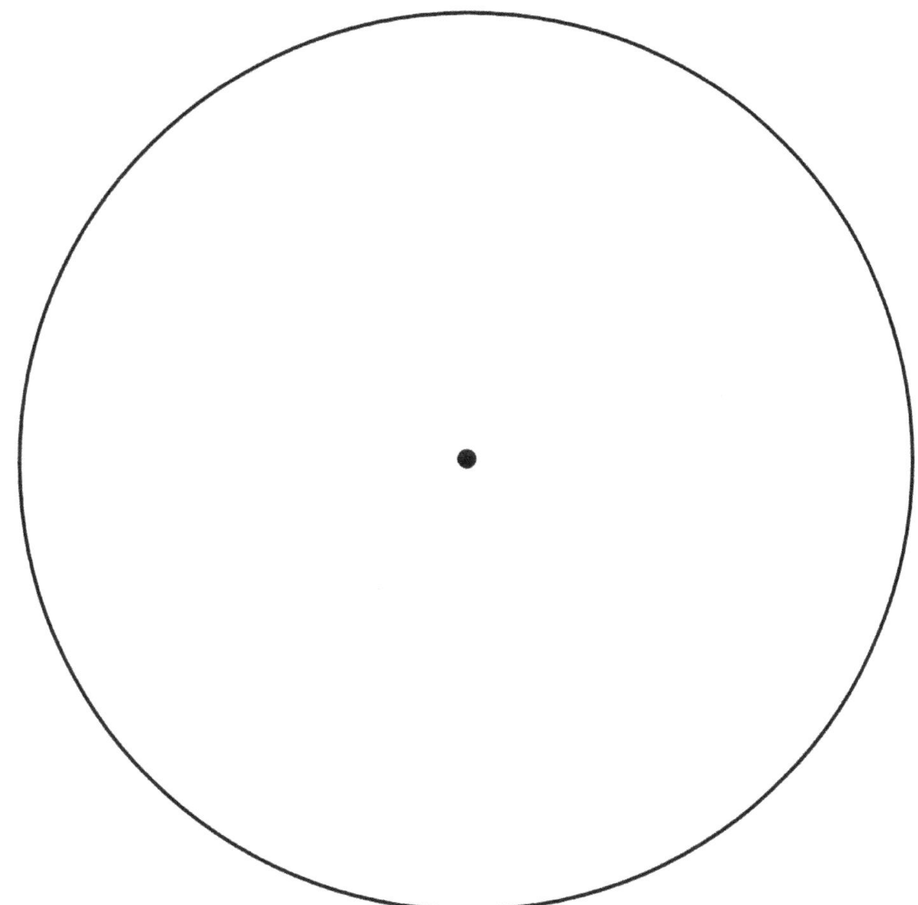

Are you happy with the balance between the time you spend talking and the time you spend listening?

If not, what can you change?

____

____

____

Finding Common Interests

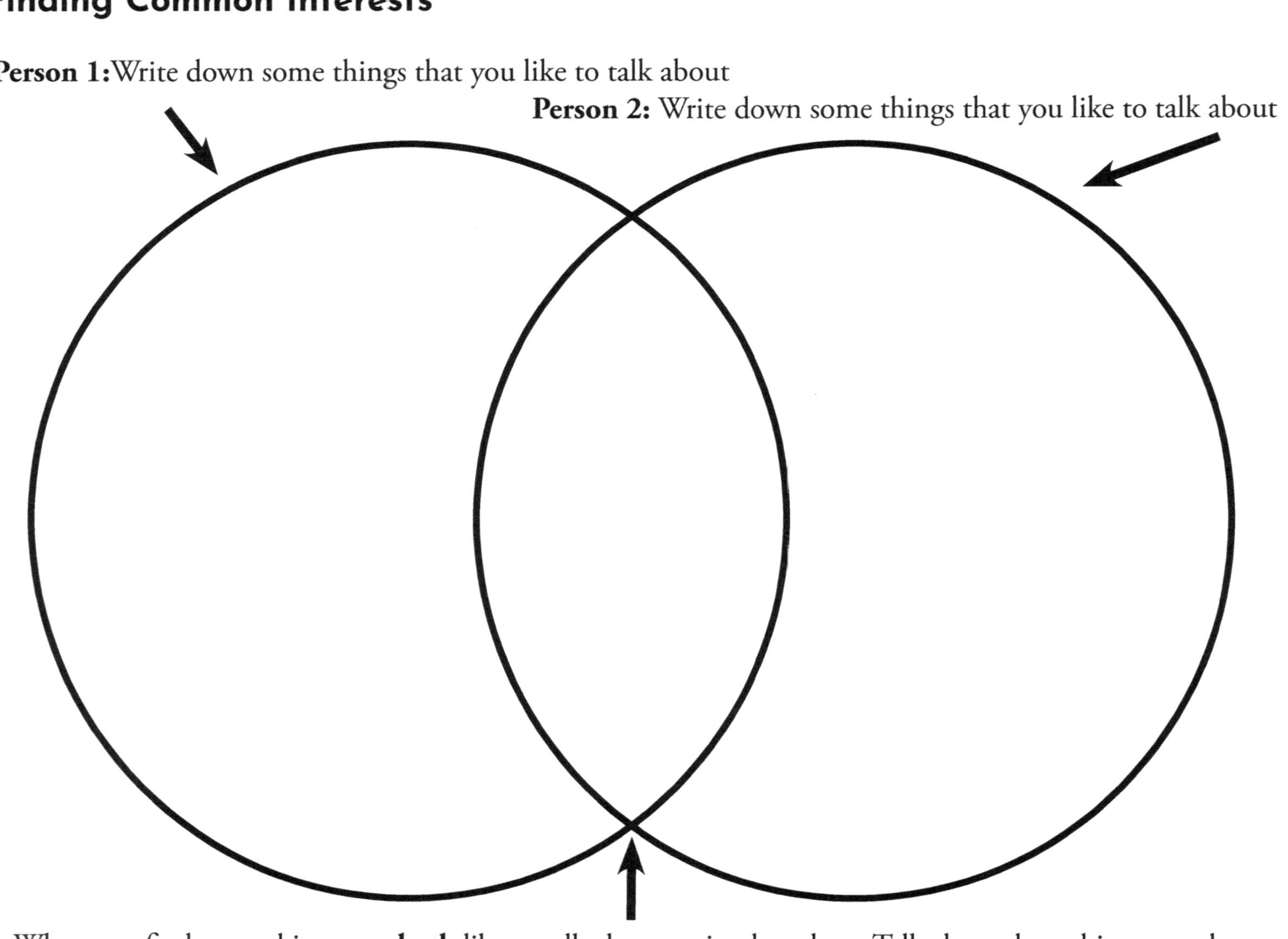

Topic 3: It's Okay to Say No

> ***When you say 'Yes' to others, make sure you are not saying 'No' to yourself.***
> ***-Paulo Coehlo***

Why Is it Hard to Say No?

We are all born assertive. Anyone who has spent any time around a toddler knows that they have no trouble saying 'no!' However, as we grow older, we learn from our environment and our experience that it is not always appropriate to say no. We can end up with several unhelpful beliefs about saying no that make it difficult for us to use this word. Some of these beliefs are listed below. Check the ones that apply to you:

Unhelpful beliefs about saying no:

- ☐ Saying no is rude and aggressive.
- ☐ Saying no is unkind, uncaring and selfish.
- ☐ Saying no will hurt and upset others and make them feel rejected.
- ☐ If I say no to somebody, they won't like me anymore.
- ☐ Others' needs are more important than mine.
- ☐ I should always try to please others and be helpful.
- ☐ Saying no over little things is small-minded and petty.

Add your own:

____

____

____

Even though saying no can be difficult for some people, there are some basic principles you can apply when you want to say no assertively. These are:

- be straightforward and honest so that you can make the point effectively (but don't be rude!)
- keep it short and succinct
- be open and honest, and inform the person if you are finding it difficult
- be polite – say something like, 'I appreciate you asking'
- speak slowly with warmth, otherwise it may sound abrupt
- don't apologise or give elaborate reasons for saying no. It is your right to say no if you don't want to do things
- remember that it is better in the long run to be truthful than breed resentment and bitterness within yourself.

Ways of Saying No

Direct no: When someone asks you to do something you don't want to do, just say no. The aim is to say no without apologising. The other person has the problem, but you do not have to allow them to pass it on to you. This technique can be quite forceful but is often effective.

Reflecting no: This technique involves acknowledging the content and feeling of the request, then adding your assertive refusal at the end. For example, 'I know you want to go to the beach today, but I cannot go to the beach this weekend'. Or, 'I know you're looking forward to a bike ride this afternoon, but I can't come'.

Reasoned no: In this technique, you give a very brief and genuine reason for why you are saying no. For example, 'I can't go to the beach with you because I have an assignment that needs to be finished by tomorrow'.

Raincheck no: This is not a definite no. It is a way of saying no to the request at the present moment but leaves room for saying yes in the future. Only use it if you genuinely want to meet the request. For example, 'I can't go to the beach with you this weekend, but I could make it next weekend'.

Enquiring no: As with the raincheck no, this is not a definite no. It is a way of opening up the request to see if there is another way it could be met. For example, 'Is there any other time you'd like to go?'

Broken record no: This can be used in a wide range of situations. You just repeat the simple statement of refusal repeatedly. No explanation, just repeat it. It is particularly good for persistent requests. For example:

Olivia: Come to the beach with me today.

Phil: No, I can't go to the beach today.

Olivia: Please, it is such a beautiful day.

Phil: No, I can't go to the beach today.

Olivia: Oh, come on, I'll pay for lunch.

Phil: No, I can't go to the beach today.

(Adapted from: Assert Yourself, CCI 2008)

Topic 4: Social Relationships

The most important thing in communication is hearing what isn't said.
~Peter F. Drucker

Did You Know? Social relationships, whether they are with your peers at school, casual friends or close family members, are based on good communication. Letting others know what you need or want in an assertive and respectful manner is important in any relationship. Unfortunately, children with ADHD have trouble expressing their needs, and seldom look internally for answers to their personal needs. In frustration, they may shut down, leave the situation or, worse, lash out. Remember that you have the right to ask for extra time to think things over before responding.

Children with ADHD and other learning disabilities often struggle to understand what other people do, say or show. They have difficulties with:

- listening (understanding what someone has told them)
- talking (saying what they mean)
- noticing and interpreting facial expression and body language (social cues)
- planning and controlling what they do.

Do you have difficulties with any of the above? If so, how are you managing it?

____

____

____

Did You Know? Many children with ADHD struggle with appropriate behaviour in social settings and situations where they must interact with others. Sometimes this is because they haven't received training in the home, or perhaps they learned another system of values and behaviours. Perhaps they did have good role models in the home and neighbourhood who promoted and modelled appropriate behaviour, but they didn't pick it up as well as most children – just like some children learn to read without formal instruction prior to school and some need the structured process of reading instruction.

Feeling isolated, different, unlikeable and alone, or being rejected by your peer group, are painful aspects of ADHD-related issues that create long-lasting effects. For friendships to grow and be maintained (providing the positive connections with others that are so important), children need certain skills. These include being able to control impulses, take turns, share, listen, be empathetic, attentive and focused, communicate effectively with others, be aware of and respond to social cues, and have be able to problem-solve situations and resolve conflicts as they arise. Unfortunately, these are all skill areas that can be challenging for a child with ADHD.

Do you find understanding social cues challenging?

____

____

____

Do you often feel misunderstood? Yes No

If yes, what has it cost you in terms of relationships?

____

____

____

Did You Know? Once a child is labelled by their peer group in a negative way because of social skills deficits, it can be very hard to dispel this reputation. In fact, having a negative reputation is one of the main obstacles children have to overcome socially. Studies have found that the negative peer status of children with ADHD is often already established by early- to middle-primary school years, and this reputation can stick with the child even as they begin to make positive changes in their social skills.

Have you been labelled negatively because of your ADHD-related social skills challenges?

____

____

Exercise: Read through the list of social skills below. Tick the ones you find challenging. Add any other social skills you have struggled with.

- ☐ Approaching others in socially acceptable ways
- ☐ Listening – paying attention to someone who is talking
- ☐ Introducing other people
- ☐ Starting a conversation
- ☐ Asking questions
- ☐ Saying thank you
- ☐ Giving compliments
- ☐ Making and keeping friends
- ☐ Introducing yourself
- ☐ Seeking attention properly
- ☐ Accepting the consequences of one's behaviour
- ☐ Handling frustration/anger
- ☐ Resolving conflict with others appropriately
- ☐ Using words instead of physical contact

- [ ] Asking for help
- [ ] Being attentive and polite
- [ ] Repeating important communication to check you have heard correctly
- [ ] Putting things in your diary/calendar as soon as you hear about them
- [ ] Writing things down/making notes
- [ ] Knowing when and how to say sorry
- [ ] Recognising and naming your emotions
- [ ] Expressing your feelings to others
- [ ] Understanding other people's feelings

Others:

____

____

____

Are You an Introvert or an Extrovert?

> ***Your vision will become clear only when you can look into your own heart. Who looks outside, dreams; who looks inside, awakes.***
> ***–Carl Jung***

You probably know people who are outgoing, and people who are shy. Those who are outgoing are named extroverts and those who are quiet and prefer small groups are named introverts. In your view, is it better to be an extrovert or an introvert? The answer is neither! The world needs both types of people, and people who fall everywhere in between. If you would like to know a bit more about your preferred style, read the pairs of statements in the questionnaire on the next page and circle the one that sounds most like you.

Introvert/Extrovert Questionnaire

Circle A or B for each one. Do not overthink your answer.

1	A	I am not easily bored	B	I am easily bored
2	A	I don't like fast, scary rides	B	I love being scared by fast rides
3	A	I would rather spend the evening at home quietly with a few friends	B	I would rather spend the evening at a loud party with lots of people
4	A	I enjoy being alone at times	B	I hate to be alone
5	A	I like to have a few close friends	B	I like to have many casual friends
6	A	I would rather write a book than sell things to people	B	I would rather sell things to people than write a book
7	A	I'm not likely to take a dare	B	I'll take almost any dare
8	A	I think April Fool's Day is stupid	B	I think April Fool's Day is fun
9	A	You won't find me watching *Mr Bean*	B	I think *Mr Bean* is funny
10	A	I enjoy talking about ideas	B	I would rather do things than discuss them
11	A	In hide-and-seek, you'll find me behind the tree	B	In hide-and-seek, you'll find me in the tree
12	A	I avoid crowds	B	I like crowds
13	A	I don't like to dance	B	I like to dance
14	A	Convertibles aren't safe; you shouldn't ride in one	B	Convertibles are fun; you should ride in one
15	A	I enjoy working behind the scenes	B	I want to be on stage

What is your style? Total your As and Bs: A __ B __

Score as follows:

- 10 or more As suggest you may be an introvert. This means that you are more comfortable in small groups or one-on-one social settings. You may also feel that people drain your energy.
- 10 or more Bs mean you may be an extrovert. You're happiest when you're with others and feel energised from being around others.
- If you got similar scores for As and Bs, you probably feel comfortable wherever you are, with people or alone.

Find out more

- Give this questionnaire to other members of your family and see how they score. Are they extroverts or introverts?

Should you change your style?

Some introverts think they're too shy and wish they could be different. But there is nothing wrong with being quiet, enjoying solitude, or being a thinker. However, if being introverted worries you, speak to an adult you trust.

Some extroverts are funny. But after a while, they can get tired of being the life of the party. If this is you, take a break. Let your family and friends know that you'd like to engage in some solitary activities for a while.

Remember that you do not have to be the same all the time. What's most important is to talk about these things and to be yourself.

Working in Groups

> ***We can accomplish more together than we can alone.***
> ***~Max De Pree***

Did You Know? Although it is not always easy for children with ADHD to work in groups, significant social and academic gains can be made in group learning settings. A group environment provides a structured setting in which children can discuss feelings and situations, develop an understanding of the feelings of others, and realise that they are not the only ones who face challenges. New skills can also be more fun when learned and practised in a group setting. Having a sense of belonging to a group can be particularly helpful to ADHD children.

Based on your own experiences, what is the best and the worst thing about working in groups?

____

____

____

Which of the following skills do you think are important for effective group work? And why?

- ☐ Punctuality ______________________________
- ☐ Organisation ____________________________
- ☐ Prioritising ______________________________
- ☐ Managing conflict _________________________
- ☐ Problem-solving __________________________
- ☐ Assertiveness ____________________________
- ☐ Confidence ______________________________
- ☐ Giving and receiving feedback ____________________

Topic 5: Bullying

Strong people stand up for themselves, stronger people stand up for others.
~Chris Gardner

Did You Know? It's important that you learn to protect yourself from bullies in an assertive and confident manner. It is also important that you know the difference between disagreements or conflict between classmates and bullying. Bullying is when a person deliberately and repeatedly hurts another. The hurt can be physical or emotional and can include hitting, pushing, name calling, exclusion and teasing. One way to stand up to bullies is to stand tall, look the bully in the eye, and say 'stop' in a strong and confident way. This works because bullies avoid people who come across as confident and sure of themselves. Even if you don't feel confident, you can pretend to be by the way that you respond. Always remember that what is most important is your safety, so where you can, avoid the bully. Where possible 'buddy up' with a friend on the bus, in the hallways and during recess. If the bully does not stop, speak to your parents or a teacher.

Scenario

Peter is 13 years old. He is a hiker and boy scout and was being bullied. Peter has ADHD as well as Asperger's, a minor form of autism that makes socialising difficult. Since year three, Peter has been known as a nerd. In high school, he had a group of four friends with similar interests. They were labelled the nerdy group. Peter enjoyed doing math quizzes and building Lego. He loved going to school to see his friends and occasionally would have all four come over to build Lego and eat pizza. But in year nine, all that changed. The others were done with math quizzes and Lego, but Peter wasn't. Then one day, the group just ditched him. He was heartbroken but didn't know what to do. The group of four started to torment him. They knew about his Asperger's and used it to their advantage. They called him terrible names. They stole his lunch, chased him and spread rumours about his sexuality. One day after school, he ran to his room and cried like crazy. He had lost all his friends.

His mum knocked on the door and asked if he was up for a chat. He begged his mother to move him to another school. His mother was surprised and asked him what was troubling him so much. They had a long chat, which made Peter feel loved and understood.

His mother encouraged him to find a new group of friends and reminded him of other boys that he had been friends with in the past. Peter knew that it was going to be difficult to make new friends. Luckily, the end of the school year was only two weeks away and Peter planned on reconnecting with other boys and girls during the school holidays in preparation for the new school year.

When the new school year started, Peter was happy to have a new friend called Jaden, whom he had known since primary school but had never really gotten to know. Jaden stood up for Peter when he was bullied and defended him. He had a good group of friends, mainly girls, and they all started having recess together. When the bullies were mean to Peter, the girls would tell them to grow up and stop being childish. Peter finally felt good, knowing that he had real friends. The victory came when John's, mother called Peter's mother and said that John (who was one of the bullies) had something to say to Peter. John spoke on the phone and apologised to Peter for what had happened and his part in the bullying. He asked if Peter would like to go over to his house to play Minecraft and eat pizza. To which Peter replied, 'Why not?'

Why People Bully Others

There are many reasons why someone might bully others. Whatever the reason, bullying is never okay.

Bullying can be very hurtful. You may:

- have trouble sleeping
- lose your appetite
- have trouble concentrating
- feel down about yourself
- find it hard to cope
- have thoughts about hurting yourself
- feel suicidal
- have trouble with schoolwork
- feel physically sick
- feel hopeless or powerless
- feel alone, sad, angry or confused
- feel unsafe or afraid.

Are you being bullied or have you been bullied? If so, what happened?

____

____

____

Who in your Circle of Support would you ask for help if you were ever bullied?

____

____

____

The Impact of Bullying

> ***Right is right even if no one is doing it; wrong is wrong even if everyone is doing it.***
> ***~Saint Augustine***

The single student who bullies can have a wide-ranging impact on the students they bully, students who observe bullying and the overall climate of the school and community.

Students Who Are Bullied

Students deserve to feel safe a school. But when they experience bullying, these types of effects can last long into their future:

- Depression
- Low self-esteem
- Suicidal thoughts
- Health problems
- Poor grades

Students Who Bully Others

Students who intentionally bully others should be held accountable for their actions. Those who bully their peers are also more likely to:

- Get into frequent fights
- Drink alcohol and smoke
- Perceive a negative climate at school
- Steal and vandalise property
- Report poor grades
- Carry a weapon

Observers of Bullying

Students who see bullying happen may also feel that they are in an unsafe environment. Effects may include feeling:

- Fearful
- Guilty for not acting
- Powerless to act
- Tempted to participate

Schools With Bullying Issues

When bullying continues and a school does not take action, the entire school climate can be affected in the following ways:

- The school develops an environment of fear and disrespect.
- Students have difficulty learning.
- Students feel insecure.
- Students dislike school.
- Students feel teachers and staff have little control and don't care about them.

It is important to note that not all students who bully others have obvious behaviour problems or are engaged in rule-breaking activities. Some of them are highly skilled socially and good at ingratiating themselves with their teacher and other adults. This is true of some boys who bully, but is perhaps even more common among bullying girls. For this reason, it is often difficult for adults to discover or even imagine that these students engage in bullying behaviour.

What to Do if You're Being Bullied

There's always something you can do. Here are some ideas:

- Keep your distance from the bullies.
- Don't bully them back.
- Tell them what they are doing is not okay.
- Talk to an adult you trust.
- Take time to do something nice for yourself.
- Have someone help you report cyberbullying or assault.

Strategies for Standing Up to Bullies

Standing up to bullies can be difficult. Learning ways to respond to a bully without escalating the situation can be helpful.

One way of doing this is **Fogging** – responding with neutral statements or agreeing with what the bully says. For example, 'Thanks for noticing' or 'maybe I will'. The idea is to show the bully that what they are saying is not bothering you.

The other is **Bold Talk** – standing up for what you believe in. Going against what a friend says or does is often scary but there are ways to be true to yourself without starting a fight. It takes courage because you have to feel brave to use it.

Fogging

When a bully says:

Everyone hates you

You're such a loser

You're actually so dumb

How does it feel to have no friends?

You have stupid hair

You're such a nerd

Your fogging response could be:

Thanks for noticing

Oh, okay

That's interesting

Whatever

You're probably right

That's your opinion

Why do you care?

Use Bold Talk When You Are:	To Get Result When Using Bold Talk	Bold Talk Statements That Work
• Telling someone to stop doing something • Politely saying no to someone • Disagreeing with bullying or gossip	• Look the person in the eye. • Use an assertive tone of voice (not too harsh but not too soft). • Your face needs to reflect your message; look serious but not mean. • Own what you say by using 'I' statements (e.g. 'I feel … when…'). • Role play with someone in your Circle of Support. Have the other person be rude, mean or make you do something you know is wrong. You will feel strange at first, but with practice, it gets easier. • Report ongoing behaviour before it goes too far. Using bold talk does not mean that the other person will stop the first, second or third time, but keep at it. Using bold talk will help you feel better and more confident.	• 'Stop.' • 'I told you to stop.' • 'Don't talk to me like that.' • 'I think that is mean.' • 'No thanks.' • 'I don't want to do that.' • 'I don't like how you are playing.' • 'I don't like talking about people who aren't here.' • 'That is harsh. How would you like it if they did that to you?' • 'How about if I think my way and you think your way?' Agree to disagree.

Bold Talk for Peer Pressure Things you can say when you don't want to do what a friend wants you to do:	**Bold Talk for Gossip** Things that you can say when a friend is gossiping, and you don't like it:	**Bold Talk for Hurt Feelings** Things you can say when a friend hurts your feelings:
• 'I don't really want to do this.' • 'This is mean. I don't want to do this.' • 'I changed my mind – I don't want to do this.' • 'This is making me feel bad. I don't want to say that.' • 'I am feeling worried about this – I want to be left out of this.' • 'This does not sound like a good idea. I want out.' • 'This is not cool. I don't want to do this.' • 'I can just tell that this is going to go wrong, and I am going to get busted. I am out!' • 'I think this is going to hurt someone else's feelings. Let's not do it.'	• 'Are you sure you should be saying this? I don't think this is right.' • 'This sounds like gossip. Let's change the subject.' • 'Hey – I don't want to talk like this. It's not who I am!' • 'Come on guys. This is how rumours get started.' • 'Oh, come on, let's stop the drama and change the subject.'	• 'I feel upset. You seem mad at me and I don't understand why.' • 'I was really sad when you didn't invite me. It was embarrassing.' • 'I am angry because you broke your promise and told my secret.' • 'I am confused. We were together all weekend and now you aren't acting like my friend.'

Bold Talk: Role Play

Friend: Hey can I use your phone to text Sarah and pretend that it's Sam?

You: Why?

Friend: She's totally obsessed with him. It'll be funny. You'll see.

You: No thanks. My mum reads all of my texts. Besides, I don't like drama.

Friend: You know you can delete all of your texts. Come on!

You: Look, I don't want any part of this. It sounds mean and stupid. Use your own phone and keep me out of this.

Friend: You're so lame.

You: Whatever. If I was with her, I wouldn't text you and pretend to be someone else. What you want to do is mean and dumb.

Remember, the bully needs you to **care** about what they say and do.
You have the **power** to follow or not. The power is yours to give!

Quiz 4 (see answers in Appendix E)

1. **JP wants to be friends with Jane, a new girl at school. What should he do?**

   A. Introduce himself to Jane and offer to show her around the school.

   B. Act cool and brag about being the best at Maths.

   C. Interrupt Jane when she is talking to another girl.

2. **Tristan likes playing football with the other boys at school, but they don't seem to want to play with him. Whenever Tristan asks if he can play, someone says, 'We have enough players already'. What could Tristan do?**

   A. Shout 'loser' whenever someone drops the ball.

   B. Threaten to beat them up after school.

   C. Watch the game and compliment good play. Take note of how the other boys behave on the field and see if he could change some of his ways that may be annoying to others; for example, bragging about winning.

3. **Several times you've watched a boy in year 10 grab a younger boy's lunch box and kick it around as if it were a football, shouting, 'Come and get it, you loser'. What can you do?**

   A. Trip the bully and punch him on the nose.

   B. Tell the bully that he should be ashamed for engaging in such behaviour and run off.

   C. Approach the boy who is being bullied and ask him if he has done something about it. Encourage him to speak to a teacher or his parents.

4. **You've been teasing one of your friends who is really bad at reading and writing. Now they've started to sit alone and once you noticed tears in their eyes. What should you do?**

   A. Nothing. They were probably just having a bad day and it has nothing to do with you.

   B. Stop teasing your friend and ask them why they were crying.

   C. Tell your friend that you won't tease them in front of anyone anymore, but that they really are stupid and should get some extra lessons.

5. **You want to make a complaint to your teacher about a boy who keeps tripping you, making you fall twice. What's the best way to go about it?**

   A. Stay calm and stick to the facts.

   B. Get angry and shout.

   C. Start crying and walk away.

6. **You don't agree with your friend on a review of a new game. What do you say?**

   A. You are wrong.

   B. I don't agree, but you have the right to your opinion.

   C. Stop talking rubbish.

7. **You have a discussion with a friend about optimal screen time. You don't agree with them. What should you do?**

   A. Change the subject.

   B. Say what you believe respectfully.

   C. Get angry with your friend.

8. **Your friends start calling you names, sending you nasty text messages and forcing you to give them things. You don't feel good when these things happen. What should you do?**

   A. Nothing. You must have done something wrong to make your friends act like that.

   B. Start calling them names in return and threaten them.

   C. Speak to your parents or teacher and tell them what is happening.

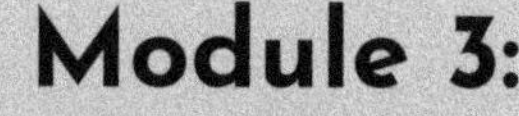

Module 3:

Practical Coping Skills

Section 4:

Making Change

Topic 1: Doing Things Differently

The secret of change is to focus your energy not on the old, but on building the new.
~Socrates

Did You Know? There is an old saying, 'If you always do what you've always done, you will always get what you've always got'. Change involves doing things differently, it involves taking action, and that can be hard to do. Before you embark on the journey of change, it is helpful to ask yourself the following questions:

- Do I want change?
- How much do I really want to change?
- Do I just want to talk about change or do I want to do something about it?
- Do I want to put in the effort required to make changes in my life?
- Do I want to start doing things differently?

Change is a difficult process. Even positive changes are hard and cause stress. Just remember that you cannot change what's going on around you until you start changing what's going on within you.

STAGES OF CHANGE

Denial
I don't need to change.
Everything is fine.

Thinking
It might not be too bad if I start doing things differently.

Preparation
What do I need to make this change happen?

Action
I'm doing it! I'm making a change to reach my goal!

Maintenance
Great! All I need to do now is keep up!

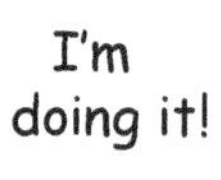

Ask yourself:

What do I want to change?

Am I ready to start?

What stage am I at in my journey of change?

Categories of Change

When we look at positive changes we have made in our lives, we can divide them into two categories:

Category 1: Someone tells us we must change and if we don't, something bad is going to happen. Your parents say that if you fail your spelling test, you will be grounded for the whole weekend. Your teacher tells you that you must complete your writing assignment by tomorrow or you will fail the class. A judge says you must go to counselling, or you will go to juvenile detention. In these cases, we change in order to avoid the bad thing that could happen if we don't change.

Category 2: At other times, we change because we want to change. We make the decision to change. We decide to change on our own. No one tells us something bad is going to happen if we don't change. We weigh the pros and cons of changing or not changing in our minds and decide for ourselves what we will do.

What are the feelings connected with these two kinds of change?

____

____

____

What is the difference between the two ways of changing?

____

____

____

Which kind of change will last longer?

____

____

____

Which kind of change is more difficult?

____

____

It is possible for one kind of change to cross over into the other. For instance, someone tells you that you should consider changing your technology habits. Your first reaction might be to resist and even tell them off. However, after getting poor results in an exam, you revisit the idea of change and decide to make adjustments to your technology use. The change you made started when someone told you to change and later you decided it was a good idea.

Think of a change you made in your life. When did you first decide there was a problem that had to be fixed? Did you realise it gradually or did it happen all at once?

____

____

____

Do you remember when you didn't think you had a problem? And how other people tried to tell you that you had a problem and you didn't believe them, or you thought they were exaggerating the problem? What feelings did you have to overcome to recognise the problem?

____

____

____

What do you understand by the statement, 'With freedom comes responsibility'?

____

____

____

Bringing About Change

Whether it is actions or behaviours, what could you stop doing, do less of, start doing and keep doing in order to bring about constructive change in your life?

Date	Stop Doing	Do Less	Start Doing	Keep Doing
3/5	Staying up super late playing games	Talking in class – especially when the teacher is explaining something	Using to-do lists to keep track of things	Studying for tests

No man is an island. No man stands alone.
~Dennis Brown

Did You Know? It can be difficult to bring about change on your own. Asking for support when you feel stuck can be the difference between surviving and thriving. The better you become at asking, the more resources and support you will find flowing into your life. Often, the main obstacle standing in the way of asking for help is the fear of getting rejected. If you can practise accepting rejections, you will overcome your fear of hearing 'no' and realise that you can't be hurt by asking for help, and that you have much to gain. The bottom line is to accept that we all need help at one point or another in our lives. Let those around you help, so that you can learn new skills that will help you change your life for the better.

You can practise asking for help in many different areas. For example, you could ask:

- your teacher to review the list of accommodations you are allowed
- a teacher for clarification of homework
- a friend to help you find a date
- another student to help you with homework
- for compassion from your parents
- your parents to help you find a part-time job
- for advice and guidance from people who have achieved something you want to achieve
- your higher power for comfort and guidance
- for honest feedback from your friends and family
- a friend to help you organise your room, then take a photo as a reminder of what an organised room looks like
- someone in your Circle of Support to help you with time management
- a teacher for productive feedback

- someone you want to befriend to spend time together outside of school
- someone on your sports team to practise with you
- a friend to exercise or walk with you.

Recall a time when you asked for help. What happened?

____

____

____

Reflect and answer the following:

I want…

____

I need help with...

____

I wish someone could help me with...

____

I need feedback on…

____

I need to understand…

____

I need to accept…

____

Reality vs Expectation

If you align expectations with reality, you will never be disappointed.
~ Terrell Owens

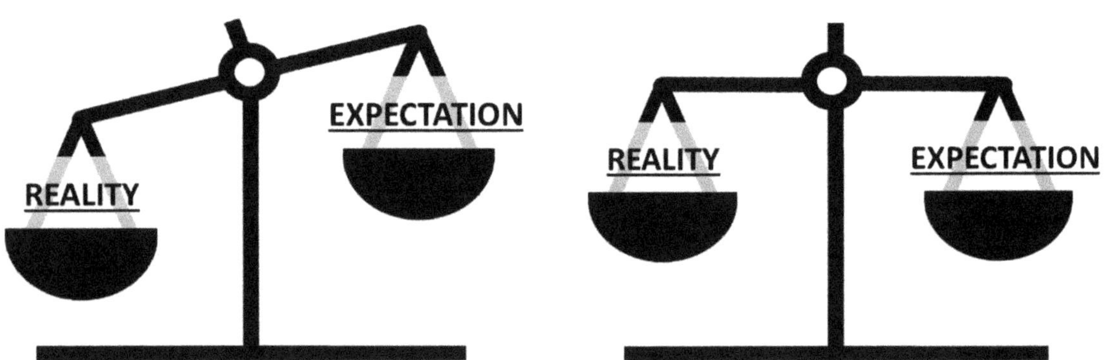

It has been said that happiness equals reality divided by expectations. If our reality is lower than how we expect life to be, then we're likely to feel unhappy or discontented.

This formula suggests that our reality needs to be equally balanced with our expectations. The more we can get them in balance, then the happier, more content, accepting and peaceful we are likely to be.

In order to make positive change, we can choose to improve our reality and/or lower our expectations.

Step 1: **Improve my Reality**	**Step 2:** **Lower my Expectations**

Topic 2: Underachievement and ADHD

In many cases, underachievement is not because a lack of knowing, but because of the lack of structure and planning.

Did You Know? Many teens with ADHD struggle with underachievement. They know they could do better, but somehow don't. Examining your current behaviours, in relation to what is needed to help you achieve your goals, can help target your needs and increase your motivation to achieve more.

There can be many reasons for underachievement. Do any of the following resonate with you?

- ☐ Stress
- ☐ Self-doubt
- ☐ Having unrealistic expectations
- ☐ Lack of family support
- ☐ Too much family pressure
- ☐ Distraction by video games, TV and other technology
- ☐ Lack of interest in school
- ☐ Preferring to spend time with friends
- ☐ Being too disorganised to create a schedule for schoolwork
- ☐ Anger at parents
- ☐ A belief that school is unimportant, that it doesn't relate to the real world
- ☐ Giving priority to other interests, such as sports and fun

Add your own:

____

____

How can an underachiever become an achiever?

____

____

How can someone with a disability succeed?

____

____

Do you know someone who successfully broke a bad habit? Ask that person how they changed. Write their story.

____

____

____

____

____

____

____

____

Write four short statements telling your parents/teachers what you would like them to understand about you. Share it with them if you want or discuss it with someone in your Circle of Support.

1. ____

2. ____

3. ____

4. ____

Did You Know? Disappointment can make you feel angry and sad. Instead of letting it make you feel that way, you can choose to use disappointment as an opportunity to grow as a person. Reflect on the situation that caused the disappointment; for example, a poor grade because you failed to manage your time effectively and not because of your level of knowledge. Turn it into a learning opportunity. You might face more disappointments because of your ADHD symptoms and learning differences, but that does not mean you have to lower your personal goals. You can choose to be bigger than your disappointments, get support and keep on going. Many children with ADHD succeed in school and other areas of their lives and go on to become extraordinary people. You can too!

Ask your parents or someone from your Circle of Support if they can put you in touch with a successful adult who has ADHD. Ask that person how they manage their ADHD. Write their answers below.

____

____

____

Imagine it is 10 years from now and someone asks you how you managed your ADHD challenges. What will you tell them?

____

____

____

I'm not telling you that it's always going to be easy –
I'm telling you it's going to be worth it.
-Art Williams

Did You Know? Every failure presents a chance to learn. Children (particularly those with ADHD) tend to overreact to failure. The biology of ADHD may cause children with ADHD to experience emotions (both good and bad) more intensely. Instead of feeling defeated, you can choose to view failure as a chance to gain information, build resilience skills and work on your problem-solving abilities. The sooner we stop shaming our failures, the easier it will be to turn them to our advantage. The only people who never experience failure are those who give up before trying.

Describe a recent failure experience that is still bothering you.

____

____

____

Rate the above failure experience on a scale of 0 to 10.

0 = not bothered at all; 10 = extremely bothered

0____________________5____________________10

What have you learned from the failure experience? Check the ones that apply to you.

- ☐ I need to learn to manage my time better.
- ☐ I need to gain skills in assertive communication.
- ☐ I need to spend more time doing homework in order to get better grades.
- ☐ Cheating isn't worth it.
- ☐ I need shouldn't be afraid to ask for the help I need to succeed.
- ☐ Instead of getting angry, I can talk with other people to gain perspective.

Write other lessons you may have learned from this experience.

____

____

____

What could you do differently next time you are in a similar situation?

____

____

____

Succeeding with ADHD

> ***I had to learn to work with my ADHD and not against it.***
> ***~Student***

Did You Know? Despite the serious challenges that individuals with ADHD face daily, many people living with this condition say that it also has its positives. As well as being inattentive, their ADHD allows them to hyper-focus, and their impulsivity can inspire creativity.

'Despite all the challenges I encounter daily, I would not trade ADHD for anything – but this only happened once I accepted my condition. At this time, I stopped wishing ADHD away and sought help. One thing that my parents and I realised soon after I was diagnosed and medicated, was that pills didn't teach skills. The medication was needed, but I also had to learn additional skills to help me manage the challenges that the new environment I had transitioned into, college, presented. Although I was never late for lectures or meetings, I had to realise that there is more to time management than being punctual for appointments. I had to accept that I was not good at using time, at prioritising or planning. Once I identified my challenges, I sought help and learned compensatory skills.'

Success means different things to different people, and it's often guided by your values. What does success mean to you ?

____

____

____

The iceberg model can also be applied to success. When you look at someone you view as a successful person, you see only the surface effects of their success. Hidden beneath the surface are the skills, attributes and actions that led them to this position of success. If you focus on developing these skills and carrying out the required actions, you too can achieve success.

Exercise: Success Iceberg

Think about the skills, attributes and actions necessary for success. Tick the ones you are already good at and circle the ones you need to work on. Write in any others you can think of.

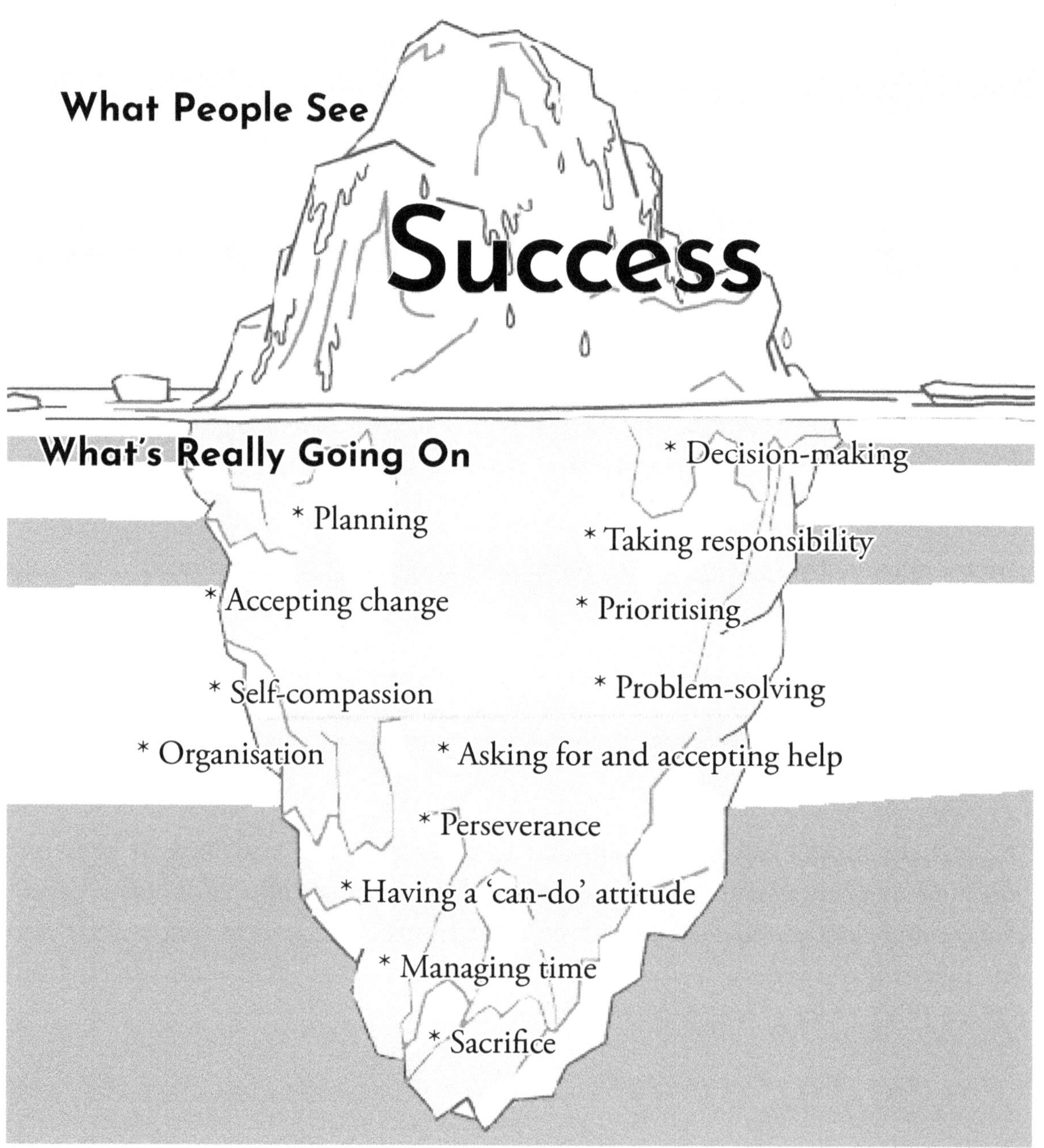

Topic 3: Screen Time and ADHD

Technology can be a weapon of mass distraction.

Did You Know? There are many benefits to technology. Like most things in life, it is not the technology that is the problem, but our inability to use it responsibly. Some individuals with ADHD are at increased risk for problematic overuse of technology. Although most cases do not reach the point where it is considered an addiction, a small percentage of children struggle to resist the temptation of technology. Valuable time is wasted on texting, social media and, obviously the big one for some children, gaming. This is time that could be used for priority tasks, such as homework, studying, and building face-to-face relationships. This not only impacts on performance, but can also lead to family conflict.

Technology is a useful servant but dangerous master.
~Christian Lous Lange

Scenario

Kate sprawled on her bed. Her laptop sat beside her, showing her favourite YouTuber making resin earrings. She was playing a matching game on her tablet, while Snapchatting with her friends on her phone.

'Have you finished your homework?' Dad called from the kitchen.

'Yes, Dad', Kate replied, not entirely truthfully. But she had plenty of time, she'd get those Science questions done later.

Her little brother Toby knocked on her door. 'Mum says set the table', he announced, swinging the door open.

'Get out of my room!' Kate shouted, throwing her pillow at him as he retreated.

'Kate! Dinner's nearly ready. Set the table now please!' Mum called.

'Yes, Mum, ,Kate answered. She plugged her earphones into her phone and opened TikTok, then went out to the dining room. She set the table one-handed, watching

videos on her phone. Once the table was set, she slumped into her chair, mindlessly glued to the small screen.

A hand fell on her shoulder and she looked up into Mum's angry face. 'Put that phone away! Can't you do anything without being attached to a screen?'

Can you relate to Kate in the above scenario?

____

____

How else could Kate have managed the situation?

____

____

Is your technology use having a negative impact on your grades? Give a reason for your answer.

____

____

Is your technology use causing conflict between you and your parents? Give a reason for your answer.

____

____

If you've answered 'yes' to the above questions, what is preventing you from using technology more responsibly?

____

____

Things to Do Without Screens

 Board games or jigsaws

 Practice a sport

 Play with a pet

 Call or visit a friend

 Draw a comic

 Origami

 Learn to juggle

 Play ping pong or frisbee

 Read a book

 Go for a walk, a run or walk the dog

 Paint something

 Call a grandparent

 Find somewhere to volunteer

 Invent a new game

 Water gun fight

 Yoga

 Practice an instrument

 Help with some chores

 Have a relaxing bath

 Ride your bike, skateboard or scooter

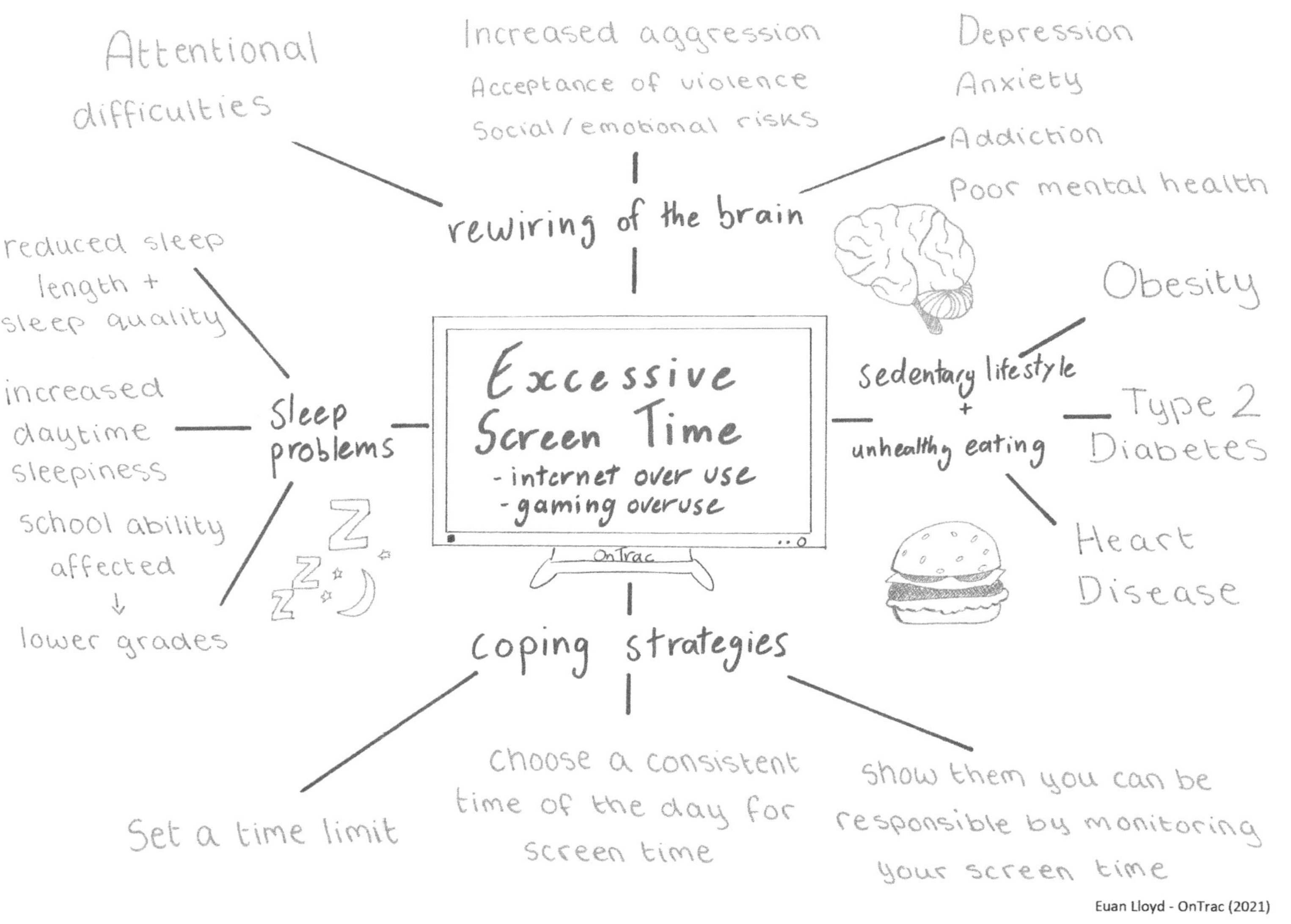
Attentional difficulties
Increased aggression
Acceptance of violence
Social / emotional risks
Depression
Anxiety
Addiction
Poor mental health
rewiring of the brain
reduced sleep length + sleep quality
increased daytime sleepiness
school ability affected → lower grades
Sleep problems
Excessive Screen Time
- internet over use
- gaming overuse
OnTrac
sedentary lifestyle + unhealthy eating
Obesity
Type 2 Diabetes
Heart Disease
coping strategies
Set a time limit
Choose a consistent time of the day for screen time
Show them you can be responsible by monitoring your screen time
Euan Lloyd - OnTrac (2021)

The following are strategies that you and your parents can implement to help you control your screen time. They can:

- set a time limit for screen time and consistently enforce limits.
- choose a time of day that is consistent. This helps you predict when you will be able to use electronics and not beg for the device 24/7. For example, 30 minutes or one hour after you complete your homework.
- help you monitor when the time to use the device is up. You might need a timer that makes a sound when it is time to put the device away. Be responsible for keeping track of your screen time. Show your parent that you can be responsible if given the chance.
- have your electronic devices in the common living area so they can monitor safe and appropriate use.
- have you store your electronics in their bedroom overnight so you are not temped to play games when you should be sleeping.
- give you praise for respecting the limits for device use and provide appropriate and reasonable consequences if you purposefully disobey limits. This may include losing device time the following day.

When your parents enforce new rules in the home, you may become upset at first until you learn the new routine. Be prepared for this and don't fight it. They have your best interest at heart. If your parents notice a decrease in your sleep or grades, or that you are choosing screen time over spending time with other children and with the family, they may suggest that you speak to someone about your use of technology.

Topic 4: Learning Styles

Every child has a different learning style and pace. Each child is unique, not only capable of learning but also capable of succeeding
~Robert John Meehan.

We all learn differently. Here are three learning styles.

Visual Learners	Auditory Learners	Kinaesthetic Learners
• express themselves through facial expressions • are interested in videos and images • use their eyes to find solutions to a particular problem	• express themselves through their words • enjoy sound and music • want to discuss the possible solutions	• express themselves through their body language • are interested in physical activities • look for solutions using their hands

Which learning style reasonates most with you? Explain why.

____

____

____

Describe your natural talents that are not given credit at school:

____

____

____

Knowing your learning style makes it easier to know what areas you could use support in. This might include classroom accommodations. See **Appendix H** for more information on the different learning styles and strategies that work for each style.

Did You Know? Students with ADHD can ask for classroom accommodations designed to increase their success. Sometimes students are embarrassed about these accommodations or afraid that others will find out that they have ADHD or other challenges.

Remember that accepting accommodations is not a sign of weakness. Accommodations are environmental supports available to students to help them meet their individual learning needs, and allow their true ability and gifts to be acknowledged and developed.

Have you been given accommodations at school?

____

____

____

Describe your feelings about using accommodations in the classroom.

____

____

____

Find out if any of the supports you need are available as accommodations.

Typical accommodations include:

- special use of computers
- note takers
- untimed tests
- extra time for timed tests and exams
- permission to make up missed work
- alternate assignments
- alternate grading, such as minimising deductions for minor errors

- homework help
- special setting assignments
- verbal (instead of written) tests
- student aid

As you learn more about yourself and the accommodations that are available, you can ask your parents to arrange a meeting with your school to determine what can be put in place to assist you.

Topic 5: Driving and ADHD

If you're going to drive, you owe it to the other road users and yourself to operate the vehicle in a safe and responsible manner.

Did You Know? Driving is a privilege and not a right. Studies show that teenagers with ADHD are four times more likely than their peers without ADHD to get speeding fines and have accidents. They are also more likely to be repeat offenders. Some of the symptoms of ADHD that play a role in driving problems include being impulsive, not paying attention, frustration, and being late and trying to make up time. The laws around driving are getting stricter in Australia; for example, with one infringement you can lose your licence for a long time. It might be worth your while to look up the laws around driving and ADHD in the country/state where you live.

The following tips will help you reduce distraction when driving:

- Limit music sources and choices.
- Pre-set your radio stations and set up any streaming devices for playlists before starting the car.
- Drive without passengers or choose passengers carefully (where you have a choice).
- Plan trips ahead of time, get directions and look over them before beginning your trip.
- Leave yourself plenty of time to get to your destination.
- If you get lost, pull over in order to look at at a map or adjust your GPS.
- Don't speed or run traffic lights to make up for lost time if you get lost.
- Don't eat or drink while driving.
- Don't drive after consuming alcohol or other drugs.

- Take driving lessons.
- Wear your seat belt.
- Consider taking your ADHD medication if you know you'll be driving.
- Minimise distractions like loud music and talking on your phone.

What is your overall opinion on road rage?

____

____

____

What do you think is happening in the image below?

____

____

____

Making Change Quiz

(see answers in Appendix E)

1. **JP asks your opinion about making changes that last. Which of the following would you advise him to do?**
   - A. It's best to keep goals quiet to prevent public failure.
   - B. Reach out and talk to someone, because support can help you stay on track.
   - C. Change is impossible; you will always relapse.

2. **Tristan tells you that he wants to break three habits, but does not know how to start. What do you tell him?**
   - A. Quit all three at once.
   - B. It's tough to change more than one thing at once. Address each habit one at a time.
   - C. Tell him to wait and change will happen by itself.

3. **JP tells you that he tried to make changes to his gaming habits, but he failed. How will you respond? Tell him that:**
   - A. When making changes, a slip-up means that you've failed.
   - B. There are no lessons in mistakes.
   - C. Everyone has lapses when trying to build healthy habits – he needs to be kind to himself and not beat himself up.

4. **Tristan tells you that he struggles to stay motivated when working on long-term assignments. What will you tell him?**
   - A. Only reward yourself when you meet your end goal.
   - B. Rewards, however small, can keep you motivated. Give yourself small rewards along the way to the end goal.
   - C. Only big rewards motivate people.

5. **JP is very smart, but he seldom completes homework and struggles to listen in class. What could JP do differently?**

   A. He shouldn't worry because he will do well in the exams.

   B. He could try to identify ways of making the task less boring; for example, JP could listen to music while doing his homework.

   C. He could try harder.

6. **Xavier would benefit from extra time during exams, an accommodation that is available at his school. However, he is ashamed and feels that it would be cheating if he got extra time to complete his exams. How can you help Xavier?**

   A. You agree with him – he should have the same time to complete the exam as all the other students.

   B. You put yourself in his position and ask him to tell you what you should do, highlighting the fact that accepting an accommodation is not a sign of weakness, but rather one of insight into what you need in order to do your best.

   C. You tell him that he is very smart and will pass, even without the accommodations.

7. **JP is disappointed because he seldom achieves the goals that he sets for himself. He tells you that he is losing faith in his ability to succeed in life. How can you help JP?**

   A. Tell him that he should only have goals after high school.

   B. Tell him that if he works harder and becomes more organised, he will achieve his goals.

   C. Ask JP if he has heard of the SMART acronym in relation to goal setting and show him how it works.

Troubleshooting Struggles

Tick the struggles that continue to be challenging for you. Apply the solutions on the right-hand side column.

Struggles		Questions to ask yourself
		Solutions to consider
Fail to give adequate attention to detail/ make careless mistakes in schoolwork or other activities		• Recheck your attention span and break activities into smaller units. • What is your learning style? • Is your worry, anxiety or anger interfering with your ability to listen?
		• Practise mindfulness. • Use your problem-solving skills to come up with ways you can slow down and pay attention.
Difficulty sustaining attention in tasks		• Is your work environment too distracting? • What is your mind telling you? • Ask yourself, 'Am I doing what I am supposed to be doing?' If not, get to the task without delay.
		• Use your problem-solving skills to come up with ways to know when your attention is drifting and bring it back to the task at hand.
Fail to listen when spoken to directly		• Is your worry, anxiety or anger interfering with your ability to listen?
		• Keep your eyes on the person who is speaking. Talk to someone in your Circle of Support or your mentor about ways to improve your listening. • Talk to others about how they concentrate when someone is speaking. • Practise mindfulness. • Use problem-solving skills to brainstorm ways you can focus on what the person is saying.

Difficulty in organising, planning and prioritising tasks		• Have your to-do list in your diary. Avoid sticky notes. • Prioritise from your to-do list. Use the Pebble Jar concept from page 223. • Carry over to the next day what you don't get done today. • Use your problem-solving skills to come up with an action plan and organise your work.
Procrastination		• What has procrastination cost you? • What excuses do you use for your procrastination? • What is your mind telling you?
		• Identify why you procrastinate. • Use your problem-solving skills to manage your procrastination.
Lose things necessary for tasks or activities		• Use a single work area. • Get into the habit of placing things back in their place. • Declutter frequently. • Use your problem-solving skills to think of ways to stay organised.
Become easily distracted by external events		• Is your environment conducive to learning? • What is your learning style?
		• Choose a place to work that suits your learning style. • Minimise clutter. • Practise mindfulness. • Use problem-solving to come up with solutions to manage your distractibility.
Forgetful in daily activities		• Use a diary and to-do list. • Use a beeper system to remind you to check your diary. • Link checking your diary to activities that you do habitually (e.g. brushing your teeth, before going to bed etc.). • Use your problem-solving skills to set reminders.

Relationship conflicts (home and school)		• Are you using 'I' statements?
		• Review your communication style. • Take responsibility for your actions and apologise. Say sorry and ask how you can make the situation better. • Review what you can control. • Use problem-solving skills to identify when you are being triggered.
Unmotivated, low self-esteem and lacking confidence		• Are you motivated from the outside or from within yourself? • Are you eating and sleeping well? • Are you exercising? • Are you communicating assertively? • Are you living consistent with your values? • Use your problem-solving skills to explore what might be contributing to these feelings.
Emotion regulation		• Name what you are feeling. • Review the flipping your lid tool on page 54. • Practice mindfulness. • Use 'I' statements to communicate your feelings and your needs. • Are you living consistent with your values? • Use your problem-solving skills to explore solutions to this problem.

Did You Know? Throughout history, people have created images and displayed them on shields and banners to express what they stand for. Often people wear T-shirts to display their group affiliation, values and beliefs.

Imagine that you have been selected to design a T-shirt to celebrate International ADHD Awareness Day in October. What will your T-shirt look like? Draw it below.

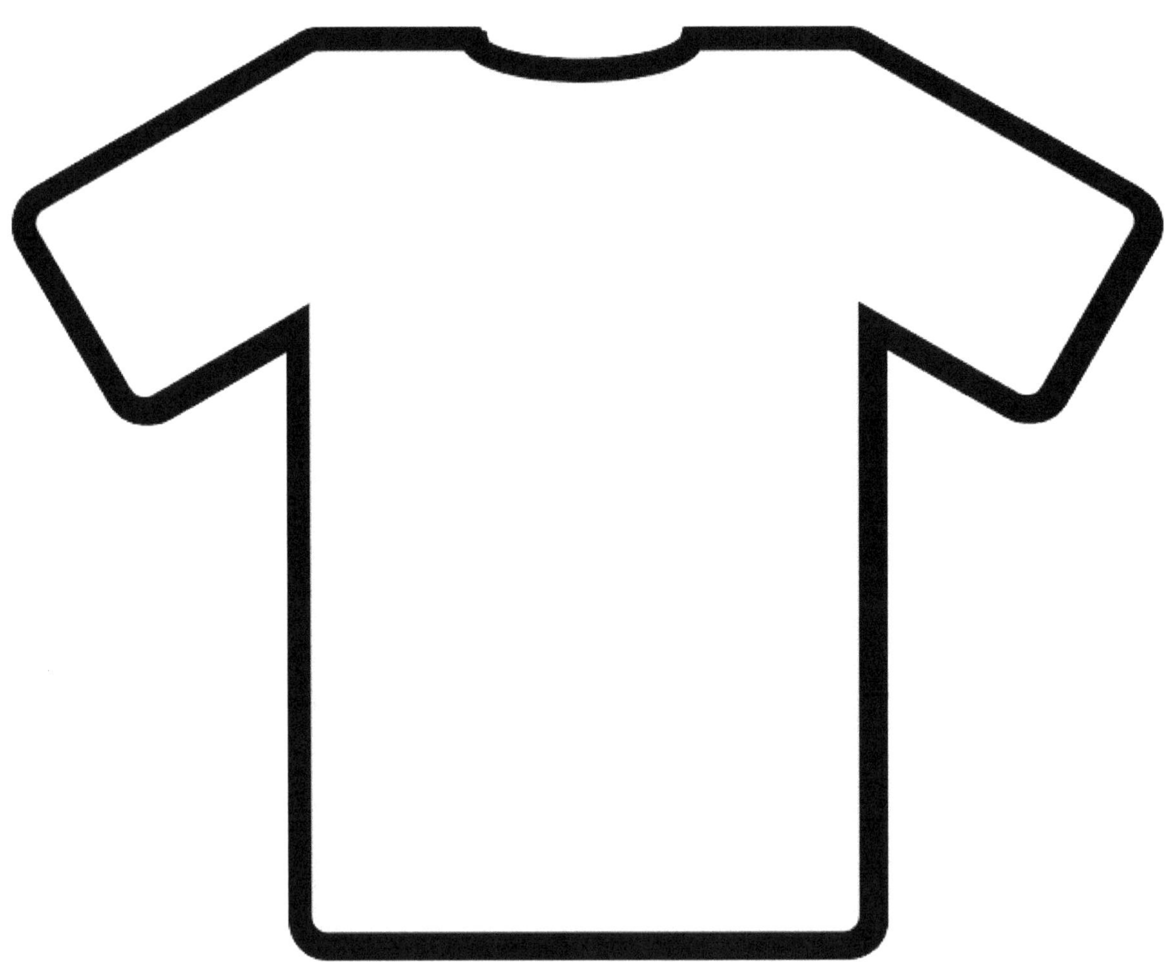

If you have completed the activities in this workbook that were important to you, you've learned a lot about your ADHD. I hope that you now have a better understanding of the aspects of you that exist beneath the surface, and that these become what you are judged by.

Remember that:

'If you don't go within, you will go without.'

References:

American Psychiatric Association (2013). *Diagnostic and Statistical Manual of Mental Health Disorders, (5th ed.).* VA: American Psychiatric Association.

Bellak-Adams, K. (2010). *AD/HD Success! Solutions for boosting self-esteem. The diary method for ages 7–17. Kerin Bellak-Adams.*

da Camara, G. (2018). *Fridays with Tristan: Understanding ADHD from a mentoring perspective. A guide for tweens, teens and their families.* Blackjack Books. Australia

Shapiro, L. E. (2010). T*he ADHD workbook for children. Helping children gain self-confidence, social skills & self-control.* Canada: Raincoast books.

Ramsay, J. R. & Rostain A. L. (2015). *The Adult ADHD Tool Kit. Using CBT to facilitate coping inside out.* New York: Routledge.

Ramsay, J. R. *How Cognitive Behavioural Therapy Unlocks Positivity and Productivity for Adults with ADHD.* Attitude. <https://www.additudemag.com/product/cognitive-behavioral-therapy-adult-adhd-j-russell-ramsay/>

Recommended Readings

For Parents

Hallowell, E. & Ratey, J. (1996). *Driven to Distraction: Recognising and coping with attention deficit disorder from childhood through adult.* New York: Simon & Schuster.

Dendy Zeigler, C. A. (1995). *Teenagers with ADD: A parent's guide.* Bethesda, Woodbine House.

Goldstein, S., Brook, R., & Weiss, S. (2004). *Angry Children, Worried Parents: Seven steps to help families manage anger.* North Branch, MN: Specialty Press.

Greene, R. (2005). *The Explosive Child* (3rd ed.). New York: Harper Collins.

Lougy, R. A., DeRuvo, S. L., Rosenthal, D., (2009). *The School Counselor's Guide to ADHD: What to do and know to help your students.* Corwin.

For Teens

Zeigler Dendy, C. A. & Zeigler, A. (2003, 2007). *A Bird's-Eye View of Life with ADD and ADHD: Advice from young survivors. A survival guide for children and teens.* Chris A. Zeigler Dendy Consulting LLC.

da Camara, G. (2018). *Fridays with Tristan: Understanding ADHD from a mentoring perspective. A guide for tweens, teens and their families.* Australia: Blackjack Books.

Gehret, J. (1992). *I'm somebody too.* Fairport, New York: GSI.

Other Resources

Australian Guidelines for ADHD: https://aadpa.com.au/guideline/

Attention Deficit Disorder Association (ADDA): https://add.org

Children and Adults with Attention Deficit Disorder (CHADD): https://chadd.org

ADHD Aware: https://adhdaware.org.uk

ADDISS: www.addiss.co.uk

Understood: https://www.understood.org

Additude Magazine: https://www.additudemag.com

Canadian ADHD Resources Alliance (CADDRA): https://www.caddra.ca

Center on the Developing Child Harvard University: https://developingchild.harvard.edu

Appendices

Appendix A: DSM-5 Diagnostic Criteria for ADHD

Diagnostic Criteria for ADHD

A. Persistent pattern of inattention and/or hyperactivity/impulsivity that interferes with functioning or development, as characterised by (1) and/or (2).

Six or more of the following symptoms of inattention, or six or more of the following symptoms of hyperactivity/impulsivity must be present, for at least six months, to a degree that is inconsistent with developmental level, and that negatively impacts directly on social and academic/occupational activities.

Note: The symptoms are not solely a manifestation of oppositional behaviour, defiance, hostility, or failure to understand tasks or instructions. For individuals aged of 17 and older, at least five symptoms are required.

1. Symptoms of Inattention	2. Symptoms of Hyperactivity/Impulsivity
• Often fails to pay close attention to details or makes careless mistakes in schoolwork, work or other activities • Often has difficulty sustaining attention in tasks or play activities • Often does not seem to listen when spoken to directly • Often does not follow through on instructions and fails to finish schoolwork, chores, or duties in the workplace (not because of oppositional behaviour or failure to understand instructions)	• Often fidgets with hands or feet, or squirms in their seat • Often leaves their seat in the classroom or in other situations in which remaining seated is expected • Often runs about or climbs excessively in situations in which it is inappropriate (in adolescents or adults it may be limited to subjective feelings of restlessness) • Often has difficulty playing or engaging in leisure activities quietly

• Often has difficulty organising tasks and activities • Often avoids, dislikes or is reluctant to engage in tasks that require sustained mental effort • Often loses things necessary for tasks or activities • Is often easily distracted by extraneous stimuli • Is often forgetful in daily activities	• Is often 'on the go' or often acts as if 'driven by motor' • Often talks excessively • Often blurts out answers before questions have been completed • Often has difficulty waiting their turn • Often interrupts or intrudes on others

B. Several inattentive or hyperactive-impulsive symptoms were present before the age of 12 years.

C. Several inattentive or hyperactive-impulsive symptoms are present in two or more settings (e.g. at home, school, work, with friends or relatives, and in other activities).

D. There is clear evidence that the symptoms interfere with, or reduce the quality of, social, academic, or occupational functioning.

E. The symptoms do not occur exclusively during the course of schizophrenia, or another psychotic disorder and are not better explained by another mental disorder (e.g. mood disorder, anxiety disorder, dissociative disorder or personality disorder, substance intoxication, or withdrawal).

Prevalence

Population surveys suggest that ADHD occurs in most cultures in about 5% of children and 2.5% of adults.

Gender-related Diagnostic Issues

ADHD is more frequent in males than in females in the general population, with a ratio of approximately 2:1 in children and 1.6:1 in adults. Females are more likely than males to present primarily with inattentive features.

Frequently Asked Questions

How many subtypes of ADHD are there?

ADHD is the umbrella word for the following three subtypes:

1. predominantly hyperactive and impulsive
2. predominantly inattentive
3. combined type.

Who gets ADHD?

- Both children and adults can have ADHD.
- Research shows that boys outnumber girls diagnosed with ADHD by 2:1.
- ADHD is diagnosed all around the world with similar rates to those found in the United States.

Does having ADHD mean I'm not smart?

Not at all. It means that you do things a little differently to other people. Sometimes people with ADHD must work a little harder or in a different way to get things done.

Why can I pay attention sometimes?

Sometimes people might ask why you can concentrate so well on video games and not on your homework. Paying attention is not a problem when you are really interested in what you are doing. It is much more difficult for someone with ADHD to pay attention if the subject matter isn't exciting or is difficult to understand.

What are some good things about ADHD?

People with ADHD are usually talented, creative and spontaneous. They have lots of energy, are kind natured and are open to trying new things.

Will I always have ADHD?

It is unlikely that you will ever entirely outgrow ADHD. However, some individuals with ADHD do not have major difficulties associated with ADHD when they are adults. Those individuals who find jobs that suit their higher activity level and a partner who is understanding and supportive generally manage well. For others, the symptoms lessen with age or they simply learn strategies to cope with their ADHD challenges.

Will taking medication make me a drug addict?

There is no evidence that ADHD medication (stimulants) use in adolescence causes substance abuse or addiction. In fact, it may even decrease the risk of this problem since your life will be more 'in control' with medication. Also, your need to self-medicate with drugs and other substances will be less.

Appendix B: EF Word Finder Answer Key

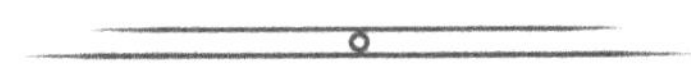

D	G		G		E									P
I	N			N		M	L					P	R	W
S	I				I	O	I				U	O		O
O	N				S	N		T		N	C	G		L
R	O			I			E		C	R		N		S
G	I	U	N	D	E	R	S	T	A	N	D	I	N	G
A	T	G					U	S	S			W		
N	I					A	T			I		O	S	
I	S				L	I					L	L	T	
S	N			I	N	Y	S	S	E	M		L	A	
E	A		T	A								O	R	
D	R	Y	T	P	L	A	N	N	I	N	G	F	T	
Y	T	I	L	I	B	I	T	C	A	R	T	S	I	D
	O		L	U	F	T	E	G	R	O	F		N	
N													G	

Appendix C: Fight-Flight Response

When we see something scary, or think frightening thoughts, our body gets us ready to take some form of action. When this happens, the fight or flight response is automatically triggered, and several physiological changes prepare us to act.

This can either be to run away (flight) or to stay and defend yourself (fight).

To do this, your body produces the chemicals adrenaline and cortisol. These chemicals make your heart beat faster so blood can be pumped around your body to the muscles. The muscles need oxygen and so we start to breathe faster in order to provide them with the fuel/energy they need. This helps us to become very alert and able to focus on the threat.

Blood gets diverted away from those parts of the body that aren't being used, for example, the stomach. Other bodily functions shut down. We don't need to eat at times like this, so you may notice your mouth becoming dry and it being difficult to swallow.

Your body is now working very hard. It starts to become hot.

To regulate temperature/cool down, your body begins to sweat, and pushes the blood vessels to the surface of the body, resulting in some people becoming flushed or red in the face. Sometimes your body may take in too much oxygen, resulting in people feeling faint, light-headed or as if they have wobbly or jelly legs.

The fight or flight response is not bad, and we all experience it at times to varying degrees. Usually it's natural and not a problem. However, when the fight or flight response leads to excessive anger, anxiety or other prolonged problems, it might be time to intervene.

Appendix D: Anger Word Finder Answer Key

L	O	N	E	L	Y									A				
	F	E	M	B	A	R	R	A	S	S	E	D		F				
	F	R	U	S	T	R	A	T	E	D				R				
	E	V			R		N				D	E	Y	A	R	T	E	B
	N	O			I		X				I			I				
	D	U			C		I				S		A	D				
	E	S			K		O				R		T					
	D				E		U				E		T		R			
					D		S				S	H	A	M	E	F	U	L
U	N	I	M	P	O	R	T	A	N	T	P		C		J			
											E		K		E			
A	B	A	N	D	O	N	E	D			C		E		C			
								H	U	R	T		D		T			
W	O	R	T	H	L	E	S	S			E				E			
D	I	S	B	E	L	I	E	F			D				D			
		G	U	I	L	T	Y											
U	N	S	U	P	P	O	R	T	E	D								

Appendix E: Answers to Quizzes

Quiz 1 page 103-104

1. B, 2. C, 3. A, 4. C, 5. B, 6. A, 7. B, 8. C, 9. B

Quiz 2 page 180-181

1. B, 2. A, 3. C, 4. C, 5. C

Quiz 3 page 218

1. B, 2. C, 3. C, 4. B

Quiz 4 page 297-298

1. A, 2. C, 3. C, 4. B, 5. A, 6. B, 7. B, 8. C

Quiz 5 page 326-327

1. B, 2. B, 3. C, 4, B, 5. B, 6. B, 7. C

Appendix F: Organisation Strategies

Children with ADHD rarely keep their backpacks tidy, and that sometimes has serious consequences on their overall academic performance. Organisation strategies can help children build the skills they need to stay neat – or at least neater!

What organisation skills matter the most for students with ADHD?

Students with good organisational skills have the ability to create and maintain systems to keep track of information or materials. A young child can, with a reminder, put school materials in a designated place. An adolescent can organise and locate sports equipment. Unfortunately, children with ADHD have problems with these tasks. To be organised requires time, effort and sustained attention. Of these, your children may have only time – and they'd prefer to be doing something else with it.

Learning organisation skills at school (how your teacher can help)

- Make desk-cleaning a part of the daily routine. Half an hour before dismissal, a teacher might say, 'Okay, let's do a speed clean!' to her first-grade class, prompting children to tidy up their desks and other common spaces. When the classroom is tidy, they can play a short group game before getting ready to go home for the day.
- Talk about it. Have a class discussion about what it means to be organised. Ask children to design a system for cleaning up their cubbies or a common play area. Talk about how to organise classroom routines to make them go more smoothly. Set up a suggestion box children can use if they think of other ideas.

- Instruct the class on how to set up and organise a notebook and binder. Each time you tell students something that should go in the notebook or binder, tell them exactly where it goes and supervise them to make sure it gets there. Work in pairs to ensure each student follows the plan.
- Use brightly coloured paper for project assignments, providing details and due dates. Give each student two copies; one for the notebook and one to be posted at home.
- Stay organised yourself by having classroom systems in place for daily routines – turning in homework assignments, collecting lunch money and permission slips, and so on. Teach students the systems and appoint student monitors to make sure the routines are followed as much as possible.
- Make organisation a team effort. Divide the class into two teams, appoint team leaders, and award points for keeping desks clean, cubbies or lockers organised, or notebooks neat. With the class, create a checklist that can be used for inspections. Hold daily or random spot checks and award points based on the checklist. The team with the most points at the end of the week gets to choose the class reward from a rewards menu.
- Keep classroom systems simple. Use two colour-coded folders – red for incomplete homework assignments, green for completed assignments. Use this for class work as well and teach the class to move their work from red to green as the morning progresses. Make sure they pack the folders before they go home. First thing in the morning, ask them to get out their green folders with completed homework and place them on top of their desk for review.
- Give bonus points, or some other reward, for improved organisational skills. Reward disorganised students when they can quickly locate a certain book or paper in their desk or notebooks.
- Take photos of what an organised desk, locker, classroom looks like and display them in the classroom so that the students know what neat looks like.

Learning Organisational Skills at Home (How Parents Can Help)

- Label where things should go. Attach pictures or text on clear plastic containers to show what goes in each container.
- Schedule an after-dinner clean up. Set aside five minutes after dinner to clean up the common areas in the house (living room, counter tops, mudroom). Set a timer, put on some lively music, and have the family pitch in. Make it a daily routine.
- Have your child stay put when cleaning up their work area. Instead of taking away the stuff that belongs in other rooms, have them make piles: one for the bedroom, one for the kitchen, one for the playroom. If they walk off to another area, chances are, they will get side-tracked.
- Buy your child a cork board and pins for hanging up important papers that might get lost on a cluttered desk.
- Assemble a homework supply kit. In a see-through plastic container with a lid, place everything they will need to complete assignments, from crayons and a glue stick to a calculator and dictionary. With this system, it does not matter where your child chooses to study. The necessary supplies can accompany them anywhere.
- Insert plastic sleeves into your child's notebooks or binders for storing important papers that are not hole-punched.
- Colour-code entries on a calendar; one colour for school-related activities, another for sports, a third for social activities.
- Take a photograph of what neatness should look like, whether it's in a backpack or your child's workspace. Have your child compare their work to the photograph and critique themself. Did they do a five-star job (their work looks exactly like the photo), a three-star job (only a couple of things out of place), or a one-star job (they tried but seemed to run out of steam)?
- Put up a large whiteboard that includes a space for a calendar. Give each family member a different-coloured marker to write tasks and events for the week, so each can easily spot their own.

- Have your child design a system that works for them. An organisational system that works for you is unlikely to work as well for your child.
- Take out the academic component. When helping your child organise their backpack or workspace, don't say anything about their terrible handwriting, or a paper their teacher has marked up with comments; continue organising. You are working on organisation, not academics.
- Ask permission before going into their backpack to assist with organising it. You wouldn't want them going into your purse or briefcase without asking first.
- Make organisation a family affair. Sometimes entire families are organisationally challenged. If so, admit your difficulties and ask the family to choose a problem to tackle. Design a system and get a commitment from family members to stick with the program for a few weeks to see if it helps. Hold a meeting after one week to evaluate and fine-tune the system; decide on a reward if everyone makes it through week two.
- Tackle one mess at a time. A parent's biggest downfall is having children organise their room, backpack and homework space all at once. Choose one task, get that system up and running, and after a month or two, move on to another task.

Appendix G: Impulsivity Word Finder Answer Key

			T									A						
	R		A			C	O	P	I	N	G	S	K	I	L	L	S	
	A		K									K			E		E	
T	I	M	E	O	U	T						F			T		L	
	S		T									O			G		F	
	E		U									R			O		T	
	H		R									H		S		K	A	
	A		N									E		H		A	L	
	N		S									L		T		E	K	
	D	O	N	T	I	N	T	E	R	R	U	P	T	A		P		M
														E		S		L
														R		O		A
S	T	O	P	T	H	I	N	K						B		T		C
														P		T		Y
														E		I		A
														E		A		T
										S	L	O	W	D	O	W	N	S

Appendix H: Learning Style Strategies

Strategies for Visual Learners. Visual learners learn best by seeing or watching others do something before they try it themselves. Strategies include:

- Organising their work and living space to avoid distractions.
- Sitting in the front of the room to avoid distraction, and away from doors or windows where the action takes place. Sit away from wall maps or bulletin boards.
- Using neatly organised or typed material.
- Using visual association, visual imagery, written repetition, flash cards and clustering strategies for improved memory.
- Reconstructing images in different ways – try different spatial arrangements and taking advantage of blank spaces on the page.
- Using note pads, to-do lists and other forms of reminders.
- Using organisational format outlining for recording notes. Use underlining, highlighting in different colours, symbols, flow charts, graphs or pictures in your notes.
- Practising turning visual cues back into words as you prepare for exams.
- Allowing enough time for planning and recording thoughts when doing problem-solving tasks.
- Using test preparation strategies that emphasise organisation of information and visual encoding and recall.
- Participating actively in class or group activities.
- Developing written or pictorial outlines of responses before answering essay questions

Strategies for Auditory Learners. Auditory learners learn best by listening to instructions before they try it themselves. Strategies include:

- Working in quiet areas to reduce distractions; avoiding areas with conversation, music and television.
- Sitting away from doors or windows where noises may enter the classroom
- Rehearsing information orally.
- Attending lectures and tutorials regularly.
- Discussing topics with other students, teachers and parents. Ask others to listen to your understanding of the material.
- Using mnemonics, rhymes, jingles and auditory repetition through audio recording to improve memory.
- Practising verbal interaction to improve motivation and self-monitoring.
- Using audio recorders to document lectures and for reading materials.
- Remembering to examine illustrations in textbooks and convert them into verbal descriptions.
- Reading the directions for tests or assignments aloud, or have someone read them to you, especially if the directions are long and complicated.
- Reminding yourself to review details.
- Using time managers and translating written appointment reminders into verbal cues.
- Using verbal brainstorming and audio recording for writing and proofing.
- Leaving spaces in your lecture notes for later recall and 'filing'. Expand your notes by talking with others and collecting notes from the textbook.
- Reading your notes aloud.
- Practising writing your answers using old exams and speaking your answers out loud.

Strategies for Kinaesthetic Learners. Kinaesthetic learners learn best if they are involved directly in whatever is being taught/done. Strategies include:

- Keeping verbal discourse short and to the point.
- Actively participating in discussions.
- Using all your senses: sight, touch, taste, smell, hearing.
- Using direct involvement, physical manipulation, imagery and 'hands on' activities to improve motivation, interest and memory.
- Organising information into the steps that were used to physically complete a task.
- Seeking out courses that have laboratories, field trips, etc. and lecturers who give real-life examples.
- Using case studies and applications (examples) to help with principles and abstract concepts.
- Allowing for physical action in solving problems.
- Reading or summarising directions, especially if they are lengthy and complicated, to discourage starting a task without instructions.
- Using recorded reading materials.
- Using practice, play acting and modelling to prepare for tests.
- Allowing for physical movement and periodic breaks during tests, while reading or while composing written assignments.
- Role-playing the exam situation.
- Teaching the material to someone else.
- Writing practice answers, paragraphs or essays.

Glossary

Accommodations: Changes made to the learning environment curriculum in order to better serve children with special needs or learning differences. Accommodations can include, but are not limited, to test presentation, extended time, different testing locations and variation in the way material is presented and/or taught to students.

ADD: This refers to 'Attention Deficit Disorder,' an older term for ADHD that some people still use, especially in reference to the presentation of ADHD that has less hyperactivity and is more characterised by inattention. This term has been replaced with the term 'ADHD' to include all presentations of this disorder.

ADHD: This refers to Attention-Deficit/Hyperactivity Disorder, the official name given this condition by the American Psychiatric Association. It is described in the Diagnostic and Statistical Manual of Mental Disorders as a persistent condition that impairs functioning or development, and characterised by chronic inattention, hyperactivity, and often impulsivity.

ADHD Coach: A professional who is trained in both the field of coaching and ADHD who works primarily with adults and older teens to get past obstacles and reach their goals. Coaches often help those with ADHD with organisational and executive functioning challenges.

ADHD – Combined Type (ADHD-C): A subtype of ADHD characterised by both inattentive and hyperactive/impulsive symptoms of ADHD.

ADHD – Not Otherwise Specified (ADHD-NOS): A subtype of ADHD diagnosed when the inattention, hyperactivity and impulsivity symptoms are present, but the individual does not meet the full criteria for the other subtypes of ADHD.

ADHD – Predominantly Hyperactive-Impulsive (ADHD PH-I): A subtype of ADHD characterised by impulsivity and hyperactivity but lacking the symptoms of inattention.

ADHD – Predominantly Inattentive (ADHD-PI): A subtype of ADHD characterised by inattentive symptoms, but lacking hyperactivity and impulsivity symptoms.

Anxiety: Uneasiness of the mind, typically shown by apprehension, worry and fear about everyday situations. Anxiety can co-exist with ADHD.

Attentional Bias: Preferring to pay attention to certain objects, thoughts and activities that one finds interesting.

Behaviour Modification (or Behaviour Therapy): A type of treatment provided by a trained mental health professional that teaches clients how to identify the interconnection between thoughts, feelings and behaviours, and learn new skills that replace negative behaviours with positive ones.

Behavioural Contract: A simple positive-reinforcement contract between student and teacher, or between parent and child, that is designed to change behaviour. The contract explains the desired behaviour that will be increased and the reinforcement that will be earned. In addition, inappropriate behaviour is often listed, including the consequences for the behaviour.

CHADD – Children and Adults with Attention-Deficit/Hyperactivity Disorder: A non-profit organisation committed to helping people with ADHD, their families and the professionals who work with them.

Child Behaviour Checklist: A behavioural rating scale used by parents and teachers to evaluate emotional and behavioural problems in children.

Classroom Behaviour Management: Strategies and techniques used by teachers to manage the behaviour of students in the classroom and reduce classroom disruption.

Clinical Trial: Also called a research study, a clinical trial is designed to test an intervention, treatment or new approach. Clinical trials may compare a new treatment to a treatment that is already available.

Co-Existing Conditions: When two or more mental health conditions are present in the same individual, they are said to be co-existing (also called co-occurring or co-morbid); for example, ADHD can co-exist with depression or anxiety.

Cognitive Restructuring: Changing self-defeating thought patterns brought about by earlier life experiences.

Comorbidity: Two or more disorders occurring in an individual at the same time.

Comprehensive Assessment: An evaluation process that takes into consideration any factors that contribute to an individual's current problems or functioning difficulties. These can include behaviours, education or employment skills, family history and relationships, emotional well-being, social skills, traumatic events and co-existing mental health conditions. Strengths and abilities are also assessed. The process forms the basis for a diagnosis and treatment plan.

Conduct Disorder: A group of behavioural and emotional problems in children and adolescents that can be exhibited as aggressive behaviour towards people and animals, destruction of property, lying, stealing, deceitfulness,and serious rule violations.

Daily Behaviour Report Card (DBRC): A method of daily communication between teachers and parents in which the behaviours of the child throughout the day are reported. The card can be adapted to develop behaviour goals, monitor the child's progress, or determine if behaviour interventions are working to improve the child's behaviour.

Distractibility: The inability to sustain attention on the task at hand so that it disrupts a person's concentration.

DSM-5 Diagnostic and Statistical Manual of Mental Disorders: This manual, written by the American Psychiatric Association, describes how mental health disorders are classified, including the symptoms used for diagnosis. It is used by various health care professionals and insurance companies across a wide range of settings to classify mental disorders for diagnosis and insurance purposes.

Dyslexia: A specific learning disability that impairs a person's ability to read. It is characterised by spelling challenges, word retrieval while speaking and a lack of fluency, causing reading to be slower and require much effort.

Executive Functions: Mental skills that allow us to control and coordinate other mental functions and abilities, such as planning or task completion. This deficit is common in those with ADHD.

Functional Impairment Difficulties: These are life challenges that interfere with a person's ability to function in major life activities, including social situations, school, employment and in the community.

Hyperactivity: Having increased movement, impulsive actions and a shorter attention span. A hyperactive person has constant activity and is easily distracted and impulsive. Other characteristics of hyperactive behaviour also include an inability to concentrate and aggressiveness.

Hyperfocus: A deep and intense mental concentration fixated on an activity, specific event or topic.

Impulsivity: Acting with little or no thought of the consequences or reacting rapidly without considering the negative consequences of the reaction.

Inattention: Failure to pay attention to a specified object or task.

Independent Educational Evaluation (IEE): An assessment conducted by a qualified examiner not employed by a school district to determine if a student may be eligible for special education. An IEE is conducted if parents disagree with a school district's assessment of their child's eligibility for special education.

Individualised Education Plan (IEP): A written document that describes the educational goals at school, and the methods of achieving these goals, for eligible children under IDEA (U.S. Department of Education's Individuals with Disabilities Education Act). This plan is based on the child's current level of performance.

Intervention: A structured process (or action) that has the effect of modifying an individual's behaviour, cognition or emotional state.

Limited English Proficient (LEP): The term used by the federal government, most states and local school districts to identify students whose difficulty in speaking, reading, writing or understanding the English language will make it difficult to succeed in English-only classrooms.

Medication Holiday: A planned period of time, for medical or evaluation purposes, when prescribed medication therapy is temporarily discontinued. This should be undertaken only with the guidance of the prescribing medical practitioner.

Mental Health Therapist: A master's or doctoral level, licensed professional who is trained in assessment, diagnosis and treatment of mental health disorders. Most mental health therapists' practice in areas of specialty, which can include ADHD and related disorders. They are trained in a broad range of therapies such as cognitive-behavioural, psychodynamic, marital, family, parent-child interaction, coaching, to name a few. They can include psychiatrists, psychologists, clinical social workers, professional counsellors, and marriage and family therapists.

Modification: Adjustments made to an assignment, test, or the general curriculum to meet the needs of a student when the expectations of the curriculum are beyond the student's ability. Modifications are written into the student's IEP or Section 504 Plan.

Multimodal Treatment: ADHD in children often requires a comprehensive approach to treatment. This 'multimodal' approach includes multiple interventions working together, tailored to the unique needs of the child, including parent training, medication and behavioural therapy.

Negative Self-Talk: Negative inner dialogue that brings out emotions such as guilt, fear, pessimism, anger, frustration, anxiety and depression. These thoughts often damage self-esteem and can appear in times of increased stress or emotional turmoil.

Neurobehavioural: Related to the relationship between the brain and behaviour.

Neurologist: A health care professional trained to diagnose and manage brain disorders.

Neuropsychologist: A psychologist trained in how the brain and the rest of the nervous system affect a person's behaviour and cognition. They are able to administer neuropsychological testing, which aims to identify any challenges to full brain functioning, including identifying learning disabilities or the impact of illnesses or injuries to the brain.

Neurotransmitter: A chemical in the brain that functions as a messenger to transmit nerve impulses between nerve cells (neurons) within the nervous system.

Non-stimulant Medication: A medication that has been approved to treat ADHD (generally considered second-line medication) prescribed to those who have an incomplete response or no response to stimulants, cannot tolerate stimulants, or have certain co-existing psychiatric conditions.

Occupational Therapist: A licensed health care professional who provides therapy centred on sensory integration to address the physical, behavioural and emotional effects of ADHD, and identifies goals to help the child succeed at school and at home.

Peer Rejection: When someone is purposely excluded from a social relationship or social interaction by peers.

Planned Ignoring: A behavioural intervention strategy in which one provides no attention to negative and maladaptive behaviour to reduce inappropriate behaviours.

Positive Behavioural Support (PBS): Rooted in research, PBS provides a systemic approach to decreasing problem behaviours and increasing socially acceptable behaviours in the individual and in the system, such as a school.

Prefrontal Cortex: The front part of the frontal lobe in the brain that plays a role in controlling attention, behaviour, judgment and emotion.

Progress Monitoring: A practice to assess a student's academic performance, record performance data, and evaluate how well the student is responding to instruction as well as the effectiveness of the instruction.

Prosocial Behaviour: Positive actions to help others, motivated by a sense of empathy and caring, rather than for personal gain.

Psychoeducational Testing: An assessment process that includes tests, observations and history taking to identify a student's cognitive strengths and challenges, in order to develop a plan for the student's success in the classroom.

Psychologist: A licensed mental health professional trained in the study of behaviour, emotions and functioning. Psychologists are trained in psychological therapy, consultation and testing.

Rebound Effect: The tendency in some medications (including some ADHD medications), when withdrawn from use, to lead to symptoms of greater severity than were present before the medication was initiated.

Response to Intervention (RTI): A multilevel prevention system used by schools to maximise student achievement and reduce behaviour problems. RTI is used to identify students at risk for learning failures, monitor student progress, provide evidence-based interventions, and adjust the interventions based on students' responsiveness.

Self-Regulation: Managing (regulating) one's own behaviour with appropriate behaviour and actions in order to attain one's goals.

Sensory Integration Disorder (SID): Also known as Sensory Processing Disorder, SID is a condition in which the brain and nervous system are unable to correctly receive, organise and process information coming in from the senses, causing learning and behavioural problems.

Specific Learning Disability (SLD/LD): A disorder in learning processes involved in understanding and using spoken or written language that significantly interferes with a person's ability to listen, think, speak, read, write, spell or do mathematics.

Speech or Language Impairment: A communication disorder including difficulties with articulation, stuttering, or a language impairment that adversely affects a person's educational performance.

Stimulant Medication: Medication that 'stimulate' (increase) certain activity in the body's central nervous system, including the production and activity of neurotransmitters. Most medications approved for the treatment of ADHD are stimulant medications. When taken as prescribed, they generally help improve the symptoms of ADHD by promoting alertness, awareness and the ability to focus.

Target Behaviour: A specific behaviour that has been chosen or 'targeted' either to increase in frequency (if it is a positive behaviour) or decrease in frequency (if it is a negative behaviour).

Token Economy System: A behaviour modification system in which a student earns tokens for exhibiting the desired behaviour. The tokens are exchanged at a later time for a reinforcer, which is typically selected by the student.

Working Memory: A system in the brain that temporarily stores and processes the information needed for much more complex tasks such as reasoning, comprehension and learning.

Notes

Notes

Notes

Notes

Notes

www.ingramcontent.com/pod-product-compliance
Lightning Source LLC
LaVergne TN
LVHW060629110826
845147LV00014B/874

9781760802585